Glanz und Abglanz

Two Centuries of German Studies in the University of London

Glanz und Abglanz

Two Centuries of German Studies in the University of London

by

John L. Flood and Anne Simon

Published by the
Institute of Modern Languages Research
School of Advanced Study, University of London
Senate House, Malet Street, London WC1E 7HU
http://www.modernlanguages.sas.ac.uk

Cover Image

Plate from Goethe's *Farbenlehre* (1810) from the Germanic Studies Collection, London (digitization: Senate House Library).

First published 2017
ISBN 978 0 85457 263 2

Contents

Foreword

As convenor of German Studies at the Institute of Modern Languages Research, successor in title to the Institute of Germanic & Romance Studies and its forerunner, the Institute of Germanic Studies, I have always been acutely conscious of the work that my predecessors and colleagues have done for the discipline at the Institute – and more widely in the federal University of London. It is with warmest thanks to the authors of the three essays collected here that I commend this volume to all readers, whether they regard themselves as members of the German Studies community or take an interest from the 'outside'.

It is impossible not to feel a sense of pride and admiration for the spirited and dedicated work done in the name of German Studies since the University's foundation in the early nineteenth century, whether at UCL ('the godless institution of Gower Street'), its rival KCL, or any of the other Colleges that followed suit in offering German. John Flood's historical overview should be mandatory reading for anyone working with the Institute, as he tells the stories behind the names we still encounter daily: whether as donors to the library, as benefactors whose endowed funds finance a high-profile public lecture programme, or as outstanding researchers who have laid the intellectual foundations for our work today. In his second essay, John turns to the legacy of two of these 'ancestors' in the field, Robert Priebsch and August Closs, describing the treasures to be found in the collection of first editions and other bibliophiles' delights that is the Priebsch-Closs Collection.

Anne Simon's history of the Institute of Germanic Studies (IGS), the second essay in this volume, of course does not stop with the amalgamation of the IGS with the Institute of Romance Studies in 2004, but goes on to chart the history of the two subsequent enlarged versions of the core Institute: the IGRS and IMLR. Anne provides us with a timely reminder of the European spirit that led to the Institute's foundation in 1950 (after first proposals for the 'ambitious project' by Leonard Willoughby in 1943!) and of the work that has been done here since to initiate, support and promote research in German Studies, both with a single-language focus and as a comparative, interdisciplinary undertaking.

We – the IMLR and our collaborators in this country and abroad – will do all we can to continue the varied programme we have developed over the past decades and to remain a thriving, energetic hub of research in German literature and culture at the heart of Bloomsbury.

Dr Godela Weiss-Sussex
Reader in German, IMLR

August 2016

List of Illustrations

List of Abbreviations

ATG	The Association of Teachers of German
AUPF	The Association of University Professors of French
BL	British Library
BM	British Museum
CAOIII	Committee on Academic Organisation
CILT	Centre for Information on Language Teaching and Research
CUTG	Conference of University Teachers of German in Great Britain and Ireland
FGPC	Finance and General Purposes Committee
HEFCE	Higher Education Funding Council for England
IGS	Institute of Germanic Studies
IGRS	Institute of Germanic & Romance Studies
IMLR	Institute of Modern Languages Research
KCL	King's College London
LSE	London School of Economics and Political Science
MLA	The Modern Language Association
ODNB	*Oxford Dictionary of National Biography*
QMC	Queen Mary College
QMUL	Queen Mary, University of London
RAE	Research Assessment Exercise
RHC	Royal Holloway College
RHUL	Royal Holloway, University of London
SARC	Subject Area Review Committee
UC	University College
UCL	University College London
UL	University Library

‘Taught By Giants’

Glimpses into the First 175 Years of German Studies in the University of London

John L. Flood

For William Jervis Jones,

Scholar, Colleague and Friend

'Taught By Giants'
Glimpses into the First 175 Years of German Studies in the University of London[1]

In the early nineteenth century London was the only European capital apart from Constantinople and Madrid not to have a university and was thus, as the poet Thomas Campbell (1777–1841), who had been impressed by the new University of Bonn (founded, or rather re-established, in 1818), put it at the meeting at the London Tavern in Bishopsgate on 1 July 1825 at which the project for a university in the city was launched, 'linked in unholy alliance with the capitals of the Turk and Spaniard'.[2] Tellingly, the project's supporters' initial prospectus noted that 'the City of London is nearly equal in population, and far superior in wealth, to each of the Kingdoms of Denmark, Saxony, Hanover, and Wirtemburgh, every one of which has at least one flourishing University'.[3] The project resulted in the foundation, in 1826, of what is now University College London (UCL). Its aim was to provide higher education to young men of all religious faiths (nonconformists, Roman Catholics, Jews and others) and none – in contrast to Oxford and Cambridge which required students to be confessing members of the Church of England. The beginnings of the

1 This essay has its origin in a talk given in August 2016 at an informal reunion for former members of the University's Board of Studies in Germanic Languages and Literatures. It does not aim to be comprehensive, exhaustive or authoritative in its coverage of the history of German Studies in the individual Colleges of the University. Its focus is on selected personalities, and on structures, rather than on curriculum and content or individual noteworthy scholarly achievements. Above all, its aim is to present a personal view from the centre of the University from someone who has been associated with the University for more than fifty years. Readers interested in the development of German Studies in particular Colleges are referred to the various College histories listed in the bibliography. In writing this essay I have been fortunate to benefit from the help of several friends and colleagues, too numerous to mention individually, who all deserve my profound gratitude for their invaluable assistance.

2 Cited in *The Political and Occasional Poems of Winthrop Mackworth Praed*, ed. by Sir George Young (London: Ward, Lock & Co., 1888), p. 62, in the introduction to his poem 'The London University' (pp. 61–65). Istanbul University was established in 1933 on the basis of the *Darülfünûn* (House of Multiple Sciences) of 1846 which in turn had antecedents going back to 1453; the Universidad Complutense in Madrid was founded in 1822.

3 Reproduced in Negley Harte and John North, *The World of University College London 1828–1978* (London: University College, 1978), p. 17.

University were nothing if not controversial. Winthrop Mackworth Praed (1802–1839), Tory politician and poet – author of 'Stanzas on seeing the Speaker Asleep in his Chair' – wrote of the 'radical infidel College' in his satirical poem 'The London University. A Discourse delivered by a College Tutor at a Supper-party' in *The Morning Chronicle* (19 July 1825), and the College, which today rather grandiosely calls itself 'UCL London's Global University', was once disparaged in the ultra-Tory magazine *John Bull* (January 1826) as 'stinkomalee' in reference to its being built on the site of a swampy rubbish dump.[4] Another contemporary satirist wrote mockingly of the plan to offer new educational opportunities to working men and the method employed to fund it – the sale of shares:

> Each dustmen shall speak, both in Latin and Greek,
> And tinkers beat bishops in knowledge –
> If the opulent tribe will consent to subscribe
> To build up a new Cockney College. [...]
> This College, when formed, established, endowed,
> Will astonish each Radical's grannam,
> Who may please her young fry in the midst of the crowd
> For two pounds ten shillings per annum. [...][5]

The establishment of 'the godless institution of Gower Street' in the form of a joint stock company swiftly resulted in a counter-movement that saw the creation of King's College, a bastion of Tory Anglicanism, under the patronage of George IV in 1829. The rivalry between the two Colleges led to the foundation by Royal Charter on 28 November 1836 of an over-arching organization, the University of London, purely as an examining and degree-awarding body. In 1842 the *London University Magazine* gave an illustration of how this worked: 'It is now rather more than four years since the London University received its charter. During this period, as many as twenty colleges have been admitted to the privilege of sending candidates to be examined, and nearly one hundred students have successfully competed for the degrees in arts and laws, and about fifty more for the degrees in medicine'. This curious arrangement was certainly not without its critics: Sir George Young (an ancestor of the Sir George Young MP who was appointed Government Chief Whip in 2012), writing about the origins of the University in 1887, remarked: 'The London University which Thomas Campbell promoted [that is, University College] was a very substantial Academic Body, and a real addition to the educational machinery of the country; and that it has never [...] succeeded

4 'The Cockney College. An Invitation to Stinkomalee', reproduced in Harte and North, *The World of University College London 1828–1978*, p. 30.

5 From 'The Cockney University', originally published in *John Bull*, July 1825, and reproduced in full in Harte and North, *The World of University College London 1828–1978*, p. 30.

in making itself quite intelligible to the inhabitants of London generally, is due to the unkind way in which it was changed at nurse. Its very name has been appropriated [...] by an oddly constituted Board of Examinations, which never had a professor, or a student, in the world; and itself has been forced to survive under the appellation of "University College, London"'.[6] The University of London did not become a teaching university until 1900. The early rivalry between University College and King's foreshadowed the duplication and reduplication of effort that would characterize the teaching of many subjects, including German, in the University of London for decades to come. With hindsight, I have always thought, the University should never have been allowed to develop in the way it did, with a large number of colleges and institutes scattered over an area from the Mile End Road in the east to Egham in the west, from Hampstead in the north (not to mention the University Marine Biological Station at Millport in the Firth of Clyde) to Wye College (and the British Institute in Paris) in the south.

Although, as we shall see, German established a foothold at both University College and King's at an early date, London was not the first university in the British Isles to make provision for German: that distinction goes to Trinity College Dublin where already in 1775 German was taught to allow 'young Gentlemen of Fortune to finish their education at home'. A chair of German, the oldest in the world, was established in 1776.[7] (In this respect German in the British Isles still compared unfavourably with English in Germany: English was taught at five German universities in the late seventeenth century, and the first Chair of English was established, at Jena, in 1768.) Such a development was quite remarkable because, although it was widely recognized that modern languages were useful and even necessary, it was not considered the business of universities to make provision for them, though there might be private teachers on the periphery offering language tuition. At Cambridge, Modern Languages were introduced as a degree subject only in 1884, though already eighty-five years earlier William Render, a Lutheran pastor and freemason who had studied at Gießen, described himself on the title page of his *A Concise Practical Grammar of the German Tongue* (London, 1799) as 'teacher of German language in the University of Cambridge',[8] and at about the same

6 *The Political and Occasional Poems of Winthrop Mackworth Praed*, p. 61.

7 M. M. Raraty, 'The Chair of German at Trinity College Dublin 1775–1886', *Hermathena. A Dublin University Review*, 102 (1986), 53–72. On the Continent the first Chair of German was established at Budapest in 1784. The first Professor of German in Germany was Friedrich Heinrich von der Hagen (1780–1856) at Berlin in 1810.

8 Render, who probably hailed from or near Heppenheim, south of Darmstadt, seems to have been a travelling companion of Francis Rawdon Hastings, afterwards Marquess of Hastings, to whom, as Earl of Moira, he dedicated his *Tour through Germany* (London, 1801). Render came to England about 1790 and settled in London, teaching German and

time as the first London colleges were getting off the ground Thomas Carlyle wrote to Goethe on 22 December 1829 about some Germans finding employment as teachers of their language at Oxford and Cambridge:

> [...] I have read the *Briefwechsel* [of Goethe with Schiller], a second time, with no little satisfaction; and even today am sending off an Essay on Schiller, grounded on that work, for the *Foreign Review* [it actually appeared in *Fraser's Magazine* in March 1831]. It will gratify you to learn that a knowledge and appreciation of Foreign, especially of German Literature is spreading with increased rapidity over all the domain of the English Tongue; so that almost at the Antipodes, in New Holland [Western Australia] itself, the Wise of your country are by this time preaching their wisdom. I have heard lately that even in Oxford and Cambridge, our two English Universities, which have all along been regarded as the strongholds of Insular pride and prejudice, there is a strange stir in this matter. Your [Barthold Georg] Niebuhr [1776–1831] has found an able Translator at Cambridge; and in Oxford two or three Germans already find employment as teachers of their language; the new light contained in which may well dazzle certain eyes. Of the benefits that must in the end result from all this no man can be doubtful: let nations, like individuals, but know one another, and mutual hatred will give place to mutual helpfulness; and instead of natural enemies, as neighbouring countries are sometimes called, we shall all be natural friends. [...][9]

At Oxford, despite the architect Sir Robert Taylor (1714–1788) making munificent provision in his will for the teaching of those languages 'essential to Diplomatic or commercial pursuits' and possessing a 'sufficient' literature, French and German being the first priority, it was not until 1847 that the Taylor Institution came into being, and only in 1903 was the Honour School of Modern Languages established.[10] Carlyle's 'two or

---

other languages in several distinguished families, before also teaching in Cambridge, Oxford, and Edinburgh. He published an English version of Kotzebue's play *Count Benyowsky* (two editions in 1798), translations of Schiller's *The Robbers*, *Don Carlos*, *Maria Stuart*, and *The Armenian* (1800), and in 1801 the first English translation of Goethe's *Werther* direct from the original German. In the preface he speaks of his 'friend the baron Goethe'. Render's *Concise Practical Grammar* appeared in a fifth edition, corrected and enlarged, in 1817. As a token of his appreciation of this work, Alexander I of Russia ordered Semyon Vorontsov, his ambassador in England, to present Render with a ring and an autograph letter. Render also published a *Pocket Dictionary* (2nd edn, 1809) in English and German, and other manuals of instruction in German. For further details see 'Render, William' in *ODNB*, http://www.oxforddnb.com /view/article/23365.

9 Carlyle to Goethe, 22 December 1829 (*The Carlyle Letters Online*, V, pp. 48–51). The 'two able translators' were Julius Charles Hare (1795–1855) and Connop Thirlwall (1797–1875), of Trinity College, whose translation of Niebuhr's *History of Rome* was published in 1828.

10 For the beginnings of German at Scottish universities see Richard Wakely, 'Modern Language Studies at Scottish Universities: The Early Days', in *France and Germany in Scotland: Studies in Language and Culture. Papers from the Centenary celebrations of the Departments of*

three Germans' at Oxford were, doubtless like Render in Cambridge, just freelance teachers without any official connection with the university.

In London, however, German was already being taught at both University College and at King's College from the outset. The initial 1826 prospectus of University College lists languages first among all the subjects to be taught and states:

> Some Languages will probably be studied only by those whose peculiar destination requires such attainments, and in this department generally, it will be fit to seek for every method of abridging the labour by which the majority are to attain that proficiency to which they ought to confine themselves. But the structure of human speech is itself one of the worthiest objects of meditation: the comparison of various languages makes each of them better understood, and illustrates the affinity of nations, while it enlarges and strengthens every vigorous understanding; even the minute and seemingly unfruitful study of words is a school of discrimination and precision; and in the arts which employ language as their instrument, the contemplation of the original models not only serves to form the taste of the youth of genius, but generally conduces to expand and elevate the human faculties.[11]

German was one of the languages offered from the time the College admitted its first students in 1828. Similarly at King's College, German featured from an early date, beginning in 1831, a year before the death of Goethe.

As further institutions came into being alongside the two original Colleges – Bedford (originally the Ladies' College, opened at 47 Bedford

French and German at the University of Edinburgh 1994–1995, ed. by Richard Wakely and Philip E. Bennett (Edinburgh: The Department of French, University of Edinburgh, 1996), pp. 1–21. As Wakely shows, generally speaking, German figured here only as a marginal, extra-curricular subject and did not become more firmly established until the late nineteenth century. The first professors of Modern Languages were not appointed at Scottish universities until after World War I; at Glasgow, for instance, though a part-time lectureship in German had been established in 1887, the William Jacks Chair of Modern Languages was not endowed until 1919. The first Glasgow lecturer was Ernst Elster (later Professor at Marburg), who stayed until 1889, when he was succeeded by Hermann Georg Fiedler (later Professor at Oxford), who in turn was followed in 1890 by Dr Alexander Tille (1866–1912), a Leipzig graduate, noted as a scholar of the Faust legend and first translator of Nietzsche's *Also sprach Zarathustra* (1883–85) into English (1896); he left in 1900 owing to differences of opinion with his students over the Boer War. On him see Fritz Hellwig, 'Alexander Tille', in Peter Neumann (ed.), *Saarländische Lebensbilder*, IV (Saarbrücken: Saarbrücker Druck und Verlag, 1989), pp. 155–90. Tille wrote an extensive account of the life of Karl Buchheim (the second Professor of German at King's College London, on whom see below): 'Karl Adolf Buchheim', *Die Zukunft*, 17 (17 October 1896), 118–28.

11 Harte and North, *The World of University College London 1828–1978*, p. 17.

Square in 1849),[12] Westfield (1882),[13] East London College (1885, renamed Queen Mary College in 1934),[14] Royal Holloway (1886),[15] Birkbeck (1907, though going back to the London Mechanics Institution set up by Dr George Birkbeck in Red Lion Square in 1823), the LSE (1895), and Goldsmiths' (1905)[16] –, all preparing students for the same examination, we eventually had the somewhat ludicrous situation of numerous Departments of German, some of them with only four or five staff, all trying to do the same thing. In the 1970s, for instance, there were some fifty-five members of the University's Board of Studies in Germanic Languages and Literatures, representing some nine institutions;[17] and of course this number excluded Assistant

12 Bedford College, founded for the education of women, was incorporated as a School of the newly created teaching University of London in 1900. See Margaret Tuke, *A History of Bedford College for Women 1849–1937* (Oxford: Oxford University Press, 1939); Linna Bentley, *Educating Women: A Pictorial History of Bedford College, University of London, 1849–1985* (St Albans: Alma, 1991); J. Mordaunt Crook (ed.), *Bedford College, University of London: Memories of 150 Years* (London: Royal Holloway and Bedford New College, 2001).

13 Westfield College became a School of the University in 1902. See Janet Sondheimer, *Castle Adamant in Hampstead: a History of Westfield College 1882–1982* (London: Westfield College, University of London, 1983).

14 One of the first MAs in German in the University's records was awarded to Rachel Beck (of 'East London and Birkbeck') in 1926: she is reputed to have discovered a source for Grillparzer's *Die Jüdin von Toledo*. East London College was provisionally admitted as a School of the University in 1907.

15 Royal Holloway College was incorporated as a School of the University of London in 1900.

16 On Goldsmiths' College, which seems not to have introduced German as a degree subject until the early 1970s, see *The Forge. The History of Goldsmiths' College, 1905–1955*, ed. by Dorothy Dymond (London: Methuen, 1955); A. E. Firth, *Goldsmiths' College: a Centenary Account* (London: Athlone Press, 1991).

17 Board membership was restricted to Appointed Teachers (Professors and Readers) and Recognised Teachers (Senior Lecturers and Lecturers). It is difficult to reconstruct the membership of the Board as it changed year by year, but an approximate list for this period (*c.*1970) is as follows:
BEDFORD: Prof. R. Peacock, Dr K. Ostberg, Mrs D. Reich, Dr P. A. Howe, Dr S. A. Ranawake, Dr J. E. Sandford, Mr S. Spencer, Mr B. A. Watson. (8)
Dutch: Prof. R. P. Meijer, Mrs T. Guest, Dr P. F. Vincent. (3)
BIRKBECK: Prof. G. A. Wells, Dr C. Jolles, Dr P. V. Brady, Dr L. Huber, Miss S. C. Harris. (5)
GOLDSMITHS': Mr E. M. Batley, Dr D. E. Jenkinson, Dr H. C. Castein, Dr C. W. Edwards. (4)
IGS: Mr M. O'C. Walshe. (1)
LSE: Dr N. Denison, Mrs B. E. Hay. (2)
KING'S: Prof. K. C. King, Dr I. Graham, Mr R. J. Beckley, Mr J. L. Flood, Mr D. C. K. Glass, Dr R. B. Harrison, Mr M. H. Jones. (7)
QUEEN MARY: Prof. A. T. Hatto, Dr R. N. Combridge, Dr F. M. Fowler, Mrs M. Alexander, Mr C. Stewart. (5)
ROYAL HOLLOWAY: Prof. R. V. Tymms, Dr M. E. Gibbs, Mr D. R. McLintock, Mr P. Prochnik, Dr I. A. White. (5)
UCL: Prof. E. M. Wilkinson, Dr G. P. G. Butler, Mrs J. P. Crick, Mrs I. Frowen, Mr W. H. A. Larrett, Mr T. D. McFarland, Mr C. J. Smith, Dr A. K. Stevens, Mr A. Stillmark. (9)
WESTFIELD: Prof. C. V. Bock, Dr M. Wynn, Mr W. J. Jones, Dr A. Marshall, Miss M.-L.

Lecturers, part-time staff, tutorial students, lectors and the like; as such, the Board represented by far the largest community of Germanists anywhere in the British Isles. Had the University been differently organized, arguably as a monolithic institution, we could probably have operated perfectly satisfactorily with half as many staff and yet have offered a much more wide-ranging set of courses. Balancing this, the apparent over-provision of staff meant that there was better coverage of specialisms, more opportunities for collaboration in special subjects and postgraduate teaching, and a uniquely robust examination system in which candidates were examined by two or three experts with national or international reputations in each field. It is worth recalling that as early as 1963 the then Principal of the University, Sir Douglas Logan, argued that the University had become so large and diffuse that attempts should be made to make it more compact and to reduce its peripheral activities. These are the thoughts that in the 1980s and 1990s would ultimately result in large-scale mergers and relocations of Colleges and institutes, the reshaping of the University and the concomitant abolition of Boards of Studies and other centralized facilities.

Apparently, the Board of Studies in Germanic Languages and Literatures, whose function was to exercise oversight over the provision made for German and Dutch throughout the University, met for the last time on 8 March 1995[18] when it was chaired by Professor David Wells – I am not sure that anyone now has a clear recollection of how exactly it ceased to exist: it just seems to have fizzled out *ohne Sang und Klang*, at the time largely unlamented, as the constituent Colleges increasingly went their own ways, establishing their own curricula and running their own examinations.[19] But why and when

Waldeck, Dr J. J. White. (6)
Total: 55
(Imperial College did not have a full-time Germanist until Mrs (later Professor) Charmian Brinson was appointed in 1979.)

18 The University Archive holds Minutes of the Board of Studies in Germanic Languages and Literatures from 1922 to 1989 and two further folders of signed minutes from 1989 to 1995 (Annex Archive Box 39) and Minutes of the Board of Studies in Romance Languages and Literatures from 1943 to 1994. I am grateful to Ruth Frendo and Jane Howard of the University Archive/Records for help with my questions concerning the Board of Studies.

19 At this time, *c.*1992, degree-giving powers devolved to all Colleges, and from that date also all Colleges received their funding directly from the University Funding Council (rather than as previously through the University of London Court). Regarding the Board's demise, the University Archive catalogue has the following explanatory note: 'In December 1989 and May 1990, following the Academic Council's submission to the Strategic Issues Group, it was recognized that there was a need to make changes to the role and operation of the federal University. As a result, from this time, the process of disbanding the Boards of Studies began. As recommended by the Strategic Issues Group, Federal Faculty Boards (also known as Subject Area Boards) would replace Boards of Studies from 1 September 1994 under the terms of the Statute introduced on that date' (see http://www.ulrls.lon.ac.uk/resources/fullcatalogueAC1-AC8.pdf).

was it established? Given the proliferation of Colleges and Departments, especially once the University changed from being simply an examining and degree-awarding institution and became a teaching body, Boards of Studies had become essential to ensure consistency of policy within each subject area throughout the University. A Board for Modern Languages met for the first time in October 1896, 120 years ago. But before we look at that, let us recall the beginnings of German Studies in the University.

The Beginnings: 1826 to 1900

When University College was founded, it was strongly influenced by Wilhelm von Humboldt's model of a modern German university founded on the ideal of the unity of research and teaching, and hence it is no surprise to find German represented among the first subjects to be taught.[20] Certainly it was in London that the subject first established a firm footing – if 'firm' is the right word: in Carlyle's view, the 'projected London University' was an institution 'which, hanging as it does at the mercy of accidents, and connected with none of the permanent establishments of the country, can scarcely for a long while come to any solid good, nay may very easily, for all that has been done in it, dissolve into smoke, and pass away from the world'.[21] There was no shortage of people in the capital who thought they could teach German or other languages: all the first appointees to Chairs in modern languages were political refugees from abroad: the most notable of them was Antonio Panizzi (1797–1879), Professor of Italian at University College from 1828 to 1838, who later rose to enduring fame as 'the Prince of Librarians' as Principal Librarian of the British Museum.[22] The teaching of German began with Ludwig von Mühlenfels (1793–1861), a son-in-law of Friedrich Schleiermacher, hailing from near Greifswald, who had fought in the Napoleonic Wars, taken a doctorate in Laws at Heidelberg, and, having fallen foul of the Prussian authorities, fled to Stockholm and thence

20 See John L. Flood and Martin Swales, 'Die Förderung der Auslandsgermanistik: Großbritannien als Beispiel', in Peter Alter (ed.), *Spuren in die Zukunft. Der Deutsche Akademische Austauschdienst 1925–2000*, I: *Der DAAD in der Zeit* (Bonn: Deutscher Akademischer Austauschdienst, 2000), pp. 152–63 (p. 154); Kurt Semmelroth, *Die Gründung der Universität London und ihre historischen Voraussetzungen, unter besonderer Berücksichtigung des deutschen Einflusses* (unpublished doctoral thesis, University of Münster, 1937); F. M. L. Thompson (ed.), *The University of London and the World of Learning, 1836–1986* (London: Hambledon Press, 1990).

21 *The Carlyle Letters Online*, IV, pp. 206–08, 15 April 1827, to Nikolaus Heinrich Julius (1783–1862) in connection with the Professorship of Northern Literature.

22 See Edward Miller, *Prince of Librarians: The Life & Times of Antonio Panizzi of the British Museum* (London: André Deutsch, 1967); also P. R. Harris, 'Panizzi, Sir Anthony (1797–1879)', in *ODNB* (http://www.oxforddnb.com/view/article/21231).

Figure 1: Ludwig von Mühlenfels.

to London, intending to go on to join a band of fellow exiles in Mexico. However, he accepted instead the appointment as Professor of German and Northern Languages and Literatures at the new University. His *Introduction to a course of German Literature* (London: University of London, 1830) is an erudite but curious work: it would almost be truer to call it a conspectus of world literature from ancient Egypt and classical antiquity, with particular attention to the German Middle Ages and the Reformation, for despite passing references to Lessing, Goethe, Schiller, Tieck and Schlegel, the real emphasis is on the 'genius' of Luther, approximately forty of the book's 157 pages being devoted to him! Already in his inaugural address at University College in 1828, Mühlenfels spoke of his intention to proceed to an investigation of the German language in the footsteps of Jacob Grimm (1785–1867) and Wilhelm von Humboldt (1767–1835). Grimm had made his mark in 1819 with his *Deutsche Grammatik* (not a German grammar as such, but a comparative grammar of all the old Germanic languages) and with the investigations that he and his brother Wilhelm were making into medieval German literature. The Brothers Grimm, along with other pioneers like Friedrich Heinrich von der Hagen, Georg Friedrich Benecke and Karl Lachmann, laid the foundations for the study of the subject not only in Germany but in other countries, too. There was great enthusiasm for Grimm's work in England – witness the Cambridge Anglo-Saxon scholar John Mitchell Kemble (1807–1857) who studied under Grimm at Göttingen[23] – even though its true significance may have been imperfectly appreciated: thus R. W. Chambers (1874–1942), Professor of English at University College, wrote in 1927: 'Exactly what Grimm's Law means is not always understood. I have been told in an examination paper that "The Early Germanic Tribes decided to shift their consonants at the instigation of a man called Grimm"'.[24] Chambers emphasizes the immense importance of the work in Comparative Philology carried out by 'three great continental scholars, Franz Bopp, Jacob Grimm and Rasmus Rask' and this was fully recognized at University College from an early date.

Mühlenfels may have put down a marker, but he did not stay long – he returned to Germany in 1829 but did not officially resign until August 1831.[25] He entrusted his teaching to his colleague Friedrich August Rosen (1805–1837), Professor of Oriental Languages from 1827 to 1831.[26] Rosen,

23 See Raymond A. Wiley (ed.), *John Mitchell Kemble and Jakob Grimm: A Correspondence 1832–1852: Unpublished Letters of Kemble and Translated Answers of Grimm* (Leiden: Brill, 1971); and *John Mitchell Kemble's Review of Jakob Grimm's 'Deutsche Grammatik'*, preface by Raymond A. Wiley (Binghamton, NY: Center for Medieval and Early Renaissance Studies, State University of New York, 1981). For the reception of Wilhelm von Humboldt in Britain see the forthcoming article by John E. Joseph, 'Wilhelm von Humboldt's Reception in the Anglosphere, 1820–present', *Forum for Modern Language Studies*, 53 (2017), 7–20.

24 R. W. Chambers, *Philologists at University College* (London: University of London Press, 1927), cited by Jethro Bithell, *Advanced German Composition*, 7th edn (London: Methuen, 1949), p. 157. In itself Bithell's book, first published in 1929, essentially an anthology of passages by various authors illustrating aspects of what Bithell calls *Deutschkunde* (p. V), gives a good insight into the range of knowledge of Germany that was expected of advanced students of German in the late 1920s.

25 On Mühlenfels see Martin Herzig, *"Ich hab's gewagt!" Das Leben des Ludwig von Mühlenfels (1793–1861)* (Berlin: Nora, 2009); and Martin Herzig, 'Ludwig von Mühlenfels (1793–1861): Vom Lützower Jäger, Burschenschafter und verfolgten Demagogen zum liberalen 1848er Reichskommissar', in Walter Schmidt (ed.), *Akteure eines Umbruchs. Männer und Frauen der Revolution von 1848*, III (Berlin: Fides, 2010), pp. 463–506. In addition to his aforementioned *Introduction to a Course of German Literature*, his publications include: *An Introductory Lecture on the German and Northern Languages and Literature* (London, 1828; 2nd edn, London, 1829), *Antrittsrede, gehalten auf der Universität zu London am 30. October 1828*, trans. by Carl Heinrich Tamms (Stralsund: Löffler, 1830); and *A Manual of German Literature, Containing Classical Specimens of German Prose and Poetry, systematically arranged* (London: Taylor, 1830).

26 On him see Gregor Pelger, 'Rosen, Friedrich August', in *Neue Deutsche Biographie*, 22 (2005), pp. 50–51. Another German, Theodor Goldstücker (1821–1872) from Königsberg, was Professor of Sanskrit at University College from 1852 to 1872 (see Rosemary Ashton, 'Gottfried Kinkel and University College London', in Peter Alter and Rudolf Muhs (eds), *Exilanten und andere Deutsche in Fontanes London*, Stuttgarter Arbeiten zur Germanistik, 331 (Stuttgart: Heinz; London: IGS, 1996) [= Festschrift for Charlotte Jolles on her 85th birthday], pp. 23–40 (p. 38)).

a friend of Felix Mendelssohn, had studied in Leipzig and Berlin under Franz Bopp (1791–1867). Mühlenfels's official successor was Dr Emanuel Hausmann, in post from 1831–32 to 1835–36.[27] What happened between 1836 and 1851 is not entirely clear (University College records for this period are not complete), but at any rate, according to Negley Harte and John North, historians of University College, Mühlenfels's successors in the Chair of German 'were of little or no consequence for many years'.[28] What we do know is that Hausmann fell ill in 1834, and on 3 October that year the Senate recommended the appointment of a Mr Wittich as a replacement for the session. Hausmann wrote on 22 July 1835 to announce that he would resume his teaching that autumn. But he did not last long: by 12 May 1837 nominations for his successor were being submitted, and on 3 June the Senate recommended to Council that the professorship 'be not at present filled'. It seems that any German teaching offered was done by the aforementioned Mr Wittich who died on 19 February 1848, whereupon, according to the Annual Report for 1849:

> [the] vacancy in the Teachership of German, occasioned by the death of Mr. Wittich, as announced in the last Report, was soon afterwards filled up by the appointment of Dr. Heimann, who during the illness of Mr. Wittich had conducted the studies of the College Class [...]. On this occasion, at the recommendation of the Senate, and in consideration of wishes expressed by the Students to have a course of German Literature, the Council re-established the Professorship of German Language and Literature.

Although Wittich appears in the College records only as 'Teacher' of German, he called himself 'Professor of German at University College, London' in several of the publications under his name, Wilhelm Wittich, which survive in the British Library and elsewhere.[29] As for his successor, Dr Adolph Heimann

27 The only publication I have traced by Emanuel Hausmann is: *Der Mensch und das Leben: Ein kleines Gedicht, in drei Gesängen* (London: D. Nutt, 1854) (copy in the National Art Library, V&A Museum, London). Possibly he was the Emanuel Hausmann who had a brother Joseph (b. *c.*1791) who also moved to England; their father was Löbel Ascher Hausmann (1770–1830) of Ratibor, Silesia.

28 Harte and North, *The World of University College London 1828–1978*, p. 39.

29 These include: *German for Beginners, or Progressive Exercises in the German Language* (London: J. Taylor, 1835); 'The Seminary for schoolmasters at Königsberg in Prussia', *The Quarterly Journal of Education*, no. XX (1836); *A Key to German for Beginners* (London, 1842); *A Lexicon to Homer ... containing all the words in the Iliad and Odyssey* (London: Simpkin, Marshall & Co., 1843); *A German Grammar*, 2nd edn (London, 1847; 3rd edn 1851); *A Visit to the Western Coast of Norway* (London, 1848); *German Tales for Beginners*, 7th edn revised and corrected (London: D. Nutt, 1855; 28th edn 1887). According to entries in COPAC, Wittich's dates were 1782–1848, but it is quite evident that there has been some confusion over authors of the same name, so it is possible that he may not have been born in 1782.

(1808–1874), who took a doctorate at Berlin in 1833 with a thesis entitled *De Thycididis orationibus*, he arrived in London in 1837 and taught at University College School, then located in Gower Street, from 1841. He was appointed Professor at University College on 13 May 1848. While he described himself rather grandly as 'PhD Professor of the German language and literature in University College, London' on the title page of his *Materials for Translating from English into German* (London, 1851), his salary was so meagre (probably around £60 a year deriving exclusively from the fees paid by students attending his classes) that he and his wife Amelia, a close friend of Christina Rossetti's, rented a large house on the south side of Gordon Square with nine bedrooms so that they could take in student lodgers to supplement their income. In fact, Heimann had also been teaching at Bedford College since 1849, remaining on the staff there until 1868 when he and his French colleague Adolphe Ragon (d. 1892?) were both dismissed 'for poor teaching'.[30] At this point, apparently to make good the loss of salary, Heimann formed a plan to open his own college, Gordon College, in his house, a plan thwarted by his landlord, William Russell, 8th Duke of Bedford, on the grounds that it would lower the tone of the area 'by bringing houses down from the private to the professional rank'.[31] Heimann seems to have hung on at University College until his death in 1874. He was the author of *An Introduction to the study of German Authors. A reading-book in prose and verse ... with notes especially etymological* (1862), *Declension of German Substantives* (1860), and various other elementary materials.[32] He also contributed to the second edition of J. G. Flügel's *A complete Dictionary of the English and German and German and English Languages ...* (1838), and in 1871 published another version of Flügel's dictionary as *Complete Dictionary of the German and English Languages: in Two Parts: namely English–German and German–English, adapted to the English student with great additions and improvements*, by C. A. Feiling,[33] A. Heimann and John Oxenford – Oxenford (1812–1877) is remembered as a translator of Goethe's *Dichtung und Wahrheit* (1846) and Eckermann's conversations with Goethe.[34] Heimann's

30 On Heimann and Ragon's dismissal see Peter Armour, 'Italian', in J. Mordaunt Crook (ed.), *Bedford College, University of London: memories of 150 years* (London: Royal Holloway and Bedford New College, 2001), pp. 227–42 (p. 228); also alluded to in Eva Jacobs, 'French', ibid., pp. 109–30 (p. 110), and Patricia Howe, 'German', ibid., pp. 181–200 (p. 182).

31 Letter of William Michael Rossetti to Adolf Heimann, 28 August 1868, in Antony H. Harrison (ed.), *The Letters of Christina Rossetti* (London and Charlottesville, 1997–2004), I, p. 314 note; cited by Ashton, 'Germans in Bloomsbury'.

32 After Heimann's death his children established a silver medal in his memory to be awarded annually to the best student in the Senior Class (UCL Calendar 1876–77, p. 24).

33 C. A. Feiling published *Tales From the German, Comprising Specimens From the Most Celebrated Authors* (London: Chapman and Hall, 1844).

34 John Oxenford (ed.), *Conversations of Goethe with Eckermann and Soret*, new edn (London: G. Bell and Sons, 1875). See also *The Autobiography of Johann Wolfgang von*

successor at University College was Friedrich Althaus (1829–1897), who had taken a doctorate at Berlin with a thesis entitled *De historiae conscriptionis historia* in 1852. He held the Chair of German from 1874–75 to 1897. Of him, Rosemary Ashton has said that he 'achieved the most permanent and respectable professional position' of all the post-1848 exiles in London.[35] While that may well be the case, his successor (as we shall see) complained bitterly about how he left the teaching of German at the College in complete disarray. Althaus published *Englische Charakterbilder* (Berlin, 1869), sketches of such notable political and literary figures as Palmerston, Cobden, Disraeli, Carlyle, Thackeray and others. He also translated into German John Forster, *Charles Dickens' Leben* (3 vols, Berlin, 1872–75, repr. Berlin, 2014), and completed Josef Neuberg's translation of Thomas Carlyle, *Geschichte Friedrichs II. von Preußen, genannt Friedrich der Große* (Berlin, 1869).

Whilst it is difficult to form much of an impression of the personalities of these early professors at University College, we are perhaps a little better placed with their colleagues at King's, even though we must regret that Franz Grillparzer was not inclined to record his impressions of the first professor here when he had an opportunity to meet him in 1836. On 31 May Grillparzer went to a performance of *The Thieving Magpie* at Covent Garden. Waiting for the opera to begin, he made the acquaintance of two Viennese ladies. Thrilled to meet the eminent dramatist, they entreated him to allow them to introduce him to a 'Professor der deutschen Sprache am King's College [...], der mir u.s.w.'. Grillparzer, possibly because he did not wish to be found associating with German-speaking emigrés in London, availed himself of the opportunity afforded by the rapturous ovations at the end of the opera to make good his escape. He had in any case not been feeling well, and was thirsty, so he went to drink a glass of ginger-beer, 'was mich erquickte, und mir sehr wohl bekam. Will dieses Zeug zu meinem Getränke machen'.[36]

The man Grillparzer missed meeting, the first Professor of German at King's College, was Adolphus Bernays, born at Mainz in 1794, a nephew of Isaak Bernays (1792–1849), Chief Rabbi of Hamburg, and a cousin of the celebrated classicist Jakob Bernays (1824–1881) and the Germanist Michael Bernays (1834–1897), and a relation of Heinrich Heine. Bernays was much

---

Goethe: (Dichtung und Wahrheit), translated by John Oxenford, introduction by Gregor Sebba (London: Sidgwick and Jackson, 1971).

35 Rosemary Ashton, *Little Germany: Exile and Asylum in Victorian England* (Oxford: OUP, 1986), p. 187.

36 Franz Grillparzer, *Sämtliche Werke*, ed. by Peter Frank and Karl Pörnbacher, IV (Munich: Hanser, 1965), p. 608. The editors unfortunately confuse King's College London with King's College Cambridge.

more committed than Mühlenfels: he was in post from 1831 to 1863.[37] Around 1850 he also taught at Queen's College in Harley Street, an institution founded in 1847 by his controversial colleague at King's, Frederick Denison Maurice (1805–1872), intended initially for governesses but quickly made accessible to all women and girls who could pay the fees. Like Mühlenfels, Bernays was an admirer of Jacob Grimm. Though he was essentially concerned with teaching practical German, in his introductory lecture at King's we find him beginning with an account of medieval literature, introducing his audience to the Minnesingers and the Mastersingers, Sebastian Brant's *Narrenschiff* and Hans Sachs. He has effusive praise for Luther as 'the Dante of the German language'. To what extent medieval or early modern literature figured on the curriculum at King's or indeed at University College in the remainder of the nineteenth century is not known – one suspects that they played a very minor role, though lectures on medieval German epics were certainly on offer at King's in 1895, and it is evident that the German curriculum at British universities tended in general to follow what was deemed to be good practice at German universities. This is not surprising given that German was firmly in the hands of native German-speakers until the First World War.[38]

A remarkable thing about the early professors of German at King's is the length of time they served: Bernays from 1831 to 1863, Carl Adolf Buchheim from 1863 to 1900, Henry Gibson Atkins from 1900 to 1937, and Frederick

37 On Bernays see John L. Flood, 'Ginger beer and sugared cauliflower. Adolphus Bernays and language teaching in nineteenth-century London', in Rüdiger Görner and Helen Kelly-Holmes (eds), *Vermittlungen. German Studies at the Turn of the Century. Deutschlandstudien an der Jahrhundertwende. Festschrift für Nigel B. R. Reeves* (Munich: iudicium 1999), pp. 101–15; also John L. Flood, 'Bernays, Adolphus (1794–1864)', *ODNB* (http://www.oxforddnb.com/view/article/61615). Bernays's second son, Leopold John (1820–1882), is remembered as one of the earliest English translators of part two of Goethe's *Faust* (1839; now in the William A. Speck collection at Yale University); he became rector of St John's Church, Stanmore, Middlesex, from 1860 to 1882. Bernays Gardens, close by the church, commemorate Leopold and his son Stewart (1866–1941), who was also rector there. Another of Adolphus's sons, Albert James Bernays (1823–1892), who studied under Carl Remigius Fresenius and Justus Liebig at Gießen, was a distinguished chemist at St Thomas's Hospital in London; he took a great interest in social aspects of medicine and hygiene and gave more than a thousand free public lectures during his lifetime (see *ODNB*, http://www.oxforddnb.com/view/article/2254). Another son, Lewis Adolphus Bernays (1831–1908), served as clerk to the Legislative Assembly of Queensland, Australia, from 1860 until his death. Yet another distinguished relative, Edward Bernays (1891–1995), a great-grandson of the Hamburg rabbi and a nephew of Sigmund Freud, is credited with being a pioneer of public relations; his book *Crystallizing Public Opinion* (New York: Boni & Liveright, 1923) exerted a strong influence on Joseph Goebbels.

38 On the early history of German Studies in Britain see Michael S. Batts, 'Die englische Germanistik um 1896 – eine importierte oder eine bodenständige Disziplin?', in Frank Fürbeth et al. (eds), *Zur Geschichte und Problematik der Nationalphilologien in Europa. 150 Jahre Erste Germanistenversammlung in Frankfurt am Main (1846–1996)* (Tübingen: Niemeyer, 1999), pp. 379–88.

Figure 2: Bernhard Höfling's portrait of Gottfried Kinkel.

Norman from 1937 to 1965 – just four people in 135 years. In the same period University College had nine: Ludwig von Mühlenfels, Emanuel Hausmann, Wilhelm Wittich, Adolph Heimann, Friedrich Althaus, Robert Priebsch, Leonard Ashley Willoughby, Leonard Wilson Forster, and Elizabeth Mary Wilkinson.

There was fierce competition to succeed Bernays at King's: among the thirteen candidates were the theologian, art and literary historian Gottfried Kinkel (1815–1882), the journalist and teacher Eugene Oswald (1826–1912)[39] and the historian Adolphus Ward (1837–1924)[40] – these last two played an influential role in the early years of the English Goethe Society (founded in 1886). The appointments committee considered:

39 Oswald was one of the founder members of the English Goethe Society, and his daughter, Ella Oswald, played a role in the Society right down to her death, aged 94, in 1965. On him see John L. Flood, '"A Man of Singularly Wide Experience of Affairs": Eugene Oswald as Writer and Journalist', in Peter Alter and Rudolf Muhs (eds), *Exilanten und andere Deutsche in Fontanes London*, Stuttgarter Arbeiten zur Germanistik, 331 (Stuttgart: Heinz; London: IGS, 1996), pp. 77–100; and John L. Flood, 'Oswald, Eugene', *ODNB* (http://www.oxforddnb.com/view/article/61618).

40 Sir Adolphus Ward was appointed Professor of History and English Literature at Owens College, Manchester, in 1866 and later became Vice-Chancellor of the Victoria University of Manchester.

> that amongst these candidates Dr Kinkel stands pre-eminent in literary distinction, that he has already secured the highest reputation both at home and abroad as a scholar and a teacher, and that on almost every ground his election would add greatly to the reputation of the college. The only reason that the committee have for not recommending him is that his name seems to be universally connected with all that is most ultra-liberal both in politics and religion in Germany, and although the committee are far from believing that he would introduce into his professional work anything opposed to the religious teaching of the college [...] yet they entertain fears [...] as to the wisdom of electing to this professorship one who is looked upon with considerable suspicion by all who know them [*sic*].[41]

Understandably, they were right to be cautious. Kinkel's involvement in the 1848 revolution had led to his imprisonment at Spandau, from which he escaped in November 1850 and arrived in London in December. After a few months in America trying to raise funds in support of his political aims, he had returned to London in March 1852 and was appointed Professor of Literature at Hyde Park College and then at Bedford College which had been founded in 1849 for the education of women. Little is known of his academic activities in these institutions apart from the fact that he taught art history, Roman history, and geography at Bedford College, but Kinkel certainly tried to make his mark: he was runner-up for the position of Professor of English Grammar and Literature at University College in 1852; he lectured on art in South Kensington, in 1859 he founded the German newspaper *Hermann: Deutsches Wochenblatt aus London*, which existed until 1914, co-founded the Deutscher Verein für Kunst und Wissenschaft[42] in 1864, and he gave a

41 F. J. C. Hearnshaw, *The Centenary History of King's College, London, 1828–1928* (London: Harrap, 1929), p. 249.

42 Among the co-founders of the Deutscher Verein für Kunst und Wissenschaft, also known as the 'German Athenaeum', were Karl Heinrich Schaible (1824–1899), Karl Adolf Buchheim, Adolph Heimann, Theodor Goldstücker, and G. W. Leitner, Professor of Arabic at King's College (see Derek Glass, 'From Moravia to the Strand: The Career of Karl Adolf Buchheim', in Peter Alter and Rudolf Muhs (eds), *Exilanten und andere Deutsche in Fontanes London*, pp. 41–76 (p. 64)). It was a social organization for select members of the large German community in London, attracting German-speaking artists and scholars, the wealthy and well-connected: the majority of its 590 members in 1910 were bankers, stockbrokers, lawyers, merchants, physicians, engineers and industrialists, with a sprinkling of musicians, writers and teachers. The annual subscription was six guineas (£6.30), no mean sum in 1910 (when, for instance, a teacher might earn £175 p.a.). Among the members were Karl Breul and Hermann Fiedler, respectively professors of German at Cambridge and Oxford, as well as the London Germanist Dr Julius Steppat, and Henry Tresawna Gerrans (1858–1921), Fellow of Worcester College, Oxford, who, though a mathematician, was a keen supporter of German (in his will, he established a Gerrans Fund at the University of Oxford for the promotion of the study of the German Language and Literature). There was precious little overlap between the membership of the 'German Athenaeum' and the London branch of the Allgemeiner Deutscher Sprachverein (whose annual subscription

celebrated lecture at the Crystal Palace on 10 November 1859 to mark the centenary of Schiller's birth. Kinkel is also remembered as having funded the (ultimately unsuccessful) defence of Franz Müller at the Old Bailey in 1864 – Müller, a German immigrant, was charged and hanged for committing the first murder on the railway in Britain. (Müller fled to America on a sailing ship but found Scotland Yard waiting for him on his arrival in New York, the policeman having travelled by faster steamship.)[43]

Instead of Kinkel, King's appointed Karl Adolf Buchheim, anglicized as Carl Adolphus Buchheim, who was another post-1848 refugee – in September the Vienna police had issued a warrant for his arrest on charges of 'Aufwieglung der Volksmassen und Vereinigung gewaltsamer Mittel zum aggressiven Widerstande gegen die Executivgewalt des Staates'.[44] When applying for the

---

was only five shillings (25p)): Breul and Fiedler were members of both organizations, as were the banker Hermann Meyer, who had joined the 'German Athenaeum' in 1885, and Friedrich Wilhelm Hugo Bartels, the first secretary of the London branch of the ADS, who is described in the Athenaeum's membership list as 'Schriftsteller'. In 1902 the club was located at 93 Mortimer Street and later, by 1908, at 19 Stratford Place, on the north side of Oxford Street, where John Lewis now is. Documentation relating to the 'German Athenaeum' is thin. There is a short article on it by Dr H. Borns, in *Die deutsche Kolonie in England*, ed. by Richard Pflaum et al. (London: Anglo-German Publishing Co., 1913), pp. 54–61, and the British Library possesses one issue of its annual report: *Jahresbericht des Deutschen Vereins für Kunst und Wissenschaft in London 1910* (London, 1911). The 'Athenaeum' closed down voluntarily on 24 October 1914 (*The Times*, 26 October 1914, p. 10) and was formally struck off the police register (*The Times*, 11 November 1914, p. 11). Newspapers of the period make occasional mention of it and its activities. See also John L. Flood, 'The London Branch of the Allgemeiner Deutscher Sprachverein', in *'Proper Words in Proper Places'. Studies in Lexicology and Lexicography in honour of William Jervis Jones*, ed. by Máire C. Davies et al. (Stuttgart: Heinz; London: IGS, 2001), pp. 230–53. The 'German Athenaeum' is just one of a number of associations of various kinds for Germans in London before the First World War, most of which still await their historians. The best known of them was perhaps the Deutscher Turnverein, established in 1861, which had premises (now the German Gymnasium Restaurant) at 26 Pancras Road, London NW1, where gymnastics were arranged on four nights a week, as well as fencing and boxing; they also had a library. Other groups included the Verband deutscher Barbier- und Friseur-Gehülfen Londons and the Deutscher Radfahrer-Verein whose members regularly rode out to the King's Oak Hotel at High Beech in Epping Forest, owned in 1904 by a Herr Gumprecht. More political was the All-Deutscher Verband, meeting at Seyd's Hotel, a favourite venue of many German groups, in Finsbury Square.

43 On Kinkel see Ashton, 'Gottfried Kinkel and University College London'; also Otto Maußer, 'Kinkel, Gottfried', in *Allgemeine Deutsche Biographie*, 55 (1910), pp. 515–28; Edith Ennen, 'Kinkel, Gottfried', *Neue Deutsche Biographie*, 11 (1977), pp. 623–24; Wolfgang Beyrodt, *Gottfried Kinkel als Kunsthistoriker* (Bonn: Röhrscheid, 1979); Hermann Rösch-Sondermann, *Gottfried Kinkel als Aesthetiker, Politiker und Dichter* (Bonn: Röhrscheid, 1982). On the London Schiller celebrations see Hermann Rösch, 'Die Londoner Schillerfeier 1859', *Zeitschrift für deutsche Philologie*, 115 (1996), 94–111; Thorsten Logge, *Zur medialen Konstruktion des Nationalen. Die Schillerfeiern 1859 in Europa und Nordamerika* (Göttingen: V&R Unipress, 2014).

44 On the warrant see Glass, 'From Moravia to the Strand', p. 53. The following account

Figure 3: C. A. Buchheim.

post he supplied testimonials from the political activist Arnold Ruge (1802–1880)[45] then living in exile in Brighton, the comparative philologist Max Müller (1823–1900), who had been appointed Taylor Professor of Modern Languages at Oxford in 1854, and no less a person than Jacob Grimm, and in 1862 he had already published a widely praised edition of Schiller's *Wallenstein* trilogy. Buchheim was born near Brno in Moravia on 24 January 1822 though he also claimed to have been born on 22 January 1828. Fleeing from the Austrian authorities on account of his republican sympathies and

---

of Buchheim's activities is heavily dependent on Glass's excellent study. On Buchheim's application to King's see Hearnshaw, *The Centenary History of King's College, London, 1828–1928*, p. 312.

45 Ruge had founded the short-lived 'Agitation Union' in 1851 to which some of the squabbling refugees belonged. Buchheim and Eugene Oswald served as its secretaries in 1863 (Flood, '"A Man of Singularly Wide Experience of Affairs"', p. 90). See also Christine Lattek, *Revolutionary Refugees: German Socialism in Britain, 1840–1860* (London: Routledge, 2006).

activities, he seems to have arrived in England early in 1852. Very soon – despite having had as yet relatively little exposure to English – he published a translation of Dickens's *Hard Times*, *Schwere Zeiten* (Stuttgart: Hoffmann, 1855), under the pseudonym of Adolf Banner. For several years Buchheim taught at a variety of institutions, including Clapham Grammar School and even as Lecturer in Modern and Ancient Languages at the London and Middlesex Hospitals, as well as for five years at Bedford College, before being appointed at King's, having made up for his lack of formal qualifications by obtaining a doctorate *in absentia* from the University of Rostock on 3 June 1862 with a dissertation on Francis Bacon's *Novum organum*.[46] His inaugural lecture at King's was entitled *German Grammar: Past and Present* (London: Bell & Daldy, 1863; copy in the British Library). His teaching duties were not onerous – the advertisement for the post specified that the 'hours of attendance are from 3.15 to 4.45 on Tuesday and Friday', so theoretically he would have had plenty of time for other activities. He published prolifically, most notably with the thirteen volumes in his 'German Classics' series, issued by the Clarendon Press at Oxford, launched in 1868 with *Egmont*. In the main he focused on editions of Lessing, Goethe, Schiller and Heine, but also published a selection of the writings of Alexander von Humboldt. This work was underpinned by his belief that it was only by careful study of the German classics that German could become both a moral and an intellectual medium for the training of the mind. His greatest successes were his anthologies *Deutsche Lyrik* (London: Macmillan, 1875) which was allegedly quoted even in Indian newspapers, while his *Balladen und Romanzen* (1891) was reviewed in the *New York Times*. Together with Dr Henry Wace, Principal of King's, he also published *First Principles of the Reformation* (1883) and *Luther's Primary Works* (1896). His *The First Part of Goethe's Faust together with the prose translation, notes and appendices of ... A. Hayward ...* Revised with introduction by C. A. Buchheim (1892), I seem to remember was still being used by my own German master at school when we were reading *Faust* in the mid-1950s. Altogether, it is worth noting that Karl Breul (1860–1932), (later) Schröder Professor of German at Cambridge, praised Buchheim as the 'most successful exponent of German literature in this country' in the second half of the nineteenth century,[47] and as to his temperament, a colleague at King's testified to 'the amiability, soundness and conciliatoriness of his character as well as his power of maintaining discipline'.[48] Buchheim died on 7 June 1900, a few months after having been awarded the Order of the Red

46 Glass, 'From Moravia to the Strand', pp. 72–73. There is no evidence that he took a doctorate in Vienna as a young man, as claimed in Wikipedia.

47 Karl Breul, 'Karl Adolf Buchheim', *The Modern Language Quarterly*, 3, 1 (July 1900), 1–4 (p. 1).

48 Thus G. W. Leitner, cited by Glass, in 'From Moravia to the Strand', p. 44.

Eagle of Prussia for his services to the cause of German culture in Britain. His daughter, Emma Sophia Buchheim (*c.*1861–1951), also taught at King's, initially in the 'Department for Ladies' from 1895, but then as Lecturer from 1909 until 1930.[49]

Let us leave University College and King's aside for a moment and see what else was going on in the University. Bedford College had been founded in 1849, and German was taught there by Adolph Heimann, whom we have already met as Professor at University College, at least from 1856 to 1868. Who, if anyone, followed him is not clear. The next person I know of there was Dr Albert Wilhelm Schüddekopf (1861–1916), who had studied at Göttingen, taking a doctorate on *Sprache und Dialekt des mittelenglischen Gedichtes William of Palerne. Ein Beitrag zur mittelenglischen Grammatik* (Erlangen, 1886). He was Professor of German at Bedford from 1888 to 1890.[50] Later on, until J. G. Robertson arrived in the summer of 1903, Robert Priebsch also taught at Bedford College for five hours a week from the summer of 1899. Student numbers were small: at Bedford in 1856–57 only three students took German in their first term, but by 1859–60 there were fifteen. Pat Howe has a wonderful anecdote about Ida Samuel, a student at Bedford from 1897 to 1901, who was the only student taking German there with Walter Rippmann (1869–1947): 'Although the system of chaperons in omnibuses had at that time almost died out, my mother was very doubtful whether I should have

49 Her publications include: *German Poetry for Beginners* (Oxford: Clarendon, 1889), *Short German Plays for Reading and Acting* (Oxford: Clarendon, 1895); and an edition of Niebuhr's *Griechische Heroen-Geschichten* (Oxford: Clarendon, 1886). For further details see Glass, 'From Moravia to the Strand', p. 71, n. 69.

50 According to Batts, 'Die englische Germanistik um 1896', p. 385, Schüddekopf also taught at Manchester, but this is incorrect: the Henry Simon Chair of German there was held from 1895 to 1930 by Arvid Johannson (see Eda Sagarra and Peter Skrine, *The Department of German at the Victoria University of Manchester, A Brief History 1895–1996* (Manchester: University of Manchester, 1996)). Schüddekopf became a naturalized British Subject on 3 May 1912; he died on 11 September 1916 of a stroke, probably brought on by the stress of having been suspended from his duties as Professor of German at Leeds after the MP for York had cast doubt on his commitment to Britain since he had allegedly not wanted his son, in the Territorial Army, to be required to fight Germans abroad. (Whether this son was the Leeds surgeon Walter George Adolphus Schüddekopf who changed his name by deed poll to Shuttleworth in December 1919 (see *The London Gazette*, 12 December 1919, p. 15527), I do not know but it seems likely.) For obituaries for Schüddekopf see *The Times*, 13 September 1916, p. 11; *Yorkshire Post*, 12 September 1916, p. 4. A Leeds student publication, *Gryphon*, 20: 1 (October 1916), p. 15, gave a warm appreciation of his work. Amongst other things, he is credited with persuading the Leeds Senate to permit students to spend some time abroad as part of their course, the first university to do so. He was presumably a relative of Carl Schüddekopf (1861–1917) who spent the years 1886–89 as tutor in London and researching in the British Museum library on behalf of German scholars before returning to Germany where he became librarian to Prince Stolberg and, from 1896 to 1912, worked at the Goethe- und Schiller-Archiv at Weimar. See Christoph König (ed.), *Internationales Germanistenlexikon 1800–1950* (Berlin: de Gruyter, 2003), III, 1670–72.

lessons alone with Mr Rippmann'[51] – I suppose the tutor's name cannot have allayed the mother's fears since it was only relatively recently – 1888 – that Jack the Ripper had been carrying out his nefarious business of murdering young women, a crime then (as now) still unsolved.

At the end of the nineteenth century, then, German was taught at University College, King's and Bedford. By and large it may be said that the nineteenth-century professors were chiefly concerned with fairly elementary teaching of the German language and literature. For instance, Heimann, at University College, outlined what 'a proficient scholar in German' ought to be able to do thus: 'to explain the structure of the language; to read a German book; to speak with some fluency; and to write a letter, or to translate a part of an English book into German without the assistance of Dictionary and Grammar. The greatest number of pupils master the first three points, but very few succeed in the last.'[52] I cannot discern any significant differences between these early teachers' respective approaches to their subject. In essence, they devoted their attention to the major recent writers: Lessing, Goethe, Schiller, Heine; but did not eschew study of medieval and early modern literature, and were interested in philology. But above all they tried to ensure that their students acquired a practical command of German. I have not fully investigated the development of German as a subject in the University, but it is apparent that during the course of the nineteenth century it came to be offered at three levels: Matriculation, the examination consisting of grammar and passages for translation; Intermediate, with a more advanced exam of a similar kind; and Honours, involving translation from and into German, grammar, historical grammar and versification, general outlines of literature, with the study of prescribed texts from Old High German onwards (in 1896 including Lessing, Lenau and Geibel), dictation, and a *viva voce* exam. By the end of the century, it became apparent that teaching in the various Colleges needed to be co-ordinated to ensure effective teaching and parity of standards. To achieve this, the University established a Board of Studies in Modern Languages. It met for the first time on 20 October 1896.

'The Age of Giants': 1900 to 1930

At the turn of the century the number of teaching staff for German was small. Even in 1902–03 there were two University Professors (Robert Priebsch

51 Patricia Howe, 'German', p. 183. On Rippmann see Nicola McLelland, 'Ripman , Walter', in *ODNB*, http://www.oxforddnb.com/view/article/105009.

52 Adolph Heimann, *Materials for Translating from English into German*, preface April 1851, cited from the 9th edn (London: Nutt, 1889) by Nicola McLelland, *German through English Eyes. A History of Language Teaching and Learning in Britain 1500–2000* (Wiesbaden: Harrassowitz, 2015), p. 363.

teaching primarily at University College, and J. G. Robertson, teaching at Bedford and University College), three Readers (one was H. G. Atkins at King's; another was Dr R. A. Williams, working under Priebsch;[53] the third I have not identified[54]), and one assistant. Yet this was an important time, for the arrival of Priebsch and Robertson marked the beginning of true scholarly activity. Arguably, the period from about 1900 to the 1930s marked the high point of German Studies in London. My predecessor at the Institute, Maurice Walshe (1911–1998), who had graduated at University College in 1933, used to tell his students in a self-deprecating way that, unlike them, he had been 'taught by giants', a contrast which, according to Pat Howe, 'some viewed with scepticism and others with relief'.[55] By 'giants' Walshe must have meant Priebsch and Robertson, and their pupils and successors Leonard Willoughby, Edna Purdie and Frederick Norman under whom he had studied in the 1930s.

A real milestone in the development of our subject in London was the appointment of Robert Priebsch at University College in 1898.[56] Born in 1866, the son of the director of a silk-weaving business, he hailed from Tannwald in Bohemia. Unlike some of his predecessors in London, he was not a political exile. Priebsch had an outstanding academic pedigree: he had been taught by Johann Kelle and August Sauer at Prague, Friedrich Paulsen, Erich Schmidt, Edward Schröder and Heinrich von Treitschke at Leipzig, Anton E. Schönbach and the Wieland scholar Bernhard Seuffert at Graz, and the English specialist Bernhard ten Brink at Strasbourg, and he was a close associate of Elias von Steinmeyer (1848–1922) in Erlangen with whom he corresponded regularly for some thirty years.[57] He originally came to Britain

53 Robert Allan Williams (1876–1951) is mentioned by Priebsch in a letter dated 2 February 1903 as a pupil of Eduard Sievers and former Lektor for English at Halle, 'ein sehr netter, ernster Mann' (August Closs (ed.), *Robert Priebsch, Elias von Steinmeyer: Briefwechsel* (Berlin: Erich Schmidt, 1979), p. 114). He would be elected Schröder Professor of German at Cambridge in 1932.

54 I had thought this might have been Wilfrid Perrett (1873–1946), but he appears as Reader at UC only from 1907 to 1934. On 21 February 1903, Priebsch wrote of the possibility of having a fourth Reader (instead of a second Professor) specializing in Modern Literature, and asked Steinmeyer's opinion on the suitability of Eugen Wolff (1863–1929): 'Er scheint nicht übel Lust zu haben, hierher zu kommen' (Closs (ed.), *Robert Priebsch, Elias von Steinmeyer: Briefwechsel*, p. 116). In the event, Wolff got a chair at Kiel in 1904.

55 Howe, 'German', p. 196.

56 Further details in John L. Flood, 'Priebsch, Robert', *ODNB*, http://www.oxforddnb.com/view/article/98340.

57 A selection of their letters [see note 53 above], which are highly illuminating about academic life in Britain and revelatory about both correspondents' utter devotion to scholarship, was edited by Priebsch's son-in-law August Closs. In 1929 Closs, who had arrived in Britain in 1924, had joined Leonard Willoughby's department as Assistant Lecturer at the University of Sheffield (Gerald Newton, *German Studies at the University of Sheffield. An Historical Perspective, 1880–1988, together with a graduate list, 1910–1988* (Sheffield, 1988), p. 19).

Figure 4: Robert Priebsch.

in the 1890s to examine and catalogue German medieval manuscripts in public and private collections, including those of Lord Ashburnham at Ashburnham Place, Sussex, Sir Thomas Phillipps ('Bibliotheca Phillippica' at Cheltenham), and the Earl of Crawford ('Bibliotheca Lindesiana' at Haigh Hall, Wigan). The result was his *Deutsche Handschriften in England* (Erlangen: Junge, 1896–1901; repr. 1979) which, together with a series of articles on German manuscripts in the Royal Library at Brussels, cemented his reputation as one of the foremost palaeographers of his generation. Perhaps the most important of his many books was his study of Cotton manuscript Caligula A.vii of the Old Saxon Biblical poem *Heliand* (1925) in the British Museum (now the British Library), but, insofar as Priebsch's name is now remembered at all, he is probably best known for *The German Language* (London: Faber and Faber, 1934; 6th revised edn, 1966), co-authored with his former pupil W. E. Collinson. Prior to coming to London, Priebsch had – notwithstanding his dire command of English – been appointed Lecturer in Anglo-Saxon at Liverpool in 1896.[58] Already here he started implementing

58 With Priebsch's support, his pupil W. E. Collinson (1889–1969), his collaborator on *The German Language*, described by Margaret Richey who studied together with him in

reforms. Thus already on 1 November 1896 he reported to Steinmeyer his delight at the fact that the Senate of the Victoria University[59] had agreed to establish a separate Faculty of Arts:

> Ich freue mich über diesen Beschluß. Nun wird sich manches (nach continentalem Muster) bei uns leichter durchsetzen lassen. Ich habe jetzt auch eine Zuhörerin, die wie sie mir sagte, A[n]g[el]s[ächsisch] aus Interesse an der Sache selbst betreiben will und nicht für ein Examen. Das ist ungewöhnlich und mir sehr sympathisch. Es wird noch manchen Kampf kosten, aber wenn ich hier bleibe, hoffe ich doch das Studium der e[n]gl[ischen] Sprache auf eine höhere u. mehr wissenschaftliche Stufe heben zu können.[60]

Indeed, on 12 January 1897, he was able to tell Steinmeyer that he had more than fifty students in his lectures on 'An Introduction to the History of the English Language' and that this gave him good practice in lecturing in English.[61] From a later letter, of 13 February 1898, we learn two interesting things: first, that he was aware of the possibility of a post at University College London (whether he had been invited to apply or simply happened to have heard about it is not clear; in any case, he did not find the prospect particularly appealing), and secondly that he was making progress with his plans to reform the study of the history of the English language, notwithstanding the resistance of the Board of Studies in Liverpool:

> Wie's mit der Londoner Stellung werden wird, weiß ich noch durchaus nicht. Ausgeschrieben ist sie noch nicht u. was man so unter Hand darüber hört, lautet nicht sehr verlockend. Im übrigen habe ich mich inzwischen hier eingelebt und finde ein ersprießliches Feld der Thätigkeit vor mir. Ich hoffe, daß ich im stande sein werde, gewisse Reformen den Unterricht im Alt- [und] Mittele[n]gl[ischen] betreffend durchzuführen, obgleich ich mich auf lebhaften Widerstand von Seite des "Board of Studies", zu dem die Professoren u. Lecturer der 3 Colleges gehören, welche die Victoria-University bilden, gefaßt machen muß.[62]

1908–09 as a 'brilliant and mature-minded young man' with 'a zeal for unremitting hard work', was appointed Assistant Lecturer at Liverpool. He was promoted on 9 July 1914 from Assistant Lecturer to full Professor, succeeding Robert Petsch (1875–1945) who had taught there since 1911. Petsch went to an appointment at Posen (Poznań), before moving to Hamburg in 1919. Collinson was elected a Fellow of University College in 1916.

59 The 'Victoria University' was a short-lived arrangement for a federal university in the north of England. Established by Royal Charter in 1880, it eventually comprised Owens College, Manchester, University College Liverpool, and Yorkshire College, Leeds. Liverpool seceded in 1903 and Leeds in 1904 to become independent city universities, leaving Manchester to be granted a new charter as the Victoria University of Manchester.

60 Closs (ed.), *Robert Priebsch, Elias von Steinmeyer: Briefwechsel*, p. 45.

61 Closs (ed.), *Robert Priebsch, Elias von Steinmeyer: Briefwechsel*, p. 47.

62 Closs (ed.), *Robert Priebsch, Elias von Steinmeyer: Briefwechsel*, p. 54.

By the time Priebsch wrote to Steinmeyer on 19 August 1898 two life-changing events had befallen him. The first was that he had got married; the second that he had been appointed to University College as from October 1898. He noted:

> Als die Stellung ausgeschrieben wurde, waren die Bedingungen sehr ungünstig; aber seitdem ist man mir sehr entgegengekommen, so daß ich voraussichtlich den Tausch nicht zu bereuen haben werde. [...] Ich freue mich nun wieder das geliebte British Museum zur Verfügung zu haben.[63]

His next letter to Steinmeyer is particularly informative. Dated 23 October 1898, it tells how he has set up house in Harlesden, and then gives an extensive account of the situation he found himself confronted with at University College following the demise of Professor Althaus:

> Mein Vorgänger Prof. Althaus hat leider das Studium der "Deutschen Sprache u. Literatur" am College sehr ins Arge gebracht u. es wird wohl ein Jahr darüber hinweggehen, ehe man's wieder zu frischerem Leben bringen kann. Doch ist es mir gelungen, ein Colleg für Alt- u. Mhd. zustande zu bringen, der erste Versuch dieser Art am College. Dies ist von großer Wichtigkeit, besonders angesichts der zu gründenden "University of London". Sie wissen wahrscheinlich, daß an Stelle der bisherigen "London University", die nur ein examinierender Körper ist, eine *lehrende* Universität gesetzt werden soll, u. daß ein darauf hinzielender Antrag bereits vom Parlamente angenommen worden ist. Darauf gründe ich manche Hoffnung, vor allem die, daß man der Lehr- und Lernfreiheit mehr Spielraum geben wird. Ich bedaure unsere Studenten, die augenblicklich von einem Examen ins andere getrieben werden, ohne die geringste Zeit zu haben, sich in den gewählten Fächern umsehen zu können.[64]

In a postscript to another letter, on 12 November 1898, he tells Steinmeyer, 'Eine meiner ersten Taten am College war die ZFDA [= *Zeitschrift für Deutsches Altertum*] bestellen zu lassen (Die letzten 10 Jhgg. u. der laufende)'.[65]

63 Closs (ed.), *Robert Priebsch, Elias von Steinmeyer: Briefwechsel*, p. 57.

64 Closs (ed.), *Robert Priebsch, Elias von Steinmeyer: Briefwechsel*, p. 58.

65 Closs (ed.), *Robert Priebsch, Elias von Steinmeyer: Briefwechsel*, p. 62. The *Zeitschrift für Deutsches Altertum*, founded by Moriz Haupt in 1841, is the longest established journal in its field still in existence today. On 2 February 1903, Priebsch mentioned that he had received £350 from the University for the purchase of books for his seminar library, to which Steinmeyer responded, 'Das lasse ich mir gefallen: 350 P[fund] extra auf einmal für das Seminar zu Bücherankäufen! So etwas gibt es in unserem sparsamen Deutschland nicht. Sie haben mit einem Schlage dadurch so viel, wie ich in den 21 Jahren, die mein Seminar besteht, dafür habe aufwenden können' (Closs (ed.), *Robert Priebsch, Elias von Steinmeyer: Briefwechsel*, pp. 114–15). Steinmeyer must have turned green with envy when Priebsch told him the following month that he had been given the further sum of £195, and in February 1904 he mentions annual grants of £50 from the University and £10 from University College for his seminar library.

A month later he writes to Steinmeyer again:

> Ich meinerseits habe die Absicht, hier in Verbindung mit unserem Professor für Englisch (W. P. Ker, Verfasser von Epic and Romance [1897] u. seinem Assistenten (G. Foster [later Provost of University College]) ein englisches u. deutsches Seminar zu gründen, etwas bisher in England unerhörtes. Ich sehe darin die einzige Hoffnung, das Studium germ[anischer] Sprachen ein wenig zu heben. Unsere Seminare einfach zu copieren, gienge ja freilich nicht an, aber trotzdem wäre es mir lieb, wenn ich die Seminarstatuten einzelner deutscher Univ[ersitäten] vor mir hätte. Deshalb möchte ich Sie herzlich bitten, mir die Erlanger Statuten des deutschen u. englischen Seminars zu senden u. mir etwaige Literatur über die Aufgaben u. Ziele unserer Seminare anzugeben.[66]

Once more we hear something on this topic, on 8 April 1899:

> Ich bin nun darüber her die Seminarstatuten für Univ. College auszuarbeiten. Ich bin neugierig ob und wie sich die Sache hier gestalten wird. Meine Schuld soll's nicht sein, wenn sich Germanische Philologie hier keinen würdigern Platz erobern sollte.[67]

Thus Liverpool's loss proved very much to be London's gain.[68] The published correspondence (Closs unfortunately published only a selection) tells us little more about Priebsch's experiences at University College, though on 20 April 1899 we find him groaning:

> Du lieber Gott, ich habe nun kennen gelernt, was es heißt, für tägliches Brot zu arbeiten u. mehr steht mir bevor, da ich nun auch den deutschen Unterricht in Bedford College übernommen habe, der mir vorderhand 5 Stunden wöchentlich beschäftigen wird. In der freien Zeit werde ich am 2. Bde meiner Hss. [i.e. his *Deutsche Handschriften in England*] arbeiten. Ich habe nun durch eine Woche täglich ca. 60 Sloane Hss. [i.e. manuscripts

66 Closs (ed.), *Robert Priebsch, Elias von Steinmeyer: Briefwechsel*, p. 64. Steinmeyer provided some helpful hints in his reply of 12 December 1898 (p. 65).

67 Closs (ed.), *Robert Priebsch, Elias von Steinmeyer: Briefwechsel*, p. 69.

68 In fact, Liverpool's 'loss' at first promised to be propitious because, as reported in *The Times* (3 November 1898), it appointed the famous Henry Sweet (1845–1912) as Lecturer in English Language, in succession to Priebsch. Writing to the Danish philologist Otto Jespersen on 8 January 1899, Sweet said: 'I've lately been offered the post of lecturer in English language at University College, Liverpool, which I've accepted. But I shall not have to begin work till next Michaelmas. We [i.e. Sweet and his wife Mary] shall leave Oxford towards the middle of June, I expect. I'd made up my mind to leave Oxford this year just before I received the offer. The Liverpool College will soon become a university, I expect they are only waiting for a lot more money. Birmingham will soon have a university. Oxford and Cambridge will probably decline when there are universities in the north of England'. In the event, for reasons which are not clear, Sweet withdrew his acceptance of the appointment. (I am indebted to Prof. M. K. MacMahon (Glasgow) for this information.)

> from the collection of Sir Hans Sloane (1660–1753) in the British Museum] durchgesehen, entsetzliches Zeug, meistens des 17. Jhd., aber ich habe mir vorgenommen, die Sache gründlich zu betreiben.[69]

He seems to have been greatly relieved when John George Robertson arrived to assist him with some of his teaching burden in 1903:

> Ich habe nun einen Collegen in der Person des Dr. J. Robertson erhalten u. zwar wird er gleich nach Ostern sein Amt antreten. Er war kurze Zeit vor etwa 14 Tagen hier u. hat auf mich einen recht soliden Eindruck gemacht. Ich werde infolgedessen nicht mehr das ganze Gebiet zu behandeln haben u. hoffe mich nun in mein eigenes Fach wieder vertiefen zu können.[70]

Three final quotations from Priebsch's correspondence are of interest. The first now strikes one as mildly amusing. It seems that Steinmeyer had reported having a female student in one of his classes, to which Priebsch responded, on 19 November 1904:

> Neugierig bin ich zu erfahren, wie sich Ihre "Zuhörerin" machen wird. Ich habe deren vier in meiner Vorlesung über den Minnesang u. empfinde hie und da eine kleine Unbehaglichkeit. Aber die guten Dinger vertragen doch im allgemeinen mehr als man glauben sollte; wahrscheinlich verstehen sie nur die Hälfte von dem, was ich sage.[71]

The second, from 24 February 1907, contains a presentiment of trouble. Priebsch laments:

> Das Studium des Deutschen scheint übrigens hier immer unpopulärer zu werden im selben Grade, als die Hinneigung zu Frankreich u. der Haß gegen Deutschland wächst. Ob es wol mal zu einer Explosion kommen wird?[72]

The 'Hinneigung zu Frankreich' clearly refers to the *entente cordiale*, concluded in 1904; the half-expected 'Explosion' would become reality in 1914. Certainly, Priebsch was less than happy in England: on 6 October 1907 he lamented to Steinmeyer:

> Das Schlimmste ist das Gefühl geistiger Abspannung, Unlust zum Arbeiten; dies steigert sich besonders an trüben, regnerischen Tagen, an denen wir hier

69 Closs (ed.), *Robert Priebsch, Elias von Steinmeyer: Briefwechsel*, p. 71.

70 Closs (ed.), *Robert Priebsch, Elias von Steinmeyer: Briefwechsel*, p. 117.

71 Closs (ed.), *Robert Priebsch, Elias von Steinmeyer: Briefwechsel*, p. 138. A remark in an earlier letter, of 11 October 1903, is also interesting for the light it sheds on the numbers of students: 'Donnerstag habe ich u. Freitag hat College Robertson die Vorlesungen mit sehr wenigen Zuhörern begonnen. Na, wir müssen eben abwarten u. sehen, was wir für die wenigen, unter denen heuer wenigstens ein paar männliche Wesen sind, tun können' (p. 121).

72 Closs (ed.), *Robert Priebsch, Elias von Steinmeyer: Briefwechsel*, p. 165.

> ja keinen Mangel haben. Offen gestanden, ich sehne mich aus England fort, aber das wird ja wol nur ein frommer Wunsch bleiben.[73]

Furthermore, he was disappointed not to be considered for appointment as his old teacher Schönbach's successor at Graz in 1911.[74]

There is one aspect of Priebsch's time at Liverpool which deserves our further attention because it was to have serious consequences for him years later in London. His appointment at Liverpool had been facilitated through the support of the great German Celticist Kuno Meyer (1858–1919), who was already Lecturer in Teutonic Languages there. Even after Priebsch moved to London, they stayed in touch: a letter of 26 June 1902 to Steinmeyer mentions that Meyer was involved in Priebsch's official appointment as University Professor, and another of 12 September 1904 states that Meyer was staying with the Priebschs at their new house on Haverstock Hill, while on 8 November 1908 Priebsch tells Steinmeyer that University College had invited Meyer to deliver ten lectures on Celtic literature, the ultimate aim being to raise up to £20,000 to establish a Chair and two Readerships in Celtic in London.[75] Meyer, who received an honorary doctorate at Oxford and became an honorary citizen of Dublin in the summer of 1911, would leave Britain in the autumn to become Professor of Celtic Philology at Berlin but he held an honorary professorship at Liverpool until 1914. Though this contact with Meyer was initially enormously helpful to Priebsch, it soon proved to have unfortunate repercussions because Meyer, who was decidedly pro-German, came to be suspected of being a German spy and would be stripped of his honorary professorship at Liverpool. He had long been associated with the cause of Irish independence and, during a lecture tour of the United States, he gave a widely reported speech to the Clan-na-Gael Society of New York on 17 December 1914 in which he had spoken of a German intention to encourage Irish military prisoners in Germany to forgo their allegiance to the British Crown and to participate in an invasion of England and

73 Closs (ed.), *Robert Priebsch, Elias von Steinmeyer: Briefwechsel*, p. 176. On 9 June 1907 Priebsch told Steinmeyer that the position of Professor of German at Oxford had been advertised and asked whether Steinmeyer would support his candidature, but on 30 June he wrote, 'Ich habe jeden Gedanken, mich um O[xford] zu bewerben, aufgegeben' (pp. 170–71). In the event, H. G. Fiedler was appointed to the post.

74 Closs (ed.), *Robert Priebsch, Elias von Steinmeyer: Briefwechsel*, p. 272, letter of 20 December 1911. Schönbach (1848–1911) had died on 25 August.

75 Closs (ed.), *Robert Priebsch, Elias von Steinmeyer: Briefwechsel*, p. 105, p. 133, p. 194. The plan to establish a Chair of Celtic in London foundered on the unwillingness or inability of the Welsh and Irish to contribute funding. Nor did it help that Meyer upset Irish Catholics by declaring in a public lecture that St Patrick had never set foot in Rome (letter of 29 January 1910, p. 206).

Ireland.[76] Whether he was a spy or not, his correspondence with Priebsch was intercepted by the British intelligence services and deemed suspect. At some point during the First World War Meyer sent Priebsch a postcard via Copenhagen asking him to look up some detail in an Irish manuscript in the British Museum. This postcard, with mysterious numbers and letters (the shelfmark of the manuscript!) was intercepted by the intelligence services who suspected a coded message. They allowed it to be delivered, nevertheless. The unsuspecting Priebsch duly went to the British Museum, got out the manuscript and supplied the information requested. His reply to Meyer was intercepted and poor old Priebsch was interrogated. Perhaps most damaging was a letter beginning 'My dear Robert' dated 2 May 1917, sent by Meyer from the famous Twentieth Century Limited train en route from Chicago to New York. This letter from Meyer was intercepted by MI5 and never reached Priebsch but was used in evidence against him. Evidence in Priebsch's favour submitted by his friends and colleagues, specifically that he had pushed for British nationals rather than Germans to be appointed to Chairs of German at British universities, such as William Collinson at Liverpool, failed to sway the investigating committee. Though nothing was ever proved against him, he was stripped of his status as a naturalized British Subject (acquired on 28 October 1914) on 8 February 1919;[77] he remained under suspicion and never got over it: 'Das wurmt mich immer noch, und das wird mich immer wurmen', he used to say, and the tears ran down his cheeks because he was very sentimental and wept very easily. His distress was natural enough: after all, he had been a co-signatory of the famous 'letter of remonstrance' published in *The Times* on 14 May 1915 following the public outrage over the sinking of the 'Lusitania' by a German U-boat on 7 May, in which, along with Cambridge's Karl Breul,[78] Oxford's Hermann Fiedler, Leeds's Schüddekopf

76 See *The Times*, 24 December 1914, p. 10. Clan-na-Gael would become the largest single financier of the Easter Rising; it conspired with imperial Germany to obtain guns and munitions for use in the Rising.

77 Priebsch's naturalization was revoked on the recommendation of the Certificates of Naturalization (Revocation) Committee, established under the British Nationality and Status of Aliens Act of 1914, on 8 February 1919. See *The London Gazette*, 28 February 1919, p. 2857, reported in *The Times*, 1 March 1919, p. 5. For a very full account of the affair see the unpublished paper by Christopher T. Husbands, *German-/Austrian-origin professors of German in British universities during the First World War: the lessons of four case studies* (2013), http://eprints.lse.ac.uk/49797/1/-Husbands_German_Austrian_origin_2013.pdf [accessed 24 May 2016].

78 Breul, born in Hannover, was naturalized on 13 March 1893. On him see Roger Paulin, 'Breul, Karl Hermann', *ODNB*, http://www.oxforddnb.com/view/article/61616. Priebsch does not seem to have held Breul in great esteem as a scholar. In a letter to Steinmeyer, dated 29 December 1902, he writes: 'Bei der Versammlung der Mod[ern] Lang[uage] Association am 22. Dec. hielt Breul eine Festrede auf Herder wie man sie in einer der höheren Klassen einer Mädchenschule hätte erwarten sollen. Er hatte sich zu diesem

and others, they 'expressed our unswerving loyalty to the country of our adoption, to which we feel bound not only by gratitude, family ties, and our solemn oath of allegiance but also by a deep sympathy born of common work and intimate knowledge of the nation's life and character'. The story of British antipathy towards all things German in the First World War is well known, but as far as German Studies were concerned, one of the fiercest expressions of it came from Gilbert Waterhouse (1888–1977), Professor of German at Trinity College Dublin, in a public lecture given there on 29 May 1917. He said:

> When the present war broke out, teachers of German in this country at once found themselves in an awkward position. For reasons that have become unpleasantly clear to all of us, [...] the word 'German' has come to stand for all that is most contemptible and revolting in human experience. This popular feeling of disgust at once attached itself without discrimination to the study of the German language in our schools and universities. [...] I do not look forward to any resumption of cordial relations with German scholars after the war. [...] I believe them all to be equally intoxicated with Kaiserism. [p. 3] [...] It is worthy of passing notice that in 1914, of the twelve principal chairs of German in the United Kingdom, eight were occupied by German scholars – some naturalized, some not; one by a neutral professor, and only three by genuine British subjects. This was a state of affairs that must not recur. The Germans themselves were far more careful in these matters. At no single one of the twenty-eight universities of Germany and Austria did an Englishman occupy a chair of English. [p. 4] [...] it is not at all necessary to have actual natives of Germany as teachers, not even after the war. [pp. 21f.] [...] One benefit the war has conferred upon us: it has settled the question of British v. Foreign professors of modern languages, and it would be a bold university indeed that now ventured to appoint a German to a chair of German in this country. [...] We must have a clean start after the war, or, better, during it, with an all-British professoriate. [p. 22] [...] we do not study German to provide Germans or German-speaking neutrals with comfortable berths in the United Kingdom, nor to flatter German vanity, nor to encourage German trade, nor to aid German propaganda. We study German in order to extract from the language, the literature, the people, and the country the maximum of benefit – moral, intellectual, and material – for ourselves. We ourselves, not Germans, must decide how, when and where we shall learn German, and we must organize the study in such a way that every ounce of energy expended upon it shall contribute to the uplifting of our national life. We can only break the power of the German university – no mean factor in the present war – by providing equal opportunities for study; but with a little effort and a little

---

Zwecke sogar mit Könneckes Bilderatlas versehen!' (Closs (ed.), *Robert Priebsch, Elias von Steinmeyer: Briefwechsel*, p. 111).

foresight Germany can be beaten as decisively in the lecture-room as in the workshop, the counting-house, or on the field of battle [p. 24].[79]

To return to Priebsch, when he retired in 1931, now equipped with a Czechoslovakian passport, it was only through the energetic intervention of his admiring friends and colleagues that he was eventually awarded a meagre pension which allowed him to live, in reduced circumstances, in Dubrovnik and Vienna, where he died in 1935.[80] In a letter of 5 December 1932 written from Vienna to Frederick Norman he lamented, 'Daß mir der £-Sturz recht empfindlich ist, können Sie sich denken. Der Lebensabend nach über 30jähriger akad[emischer] Tätigkeit ist ein bißchen hart u. kärglich ausgefallen. Wie das noch mit der Welt werden will, wer weiß es'.

Priebsch was a devoted bibliophile and scholar – R. W. Chambers, Librarian and Professor of English Language and Literature at University College, once quipped, 'Priebsch really only cares about two things, the Habsburgs and Ablaut. And I am quite convinced he prefers Ablaut'. Certainly it was largely thanks to Priebsch that London came to be recognized as a centre for Medieval Studies (though it is worth remembering that already Bernays at King's covered the Middle Ages in his lectures). The impact that Priebsch (and Robertson) made on the subject in London is well illustrated if we compare the syllabuses on offer before and after their arrival. The 1853–54 Calendar of University College outlines the programmes as follows:

GERMAN LANGUAGE AND LITERATURE.
Professor ADOLPH HEIMANN, PhD
JUNIOR CLASS: Monday, Wednesday, and Friday, 6.30 to 7.30.
SUBJECTS: Grammar, Recitation, Exercises for writing and speaking, Study of easy German authors.
SENIOR CLASS: Monday, Wednesday, and Friday, from 5.30 to 6.30.

79 Gilbert Waterhouse, *The War and the Study of German. A Public Lecture delivered in Trinity College, Dublin, on Tuesday, May 29th, 1917* (Dublin: Hodges, Figges and Co. Ltd, 1917). Waterhouse was far from unique in his views: after the sinking of the 'Lusitania', on 6 November 1916 the Council of the University of Sheffield had resolved to terminate the employment of Professor Julius Freund (b. 1871), who had been there since 1908, at the end of the year, saying 'In view of the fact that he has been interned [at Douglas Camp on the Isle of Man] as an unnaturalised alien enemy since July 1915, Professor Freund has been unable to discharge the duties of his office as Professor of German, and, in the opinion of the Council, it appeared to be improbable that the state of political feeling would permit of a German subject filling a professorial post to the advantage of the University at the end of the war' (Newton, *German Studies at The University of Sheffield*, p. 68). See also Flood/Swales, in: Alter (ed.), *Spuren in die Zukunft*, vol. I, p. 156.

80 Obituary in *The Times*, 28 May 1935, p. 21; fulsome appreciations (one of them by W. E. Collinson) in *The Times*, 29 May 1935, p. 16, and 31 May 1935, p. 21.

SUBJECTS: Translation from English prose-writers; Composition on familiar and literary topics; Reading of Wieland's *Oberon*; Schiller's *Geisterseher*; and Göthe's *Wahrheit und Dichtung*;
Study of the literary history of Germany, particularly during the last 150 years.
The instruction in this Class will be conveyed only through the medium of the German Language.
Fee for each Class, £5.

(We may note that – rather as in the case of Buchheim at King's – two hours of teaching three evenings a week will have left Heimann with plenty of time for teaching elsewhere, especially seeing that there seem to have been only three students in the Senior Class and five in the Junior!) Here are some of the examination questions set that year on German literary history (all of which had to be answered):

1. Wie wiele Jahrhunderte umfaszte die dritte Periode der deutschen Literaturgeschichte?
2. Welches ist der Character der meisten Werke aus dieser Periode?
3. Was für ein Buch ist *Till Eulenspiegel*?
4. Welches waren die besten Autoren unmittelbar nach Luther?
5. Was können Sie über Ulrich von Hutten sagen?
6. Welche drei Männer waren die Gründer der deutschen Metaphysik?
7. Hat die Englische Literatur einen Einflusz auf die neuern Deutschen Dichter gehabt?
8. Welches waren die gröszten Schriftsteller im achtzehnten Jahrhundert?
9. Erzählen Sie etwas von den Jugendjahren Wieland's.
10. Wodurch ist Wieland in seinen Schriften besonders merkwürdig?
[...]

Under Heimann's successor Althaus in 1876–77 little had changed (apart from the fee!). The programme for the Senior Class was:

Wednesday, Thursday, and Friday, from 9 to 10 a.m.

SUBJECTS:-Repetition of the chief parts of Grammar; Translations from English prose-writers; Exercises in Free Composition on given themes; Reading of the more difficult works of some of the best Authors, and Lectures on the History of German Literature, special attention being given to those parts required for the first BA Examination in the University of London.

Fee for each Class: for the Session, £6 6s.; for each Term, £2 12s. 6d.

How different things were under Priebsch and Robertson in 1902–03 may be judged from the following outline of the Senior Class syllabus:

Syntax of the German language; Exercises in dictation and free composition; Translation from and into German; reading from a special author;

Figure 5: J. G. Robertson.

conversation, using K. Meyer's German Grammar [1888]; Meissner's German Prose Composition [London: Hachette, 1899]; the special authors were Lessing's *Minna von Barnhelm*, Goethe's *Gedichte* (selected by Charles Harris [Boston, Mass.: D. C. Heath, 1899]); Uhland, *Gedichte*; Grillparzer, *Sappho*.

Lectures on the history of the German language and study of a Middle High German author, for which Otto Behaghel's *Geschichte der deutschen Sprache* [2nd edn, Strasbourg: Trübner, 1898], reading passages from Viktor Michels's *Mittelhochdeutsches Elementarbuch* [Heidelberg: Winter, 1900] and Hartmann von Aue's *Der arme Heinrich* were prescribed.

Moreover, there was now a 'Higher Senior Class' which involved the study of Old High German; Middle High German with special study of Hartmann's *Iwein*, Karl Bartsch's *Deutsche Liederdichter des 12. bis 14. Jahrhunderts*, and Rochus von Liliencron's *Die historischen Volkslieder der Deutschen vom 13. bis 16. Jahrhundert*; and literature 1749–1832 with emphasis on 'Goethes u. Schillers gemeinsames Schaffen; romantische Schule; Grillparzer'. And finally Priebsch announced that he was prepared to lead students to the Department of Manuscripts of the British Museum to acquaint them with the elements of Palaeography and to illustrate the lectures on OHG and MHG by the examination of medieval German MSS. Thus, after the arrival of Priebsch Medieval Studies became unavoidable, with the result that in 1911 Margaret Tuke, Principal of Bedford College from 1907 to 1929, was complaining about the excessive number of lectures devoted to German philology – apparently as many as ten out of a weekly total of sixteen hours were devoted to grammar and philology.[81] Professor Atkins at King's felt likewise – after all, in Frederick Norman's words, 'having been brought up under the Cambridge system, he was able to escape knowing anything whatever about the medieval side at all' – but he was simply unable to prevail against Priebsch and Robertson. Priebsch's real strength lay in teaching advanced students rather than undergraduates. There was the occasion when he found himself lecturing on *Wilhelm Tell*, deputising for a colleague who was away for a term. When, towards the end of the term, he was asked how things were going, Priebsch replied, 'Well, I shall soon have finished dictating the bibliography to them'! Indeed, it was Priebsch's failure to communicate with beginners that led to the appointment of Frederick Norman: Priebsch told Gregory Foster, Provost of University College, in 1922 that Norman should be appointed so that the students would understand things better. Priebsch's love of scholarship transmitted itself to his devoted son-in-law August Closs (1898–1990) and his granddaughter Elisabeth Closs Traugott, one of the most frequently cited linguists in America today. It was certainly under Priebsch's influence that Frederick Norman and Arthur Hatto, together with their various pupils, established London as a strong force in medieval studies.[82] As August Closs put it:

> Mit Professor R. Priebsch setzte tatsächlich eine Epoche germanistischer Forschung in England ein, die an Ernst, Gediegenheit und wissenschaftlicher Vorbildlichkeit einzig ist. Nicht zufällig sind die meisten führenden

81 The dominant role of philology and Medieval Studies is evident from consideration of the specialisms of members of staff at, for instance, University College. For example, in 1918–19 the staff consisted of Robert Priebsch, Wilfrid Perrett and Julius Steppat (the latter two both Readers, Perrett teaching Gothic and Old High German and also the phonetics of German alongside the famous phonetician Daniel Jones, while Steppat taught Old and Middle High German); otherwise there was only Robertson to teach modern literature, and Adolf Georg Haltenhoff as Assistant Lecturer. The Department looked very different in 1950–51 when it comprised Leonard Forster as Professor, Elizabeth Mary Wilkinson as Reader, K.-W. Maurer as Senior Lecturer, Ilse Appelbaum (later Graham) and Werner Schwarz as Lecturers, and Paul Salmon and George Wells as Assistant Lecturers; only Schwarz and Salmon were medievalists.

82 See John L. Flood, 'German Studies', in Alan Deyermond (ed.), *A Century of British Medieval Studies*, British Academy Centenary Monographs (Oxford: OUP; London: The British Academy, 2007), pp. 427–59. On Hatto, who was Head of the German Department at Queen Mary College from 1937 to 1977, see John L. Flood, 'Arthur Thomas Hatto 1910–2010', *Proceedings of the British Academy*, 172: *Biographical Memoirs of Fellows*, X (Oxford: OUP for the British Academy, 2011), pp. 173–98.

> Germanisten des Landes durch seine Schule gegangen. Es ist und gilt für eine Auszeichnung, bei Priebsch studiert zu haben.[83]

Of Priebsch's contemporaries in London particular mention must be made of John George Robertson (1867–1933) (known as 'J.G.' and in his family and among friends as 'George'), noted chiefly for his work on Goethe and his *History of German Literature*. Robertson was born in Glasgow. In the family home, scenes from *Hermann und Dorothea* adorned the walls, and it was these that first kindled his lifelong enthusiasm for Goethe. At the age of sixteen, after reading Carlyle and Goethe's *Faust* in translation, he resolved to learn German. After studying classics and later natural sciences at Glasgow, taking his MA in 1886 and his BSc in 1889, he abandoned science for philology and literature, and set off to Leipzig where he studied German under the eminent medievalist Friedrich Zarncke (1825–1891) and the brilliant philologist Eduard Sievers (1850–1932). In 1892 he took his doctorate with a thesis on the sixteenth-century dramatist Jakob Ayrer. Hence, it is no real surprise that his *History of German Literature* begins with no fewer than fifteen chapters on pre-1500 literature. At Leipzig he became acquainted with a young Australian pianist, Ethel Richardson (1870–1946), whom he wooed by inviting her to the autumn cycle of Wagner's operas. But marriage was as yet out of the question: the impecunious Robertson had to return to Glasgow, with no immediate prospect of employment. Failing to obtain any university appointment, he returned to Germany in 1895, to live in Munich as a freelance teacher of English. In 1896 he was appointed Lecturer in English at Strasbourg (a German city then), later being promoted to Professor *extraordinarius*, a rare distinction for a foreigner. He settled down to studying German literature and Ethel, by now his wife, to translating and then to writing novels (under her pseudonym Henry Handel Richardson).[84] In 1902 Robertson published his monumental *History of German Literature*. The first of its kind in English, this work long remained a standard authority, praised for its broad sweep and for its sober assessments and reliable presentation of essential facts.[85] The

83 From Closs's obituary of Priebsch in: *Zeitschrift für deutsche Philologie*, 61 (1936), 116–17.

84 On Robertson's life in Leipzig, Munich and Strasbourg see Edna Purdie and Olga M. Roncoroni (eds), *Henry Handel Richardson: Some Personal Impressions* (Sydney: Angus and Robertson, 1957), esp. pp. 1–22; also Purdie's own recollections of the Robertsons in London (pp. 42–46). Here they lived in a large house at 90 Regent's Park Road at a remarkably low cost, their tenancy being rent-controlled since they had lived there from before 1914. An interesting detail is that when they moved to London they wanted to engage a German cook and chose a young woman called Irene Stumpp who was a great-niece of the poet Eduard Mörike. Norman described her as 'a strange German who was either a poltergeist herself, or was able to control poltergeists'.

85 Robertson himself prepared a revised edition in 1931, incorporating studies of new writers such as Thomas Mann, Rilke, Hofmannsthal, and Toller, and further editions appeared in 1959, 1962, 1966, and 1970, with a German translation in 1968.

book firmly established Robertson's reputation: he declined the immediate offer of a professorship at the University of Michigan, but in 1903 accepted appointment as University Professor of German at London, thus beginning an association with University and Bedford Colleges which was to last thirty years.[86] The appointment, which was endowed by London County Council, was expressly non-collegiate and involved jurisdiction over all the German work throughout the University: at this time the University was seeking to model itself on the University of Berlin by taking subjects out of the hands and control of the individual Colleges and exercising control through the Boards of Studies.

Robertson did not rest upon his laurels. Not only did he found and edit the *Modern Language Review* from 1905 until 1933,[87] his pen also produced a steady stream of well-researched, authoritative, yet eminently readable books – he had little patience with heavy Teutonic scholarship. His works included *Studies in the Genesis of Romantic Theory in the Eighteenth Century* (1923), a study in which he emphasized the debt of the Romantics to Italy and which is perhaps his greatest contribution to scholarship. His other books included *Schiller after a Century* (1905), *Literature in Germany* (1907), *Shakespeare on the Continent* (1910), *Outlines of the History of German Literature* (1911), *Goethe and the Twentieth Century* (1912), *The Literature of Germany* (1913), *Carlyle* (1916), *The Gods of Greece in German Poetry* (1924), *Goethe and Byron* (1925), *Goethe* (1927), and *The Life and Work of Goethe, 1749–1832* (1932).[88] So convinced was he of the leading role of London Germanistik that

86 According to Norman (transcript of a tape-recorded interview conducted on 10 June 1965, in possession of the author), the London Chair was first offered to Karl Breul (Cambridge) and then to the Heine scholar Ernst Elster (1860–1940) of Marburg (who, having taken his doctorate under Zarncke at Leipzig, had spent 1886–88 as part-time Lecturer at Glasgow; he is mentioned in the Glasgow University Calendar for 1887–88 as giving a course of twenty lectures (in German) on German literature (covering contemporaries of Goethe and Schiller, the Romantic School, Young Germany, and modern literature till the death of Heine), and another course, also of twenty lectures but in English, on philology (covering the laws of phonetic change, German accidence and syntax) (see Wakely, 'Modern Language Studies at Scottish Universities', p. 5). The possible appointment of Elster and then his rejection of the post are mentioned by Priebsch in February 1903 (see Closs (ed.), *Robert Priebsch, Elias von Steinmeyer: Briefwechsel*, p. 114 and p. 116). Norman plausibly surmises that Robertson was eventually appointed through the happy circumstance that Robertson, Priebsch and Gregory Foster (1866–1931, successively Secretary, Principal and Provost of University College, 1900–29) had all got to know one another at Strasbourg; Foster had been Lektor for English there and received a doctorate for his thesis on the Anglo-Saxon poem *Judith* in 1892 (see Elizabeth J. Morse, 'Foster, Sir (Thomas) Gregory', in *ODNB*, http://www.oxforddnb.com/view/article/33219).

87 On Robertson's editorship of *The Modern Language Review* see C. J. Sisson and A. Gillies, '1905–1955: A Retrospect', *The Modern Language Review*, 50 (1955), 385–91, especially pp. 387–91.

88 After his death a selection of his shorter writings was published under the title *Essays*

he turned down an invitation to accept the Chair of German at Cambridge in 1910. Together with Lord Haldane, he revitalized the English Goethe Society after the First World War, becoming its president from 1930 to 1933. After his death, a year before he was due to retire, he was succeeded at Bedford College by his devoted pupil Edna Purdie. Robertson also encouraged Scandinavian Studies, succeeding W. P. Ker as director of Scandinavian Studies at University College in 1924. He threw himself into the work of Bernard Shaw's Anglo-Swedish Literary Foundation, set up in 1927. His commitment was recognized by his appointment by the King of Sweden as a knight of the Order of the North Star and the award of the Order of St Olav of Norway. Other accolades he received included the medal 'Für Kunst und Wissenschaft' presented by Reichspräsident von Hindenburg. Among the many people indebted to him were the Expressionist poet Ernst Stadler and Elsie Butler, later Professor of German at Cambridge.[89] The Board of Studies established a prize in his memory, awarded triennially for the best book published in Britain in the field of Germanic Studies.[90]

A picture of life studying under Priebsch and Robertson may be gained from the reminiscences of Margaret Richey (1883–1974) of the year 1908–09 at Bedford College. 'Both were dedicated scholars', she writes:

---

and Addresses on Literature (1935), and his last work, *Lessing's Hamburgische Dramaturgie* (1939), was completed and seen through the press by Edna Purdie.

89 On Robertson see John L. Flood, 'Robertson, John George', *ODNB*, http://www.oxforddnb.com/view/article/61619; G. P. Gooch, 'John George Robertson, 1867–1933', *Proceedings of the British Academy*, 19 (1933), 360–80; *The Times* (29 May 1933); *Bedford College Old Students' Association*, Report no. 20 (July 1933); also Purdie and Roncoroni, *Henry Handel Richardson: Some Personal Impressions*; Michael Ackland, *Henry Handel Richardson: A Life* (Cambridge: CUP, 2004); Karen McLeod, *Henry Handel Richardson* (Cambridge: CUP, 1985); E. M. Butler, *Paper Boats* (London: Collins, 1959); William D. Elliott, *Henry Handel Richardson* (Boston: Twayne, 1975); J. G. Robertson, 'The art of Henry Handel Richardson', in H. H. Richardson [E. F. L. Robertson], *Myself when young* (Melbourne: Heinemann, 1948) [written *c.*1928–29]; R. Sheppard, *Ernst Stadler (1883–1914): a German Expressionist Poet at Oxford* (Oxford: Magdalen College, 1994).

90 Recipients have included Ronald Peacock for *Hölderlin* (London: Methuen, 1938); Elizabeth Mary Wilkinson for *Johann Elias Schlegel: A German Pioneer in Aesthetics* (Oxford: Blackwell, 1945), a revised version of her 1943 London PhD thesis, written under the guidance of J. G. Robertson; Hans Eichner (who had been Assistant Lecturer in German at Bedford College from 1948 to 1950) in 1960, presumably for his edition and commentary on Friedrich Schlegel's *Literary Notebooks, 1797–1801* (London: Athlone Press, 1957); R. T. Ferguson for *Enigma: The Life of Knut Hamsun* (London: Hutchinson, 1987); W. E. Yates (Exeter) jointly for *Grillparzer* and *Nestroy: Satire and Parody in Viennese Popular Comedy* (both Cambridge: CUP, 1975); Henry and Mary Garland (Exeter) for *The Oxford Companion to German Literature* (Oxford: OUP, 1976); M. S. Silk and J. P. Stern for *Nietzsche on Tragedy* (Cambridge: CUP, 1981); David Constantine (Oxford) for *Hölderlin* (Oxford: OUP, 1990); Nicholas Boyle (Cambridge) for *Goethe: The Poet and the Age* (Oxford: OUP, 1991–2000); and John Reddick (Liverpool) for *Georg Büchner: The Shattered Whole* (Oxford: Clarendon, 1994) – this list is very incomplete.

> and both had a very real personal interest in their pupils. [...] As a teacher Priebsch was the more gifted and dynamic. Robertson, always more writer than teacher, immersed in those explorations which were to lead to his major literary achievements, had little understanding for the mind of the novice. [...] Priebsch, in spite of his inexorably high standards, had a quickening influence at every stage, from the callow beginner to the fully fledged postgraduate. His lectures on mediaeval literature were unforgettable in their lucidity, their wealth of substance and depth of insight, and in their apt and beautiful phrasing.[91]

It is not clear from this whether Priebsch habitually lectured in German or in English, but this paean of praise for his lucidity and beautiful language contrasts sharply with Frederick Norman's assertion that Priebsch mystified generations of undergraduates with his claim that the best kind of German was what, with his Bohemian unrounded vowels, he called 'Bienendaitsch' – they never fathomed what it had to do with 'bees'! Richey continues:

> All this, his fine record as teacher and scholar, was transfused with the warmth of his radiant and lovable nature, and with the impact of his deeply religious feelings. Known only to the few was the fortitude with which he surmounted his physical handicap, persistent lameness accompanied more and more as years went on by severe pain.

Norman gives a slightly different impression of him. Priebsch was an omnivorous reader (it is clear from his correspondence that he read absolutely everything that was published in the journals; furthermore, he felt that one simply had to read everything, and that before one had read everything one should not attempt to write anything), and everything he read on a subject was regurgitated in his lectures, too: he would detail everything anyone had ever said about a topic, with the result that the students ended up completely bewildered as to what they were supposed to believe. A favourite trick of his was to expound some long theory about something or other and, when the students had written it all down, he would suddenly say, 'Aber das ist alles falsch' – at which point the students would sigh and tear up their notes. 'But', Norman continues, 'he was a very nice man and people liked him as a lecturer, because he clearly enjoyed it and whilst he was totally unintelligible on historical grammar, he was far more intelligible [...] on literary history'. According to Norman, Priebsch and Robertson:

> were by no means always friendly, nor did they always see eye to eye, but there was one thing of which they were quite certain, and that is that they were to run German Studies in London and no one else. As Robertson was the modernist and Priebsch the medievalist, they divided out the work

91 Transcript in possession of the author.

between them and kept everybody else at bay and commanded what should and should not be done.

Their calling the shots naturally annoyed their colleague at King's, Buchheim's successor Henry Gibson Atkins (1871–1942), who held the Chair there from 1900 to 1937. Educated at Queen Elizabeth Grammar School, Atherstone, Warwickshire, he studied privately in France and Germany and at Trinity College, Cambridge. His earliest publication in German was a selection of Goethe's poems (1902) which, according to a contemporary reviewer, was heavily influenced by the lectures of Karl Breul at Cambridge in the 1890s.[92] I find it difficult to form much of an impression of him, in that I cannot recall ever hearing anyone mention him or his work, though Norman remarked that he was 'a very upright and soldierly looking type and quite a different sort of person from Robertson and Priebsch. He did not really get on with them and he objected in particular to the medieval syllabus [...]. He thought it was grossly exaggerated and he could never get Robertson to agree because Robertson didn't really want to quarrel with Priebsch about that.' Yet Atkins is significant in our story for he seems to have been the first native Englishman to have held a Chair of German in London:[93] he was a College Professor at King's but only a Reader in the University until he was appointed University Professor in 1923.[94] Thus he was overshadowed by Priebsch and Robertson, who were both full University Professors. Priebsch used to say of Atkins, 'Er ist ein großer Mann', implying that, as he had become a member of Senate and the University Court and thus stood a good chance of becoming Vice-Chancellor, he was a good administrator – but not a good scholar.[95] Besides Goethe, he also published on Heine (1929) and Droste-Hülshoff (1933), but his particular interest was in the history of versification, publishing a book on the subject with Methuen in 1923: *A History of German Versification: Ten Centuries of Metrical Evolution*.[96] Just before he died, he wrote a book called *German Literature through Nazi Eyes* (London: Methuen, 1941; reprinted by Routledge in 2013): it represents a scathing analysis of the work of German literary historians and critics of the 1930s such as Franz Koch, Hellmuth Langenbucher, Walter Linden and Josef Nadler. He edited *The Modern Language Review* from 1936 to 1942.

92 *The Modern Language Quarterly*, 6 (1903), 85–87.

93 In this he preceded J. G. Robertson (a Scot) by three years.

94 King's College had, in fact, proposed Atkins for a University Professorship in 1919 when he was already a member of Senate and of the Academic Council. However, the application was refused by the Board of Advisers (which included Priebsch's former student W. E. Collinson and Priebsch's colleague R. A. Williams), which cannot have pleased him.

95 Source: Norman interview transcript in possession of the author.

96 This was reviewed by Edna Purdie in *The Modern Language Review*, 19 (1924), 125.

Yet despite his relatively modest scholarly achievements Atkins was evidently an able man: he was Assistant Principal at King's (1919–23 and 1925–37), a member of Senate (1918–33) and the University Court (1929–33), and he seems to have run his department with a firm hand, to judge from a story from Frederick Norman about how he (Norman) was surprised to encounter his young colleague Arthur Hatto one afternoon in about 1936: 'Hello, Hatto', he said, 'shouldn't you be teaching a German for Scientists class?' 'Yes', said Hatto, 'but last week they didn't turn up, so this week I am punishing them by not turning up myself!' To which Norman replied, 'Well, I shouldn't let Atkins hear you say that!'.

*

So far, we have focused largely on University College, King's College and Bedford College and on the University's arrangements for exerting a centralizing control over the subject. The early years of the twentieth century saw German established at other London Colleges. In 1906 it was introduced at Birkbeck,[97] where Alexander Hargreaves, who had a Heidelberg doctorate in English dialectology, was appointed,[98] but he only stayed a year before he was succeeded by Edward Leopold Milner-Barry (1867–1917) who resigned on 31 December 1909 to become Professor of German at Bangor.[99] His successor at Birkbeck was John Henry Grafton Grattan BA, author of various books on English grammar and of *Anglo Saxon Magic and Medicine: Illustrated Specially from the Semi Pagan Text 'Lacnunga'*, for the year 1909–10.[100] Grattan was succeeded in 1910 by the important figure of Jethro Trevergy Bithell (1878–1962), who moved from an Assistant Lectureship at Manchester, where he had taken a First Class degree under Arvid Johannson

97 Yet as early as 1891 one student from Birkbeck passed London Intermediate in German (University of London Historical Record 1912), apparently a solitary case. Birkbeck was not formally admitted as a School of the University until October 1920.

98 Alexander Hargreaves, author of *A Grammar of the Dialect of Adlington (Lancashire)*, Anglistische Forschungen, 13 (Heidelberg: Winter, 1904), was a Recognised Teacher of German at Birkbeck during 1906–07.

99 Edward Leopold Milner-Barry, MA Cantab., had previously taught at Mill Hill School and had been Schools Editor of the *Modern Language Quarterly*. He was a member of the London branch of the Allgemeiner Deutscher Sprachverein (see Flood, 'The London Branch of the Allgemeiner Deutscher Sprachverein', pp. 233–34). One of his sons, Sir Stuart Milner-Barry (1906–1995), a leading international chess player, became head of Hut 6 at Bletchley Park; he was one of the leading cryptographers along with Alan Turing, Gordon Welchman and Hugh Alexander; see Ralph Erskine, 'Barry, Sir (Philip) Stuart Milner-', in *ODNB*, http://www.oxford-dnb.com/view/article/58042.

100 Grattan later became Reader in English and Germanic Philology at University College and then Baines Professor of English Language and Philology at Liverpool.

Figure 6: Jethro Bithell.

in 1900. He stayed until he retired in 1938.[101] When the poet Richard

101 Bithell had been teaching at Manchester since 1906; see Sagarra and Skrine, *The Department of German at the Victoria University of Manchester*, p. 7. At Birkbeck Bithell was succeeded as Reader by Dr Reginald J. McClean (later Professor), on whom see *German Life and Letters*, n.s. 33, 1 (1979), 1–2. He, in turn, was succeeded by Dr William Douglas Robson-Scott (1903–1980) who had been the only other member of staff for German at Birkbeck since at least 1939. He had taken his doctorate in Vienna just after the *Anschluss*; his thesis was eventually published as *German Travellers in England, 1400–1800* (Oxford: Blackwell, 1953). He was a splendid raconteur. One of the subjects he took for his exam in Vienna was medieval German. One day he presented himself for examination by the eminent scholar Dietrich von Kralik (1884–1959). 'Wie heißen Sie?', asked Kralik. 'Robson-Scott', he said, to which Kralik responded, 'Das ist kein deutscher Name'. Kralik then handed him an open book, saying, 'Was ist das?'. Robson-Scott asked, 'Wie meinen Sie, Herr Professor?' 'Wie das Buch heißt, möchte ich wissen'. Since the book was open at the first page so that he could read the title, Robson-Scott replied, 'Es ist das Nibelungenlied', to which Kralik responded with 'Gut. Sie haben bestanden', and that was the end of that. When it came to the graduation ceremony the newly appointed Gauleiter of Vienna (Odilo Globocnik?) said, 'I understand we have some foreign students taking their doctorates today. I hope they will return to their home countries and tell their compatriots how things are in the glorious Reich', to which Robson-Scott muttered under his breath, 'We most certainly shall'. Robson-Scott's extensive correspondence, some five hundred letters including several from Christopher Isherwood whom he knew in Berlin, is now in the

Dehmel, who knew Bithell well, learned of his appointment to London, he wrote, 'Ich wette, die Leute werden bald merken, was für ein rares kleines Juwel Sie sind', elaborating the metaphor by evoking Bithell's ginger hair and freckled complexion: 'den seidenen Glanz Ihres sardonyxroten Haars und Ihrer topasgoldnen Sommersprossen'.[102]

Bithell was a forceful and inspiring teacher and a meticulous and wide-ranging scholar, yet he never rose beyond the rank of Reader in German (a position he reached in 1921), the College's application to the University of London for him to be made a professor being unsuccessful. This is not surprising because both Priebsch and Robertson disdained him as a popularizer who wrote textbooks and journalism and made a commercial living out of his knowledge, something that (in Norman's view) they themselves were incapable of doing.[103] Years later Leonard Willoughby claimed that Bithell did not advance to professor because he 'had not done Gothic', regarded as the basis of sound training for any Germanic philologist, but Bithell himself, in a letter of 17 October 1948 to his friend Rudolf Majut (1887–1981, Lecturer in German at University College, Leicester), asserted that the application had failed because Hermann Georg Fiedler (1862–1945), Professor of German at Oxford, believed he had not published enough – though in fact he was a remarkably prolific scholar[104] –,

Harry Ransom Center at the University of Texas. Robson-Scott enjoyed short-lived fame in the national press in December 1975 when from the vantage point of his flat at 19 Dorset Square, London NW1, he was able to witness the progress of the six-day Balcombe Street siege in which four desperados from the Provisional IRA took two people hostage in their flat at 22b Balcombe Street, Marylebone. On Robson-Scott see also Charmian Brinson and Richard Dove, 'Friends and Enemies: The Freier Deutscher Kulturbund and the British, 1938–1946', *Angermion*, 5 (2012), 135–46.

102 Richard Dehmel, *Ausgewählte Briefe* (Berlin: Fischer, 1923), no. 175.

103 Priebsch and Robertson levelled the same objections to William Rose (on him see below) who edited several well-selling volumes in the 'Benn's Sixpenny Library' series in the late 1920s and early 1930s, soliciting leading authorities in such areas as history, literature, religion, psychology, science, and economics to contribute. One of Bithell's books, his *Companion to German Studies*, I encountered in my school library over sixty years ago; although I would not say it decided me to become a Germanist, it certainly had a positive effect.

104 Not only did Bithell publish profusely (see *German Life and Letters*, n.s. 11, 4 (July 1958), 255–56; the British Library catalogue records some seventy items under his name (including *The Minnesingers* (London: Longman, Green & Co. 1909) which, interestingly, was reviewed by D. H. Lawrence (see Armin Arnold, *D. H. Lawrence and German Literature, with Two Hitherto Unknown Essays* (*Review of H. G. Fiedler's Oxford Book of German Verse. – Review of Jethro Bithell's The Minnesingers* [originally published anonymously in the *English Review*] *by D. H. Lawrence* (Montreal: H. Heinemann, 1963)), he – and indeed William Rose also – were unusual in having had direct contact with many German and other European writers, including those exiled in Britain. See Wolfgang Brenn, 'British "Germanistik" and the Problem of National Socialism', *German Life and Letters*, n.s. 42 (1988–89), 145–67 (p. 157); also William Rose, 'German Literary Exiles in England', *German Life and Letters*, o.s. 2 (1937), 33–38.

and because Robertson in particular had always been hostile towards him as Bithell, despite cutting a dignified figure with his bow-tie and gold-rimmed spectacles, 'never was a society man. I detest being respectable and social ... I am a very rough customer; a regular Lancashire lad, with the manners of a miner'.[105] He carried on regardless; as he once wrote, 'The only thing of importance in this life is duty. Nothing else is worth a button'.[106] One of Bithell's students at Birkbeck – though I think only as a subsidiary student – was William Joyce, 'Lord Haw Haw' (1906–1946), who graduated with a First in English in 1927. The amazing thing about Bithell was that, despite his shabby treatment by the University, he was so generous, leaving his estate first in trust to his wife, Alice Emily Eastlake[107] and then to the University for 'the sole and exclusive benefit of the Institute of Germanic Languages and Literatures' (as the Institute of Germanic Studies was originally called). How very lucky we were one only realizes when one discovers that in 1907 Bithell had applied for the chair of German at Sheffield – fortunately for us, he was not even shortlisted there.[108] Bithell's generosity is all the more remarkable considering that he retired in 1938, long before the idea of an institute had even been proposed, and never set foot in it when it was founded in 1950. There is, in fact, rather more to this story than the official records relate. It seems that Bithell himself had been induced by Frederick Norman to insert a clause into his will expressing the wish, 'but creating no trust in the matter, that if the income from the trust fund be sufficient', that the University

105 His 'roughness' seems to have expressed itself not least in his robust criticism of his colleagues. Thus in a letter dated 6 August 1948 to Rudolf Majut he relates how he had once submitted 'a voluminous and withering report' to a prospective publisher of August Closs's *The Genius of the German Lyric*, and declared the same author's *Die freien Rhythmen in der deutschen Lyrik* (Bern: Francke, 1947) to be 'absolutely *ghastly*: I can't imagine how a Swiss publisher found it possible to accept it'. (*The Genius of the German Lyric* was first published by Allen & Unwin in 1938 and reissued in a revised edition by the Cresset Press, London, in 1962.)

106 *The Times*, 9 March 1962. On Bithell see John L. Flood, 'Bithell, Jethro', in *ODNB*, http://www.oxforddnb.com/view/article/61617; John S. Andrews, 'Jethro Bithell (1878–1962)', *The University of Leeds Review*, 5 (1962), 146–53 (with portrait); the special number of *German Life and Letters* marking his eightieth birthday (1958); The *Times* obituary (6 March 1962); *German Life and Letters*, n.s. 15 (1962), 315; and Rodney Livingstone, 'The Contribution of German-speaking Jewish Refugees to German Studies in Britain', in Werner E. Mosse (ed.), *Second Chance. Two Centuries of German-speaking Jews in the United Kingdom* (Tübingen: J. C. B. Mohr (Paul Siebeck), 1991), pp. 137–52 (p. 144).

107 Alice Emily Eastlake (1894–1974) was a former student of Bithell's. She had graduated with a First Class degree in 1930 and taken a PhD in 1937 with a thesis entitled 'The Influence of English Literature on the German Novel and Drama 1880–1900'. During the war she had worked deciphering codes for the Foreign Office, presumably at Bletchley Park, but it was her skills as 'a good cook and stitcher' (letter to Rudolf Majut, 30 October 1949) that Bithell prized when, in 1947, she became his second wife, his first having died in 1946.

108 Newton, *German Studies at The University of Sheffield*, pp. 56–57. Other candidates not shortlisted included Mr Milner-Barry and Dr Julius Steppat.

should use the funds to establish in his memory a Bithell Professorship tied with the directorship of the Institute. In the opinion of Mrs Bithell, Norman, who at the time of Bithell's death in 1962 was director of the Institute, aimed to arrange things to his own personal advantage with the money being used to endow a lavishly funded full-time professorial post with minimal duties at the Institute. Norman several times travelled down to Paignton in Devon to browbeat Mrs Bithell into submission – she once wrote to her friend Rudolf Majut saying how terrified she was of 'the Norman invasion', and on 6 September 1962 she complained bitterly to Majut about Norman's scheming, adding, 'I always said that of all the University people I know I liked Norman the least. Now that he has revealed himself I *dislike* him intensely'.[109] It is not clear whether she eventually succumbed to Norman's wiles, but whether she did or not, it was, it seems, the University that put paid to his scheme. In any case, one can scarcely imagine that Norman, the medievalist, would really have relished being known as the Bithell Professor of German, perpetuating the name of a man who 'had not done Gothic'.

German began at Royal Holloway College with the appointment of Dr Wilhelmine Delp (1882–1978) in 1908. The daughter of Carl Delp, a German businessman in Forest Hill, London, where there was a thriving German community, she had taken a First at Girton College in 1905, with Karl Breul as one of her examiners, and had been awarded a Pfeiffer Research Scholarship at Cambridge. This took her to Paris where she presented a thesis on a medieval French romance entitled *Étude sur la langue de Guillaume de Palerne* at the Sorbonne in 1907.[110] In 1909 she also published an edition of Honoré de Balzac's *César Birotteau* (Oxford Modern French Series), the story of a Parisian parfumier who achieves success in the cosmetics business but goes bankrupt due to property speculation. In German she published an article on 'Goethe and Gessner', in *The Modern Language Review*, 20 (1925),

109 The Bithell–Majut correspondence, some two hundred letters written between August 1944 and December 1961, is held in the Institute's archive. It gives a vivid insight into academic life, the problems of publishing, and the books being read in the post-war period, as well as into Bithell's struggles with his various research projects, notably his German dictionary, for which he would plague Majut with such queries as to the German for 'friar's balsam' and 'Yale key'. Mrs Bithell's intense dislike of Norman surfaced again when she wrote to Majut on 21 November 1962 after going through her late husband's papers. She writes of Norman, 'He does not believe in paying subscriptions. I found several lists of members of various societies which Jet [= Jethro] had marked that Norman was not a member. He seems to prefer filching other people's money which, apparently, he spends on stuff sold in bottles'.

110 There is a copy in the British Library. On her see *German Life and Letters*, n.s. 26 (1972–73), 172–73. Correspondence of Wilhelmine Delp is mentioned in Lutz Trautmann, *Findbuch zum Nachlass Hugo Hepding (1878–1959) und Familie*, Berichte und Arbeiten aus der Universitätsbibliothek und dem Universitätsarchiv Gießen, 61 (Gießen: Universitätsbibliothek, 2013) – Hugo Hepding, director of Gießen University Library from 1945 to 1948, was the husband of Dr Delp's niece Aenne Quentell.

333–37, and reviews of books by Edna Purdie. Dr Delp retired in 1944 but still regularly attended lectures at the Institute of Germanic Studies in the 1960s and 1970s. During the Second World War she had a colleague in Irene Morris (1913–2007), a Belfast graduate who later taught at Cambridge and Nottingham. She was a real character, an indomitable woman who witnessed Nazi processions in Munich in the 1930s and studied at Heidelberg, Dresden and Frankfurt. She once swam Belfast Lough, greased up like an Olympic swimmer, and once nearly drowned swimming across the Rhine near Bonn to fetch a bottle of beer for a friend.[111] When Dr Delp retired she was succeeded as Head of German by Margaret Fitzgerald Richey, who wrote extensively on Wolfram von Eschenbach and Walther von der Vogelweide.

Stuck out at Royal Holloway, with virtually no public transport other than the occasional horse-drawn bus to Egham station, Dr Delp seems to have been left to her own devices, not able to participate in intercollegiate teaching. The handful of teachers in London itself – Priebsch and Robertson, Atkins and Emma Buchheim at King's, Bithell, Julius Steppat[112] and one or two others – were expected to cater for all the needs of the subject, including Science German, throughout the University. Intercollegiate teaching was very much the norm: there is evidence that Birkbeck students attended evening courses at King's, and that King's Professor Atkins taught at Birkbeck in the morning. Moreover, in 1911 the Academic Council sanctioned a joint King's and Birkbeck scheme for seven evening courses which had Steppat doing three hours on Prose composition, Gothic, and Middle High German, Jethro Bithell doing two hours on Luther and a modern German text, and Atkins lecturing on the history of literature 1740–1805 and also on the drama of *Sturm und Drang*.[113] Science German was in the hands of Adolf Georg Haltenhoff (born *c.*1868, died 21 September 1938), attested at King's

111 Elizabeth Boa, 'An Indomitable and Vivid Personality. Irene Victoria Morris (1913–2007)', *Friends of Germanic Studies Newsletter*, 2007, 34–36.

112 Franz Julius Steppat (1866–1932) had graduated in London in 1896 and then took a doctorate under Richard Heinzel (1838–1905) at Vienna. He is mentioned by Priebsch as 'mein Lector [probably in the sense of 'Reader'] Dr. Steppat' in a letter of 6 March 1904 (Closs (ed.), *Robert Priebsch, Elias von Steinmeyer: Briefwechsel*, p. 132; see also p. 270) and certainly appears as Reader in German at University College in 1918–19, teaching Old and Middle High German; he retired in 1930. He is mentioned by Michael Batts in 'Die englische Germanistik um 1896', p. 382. Steppat seems to have published nothing. The Bayerische Staatsbibliothek holds seven letters from him to Carl von Kraus (1868–1952), dating from 1902 to 1913.

113 Senate Minute 143 of 18 October 1911. Given that around 1970 colleagues were exercised by the fact that, as yet, there was no paper in the BA Examination devoted entirely to twentieth-century literature (there was only a section on what was largely a paper on nineteenth-century literature), it is interesting to note that even in 1911 the course seems not to have extended beyond the death of Schiller in 1805! In London, even in the late 1980s, the curriculum was largely based on the notion of two classical periods: the Middle High German *Blütezeit* and Weimar Classicism.

from 1912 and as Assistant at University College in 1918–19. Norman recalls that Haltenhoff was 'a very, very good businessman' who:

> produced a German Science reader and he published this himself and he had it printed in Germany, and when inflation came in Germany, of course he had it printed very cheaply and he had the foresight to have thousands of copies printed of this wretched book, and he used to sell this to students. The first thing that happened at the beginning of the Session, when he'd get about 150 chemistry, physics and mathematics students all assembled and not knowing anything about anything and all rather terrified, he would call upon one or two of the students and give them a packet of this stuff and say, 'They're 7*s*. 6*d*. a time. Go round and sell 'em!' And the students used to walk round and collect 7*s*. 6*d*. off each of the other students, and Haltenhoff used to pocket the money. Whether they then, after that, ever came anywhere near his course, was more than he cared about.[114]

Apparently Haltenhoff called himself Dr Haltenhoff but after Priebsch enquired as to how he had come by this title, he suddenly reverted to calling himself Mister. It is possible that Haltenhoff lost his job – at least temporarily – during the First World War because by 1918 Science German was also being taught by Arthur Cyril Dunstan (1878–1965), who had taken his doctorate at Königsberg with a thesis entitled *Examination of Two English Dramas: 'The Tragedy of Mariam,' by Elizabeth Carew; And 'The True Tragedy of Herod and Antipater, with the Death of Faire Marriam,' by Gervase Markham and William Sampson* in 1908.[115] He remained in Königsberg until

114 Transcript of an interview given by Norman on 10 June 1965. Haltenhoff, whose full name was Adolf Georg(e) Martin Ludwig Ernest Haltenhoff, had married in October 1900 and lived (in 1926) at 79E Harcourt Terrace, West Brompton; he was described in *The London Gazette*, 11 May 1926, p. 3135, as being of 'No Nationality'. He also taught at the LSE, and on the title page of *A New German-English Dictionary (in roman type)* (London: Hachette, n.d.) he described himself as 'Lecturer in German in the University of London, Professor of German at the Royal College of Music, Head of the Modern Language Department, Imperial College of Science and Technology, London, etc.'. On his publications see Flood, 'The London Branch of the Allgemeiner Deutscher Sprachverein', pp. 244–46.

115 From the archivist at QMUL (11.2.16): 'Dr Dunstan joined the Faculty of Arts as a Lecturer in 1915 and left at the end of the 1929–30 academic year. He remained a Lecturer throughout. Dr Dunstan was the only member of staff for German, and there was no distinct German department during his time at QMC. When he began in 1915 he taught Intermediate and Pass courses. In 1918–19 he began teaching German courses for science students. In 1920–21 he began teaching Honours courses, and in 1923–24 German courses for History students were introduced. He also taught evening classes. While at the College, Dunstan's publications included: *Englische Phonetik mit Lesestücken*, 2. Aufl. besorgt M. Kaluza (Berlin: Göschen, 1921; repr. 1931) (1st edn Berlin: Göschen, 1912); 'The German Influence on Coleridge', *Modern Language Review*, July 1922; 'Sources and Text of the Middle High German Poem "Die Hochzeit" [Part I]', *Modern Language Review*, July 1925; part II, *Modern Language Review*, April 1926; 'Beowulf, lines 223-4', *Modern Language Review*, July 1925; Review of Eduard Sievers' *Deutsche Sagversdichtungen des IX-XI Jahrhunderts*, *Modern Language*

1914 when he was arrested as an unfriendly alien and despatched to Berlin; however, he eluded his guards at the Berlin railway station and escaped with his wife and small child to Sweden and thence back to Britain. He was a lecturer in German at East London College (the later Queen Mary College) from 1915 to 1930 when he went to the University of Sheffield, succeeding Leonard Willoughby.[116] There was no German Department as such at Queen Mary until Arthur Hatto was appointed in 1937, even though Dunstan was teaching Honours courses in German in 1920–21 (how this worked I do not understand, unless it refers to intercollegiate teaching).

The Origin of the Board of Studies in Germanic Languages and Literatures

The Board of Studies in Modern Languages, established in 1896, was renamed Board of Studies in Mediaeval and Modern Languages and Literatures in 1908 and operated as such until December 1921 when it was suddenly dissolved by Senate. This came about as a direct result of an unseemly clash of personalities involving Francis Yvon Eccles (1871–1963), a new Professor of Modern French at Bedford College – he held the Chair from 1920 to 1934 – but oddly not named as a member in the relevant Senate Minute, and Louis Brandin (1874–1940), Fielden Professor of French at University College. Apparently Eccles, who claimed a close friendship with Hilaire Belloc (1870–1953), fervently shared Belloc's militant Catholicism and anti-Semitism (especially with regard to the Dreyfus Affair and on Jewish and Masonic influence over England), and Brandin was Jewish.[117]

Review, April 1926; 'The Middle High German *Adam und Eva* by Lutwin, and the Latin *Vita Adae et Evae*', *Modern Language Review*, April 1929'. Later publications include: 'Muspilli and the Apocryphal Gospels', *German Life and Letters* 11 (1958), 270–75. With W. W. Greg he edited Elizabeth Carew, *The Tragedy of Mariam*, Malone Society reprints (Oxford: OUP, 1914). He was co-author with Karl Heine of *Lehr- und Lesebuch der englischen Sprache für Mittelschulen* (Hannover and Berlin: C. Meyer, 1921). An obituary on him by R. J. McLean appeared in *German Life and Letters*, n.s. 19 (1965), 75–76.

116 Dunstan taught at Sheffield until 1945, being appointed Head of the German Department in 1933 (Newton, *German Studies at The University of Sheffield*, pp. 9–10, p. 19, pp. 78–79, p. 81).

117 'Given that in his published writings Eccles made no secret of views that would today be described as racist and fascist, his appointment to a Chair in the University of London, an institution founded with articulated liberal intentions, is a token in itself of that liberalism, and of the University's dedication to freedom of thought and speech' (Jacobs, 'French', pp. 120–21; on Eccles, pp. 119–21). At Bedford he succeeded Gustave Rudler who had moved to take up the Marshal Foch Chair of French at Oxford in 1920. Eccles published *A Century of French Poets* (1909), *Alsace-Lorraine* (1915), *La Liquidation du romantisme, et les directions actuelles de la littérature française* (1919), *Racine in England* (1922), and Hilaire Belloc, *Pour mieux comprendre l'Angleterre contemporaine* ... Préface de Francis Yvon Eccles (Paris, *c.*1938).

It seems that Eccles objected to Brandin being accorded precedence in some matter being discussed at a meeting that was being chaired by the Germanist J. G. Robertson. The meeting broke up in chaos, and Robertson was so upset that he rushed off to see the Vice-Chancellor, saying, 'I refuse to be chairman of this any longer!'. The upshot was that a motion was put to the Senate at its very next meeting that the Board of Studies in Mediaeval and Modern Languages be replaced with effect from 1 January 1922 by separate Boards of English, of Romance Languages and Literatures, and of Germanic Languages and Literatures – thus the Germanists left the Romanists to stew on their own.[118] Margaret Richey, reminiscing in 1964, remarked on how pleasant it was 'to escape from the crowded traffic of the Modern Language Board to the smaller dimensions of a family circle'[119] – the old Board had had seventy-one members, the new Germanic Board only eighteen. Of course, the smaller size did not necessarily mean that Board meetings were henceforward all sweetness and light, rather than the scene of tensions and tantrums.

Senate Minute 835 (UoL ST2/2/38) resolved: 'That the Board of Studies in the Germanic Languages and Literatures (excluding English) be constituted for 1922 as follows:

> TEACHERS: Prof. H. G. Atkins, Mr. J. Bithell, Mr O. I. Björkhagen, Mrs J. Crosland, Miss W. E. Delp, Dr A. C. Dunstan, Prof. P. Geyl, Mr I. C. Gröndahl, Mr P. Harting, Mr J. H. Helweg, Prof. W. P. Ker, Miss I. M. Massey, Dr W. Perrett, Prof. R. C. Priebsch, Miss M. F. Richey, Prof. J. G. Robertson, Dr J. Steppat. OTHER PERSONS: Dr L. A. Willoughby'.

118 At its meeting on 16 March 1921, the Senate considered the Academic Council's proposal for 'Partition of [the] Board of Studies in Mediaeval and Modern Languages and Literatures'. After noting 'several communications from the Chairman of the Board of Studies in Mediaeval and Modern Languages and Literatures [Robertson], and a final report from the Board itself, adopted after "long and careful debate", consideration was given to a recommendation that the existing Board comprising 71 members be split into three new Boards each with about 24 members. In addition, a Standing Joint Committee should be established to deal with matters of general policy affecting more Boards than one, so that divergence of method might be avoided'. Accordingly, it was resolved (UoL Archive, UoL ST2/2/37 [Senate Minute 2736/86]): 'That as from 31 December 1921 the Board of Studies of Mediaeval and Modern Languages and Literatures cease to exist'. And (SM 2737/87): 'That as from 1 January 1922 there be constituted three new Boards of Study – each to be deemed to be within the purview of the Faculty of Arts – viz., "in English Language and Literature (including Celtic)", "in the Romance Languages and Literatures", and "in the Germanic Languages and Literatures", and that it be referred to the Board of Studies in Mediaeval and Modern Languages and Literatures in their first meeting at the first Session 1921–22 to consider and report to the Senate through the Committees and Boards of Studies Revision Committee upon the constitution of these three Boards for the year 1922'.

119 Unpublished transcript of an interview given by Dr Richey in January 1964 in the possession of the author.

Of these eighteen persons, only eleven were *Germanisten* in the narrowest sense of German specialists – the remaining seven represented Dutch, Scandinavian or had wide medieval interests.[120] The eleven German specialists were: Henry Atkins (University Reader, Professor at King's), Jethro Bithell (Birkbeck), Wilhelmine Delp (RHC), Arthur Dunstan (East London College [later QMC]), Isabella Massey (Bedford College),[121] Wilfrid Perrett (UC),[122] Robert Priebsch (University Professor), Margaret Richey (RHC), J. G. Robertson (University Professor), Julius Steppat (Reader at King's), and Leonard Willoughby, who was then at the University of Sheffield and was on the Board as an 'other person' – he had already been elected a Fellow of University College (where he had been a student under Priebsch) in 1910 and thus seems to have been earmarked for recruitment when a suitable opening arose.

Not yet members of the Board but already teaching were William Rose[123] at King's and Frederick Norman at University College. This, of

120 These seven members were:
Immanuel Björkhagen (1888–1994), Lecturer in Swedish, University College, 1921–27; author of *Modern Swedish Grammar*, 2nd revd edn (Stockholm: Norstedt, 1930).
J. Crosland (d. 1947), possibly the translator of Felix Weingartner, *On the Performance of Beethoven's Symphonies* (London: Breitkopf & Härtel, 1907); *The Song of Roland.* Newly translated into English by Jessie Crosland. With an introduction by Professor L. M. Brandin (London: Gollancz, 1907); and editions and translations of various other medieval French texts (see COPAC).
Pieter Geyl (1887–1966), Professor of Dutch History, 1919–35.
I. C. Grøndahl, author of *A First Norwegian Reader* (London: Sidgwick & Jackson, n.d.).
Pieter Harting (1892–1970), founder of the Department of Dutch at Bedford College, later Reader in Dutch 1924–30 and thereafter Professor of English at Groningen.
Jakob Heinrich Helweg (1885–1941), with J. Bithell author of *English-Danish Commercial Correspondence* (London, 1927).
W. P. Ker (1855–1923), Quain Professor of English, University College, since 1889.
At a later stage, the Scandinavian specialists, all of whom were based in the Department of Scandinavian Studies at University College, seceded to form a Board of Studies in Scandinavian Languages and Literatures.

121 Isabella Mellis Massey (1885–1960), published *Text- und Quellenstudien zu dem anonymen mitteldeutschen Gedicht von den Sieben Weisen Meistern* (unpublished doctoral thesis, University of Marburg, 1913; copy in Liverpool UL). Fluent in Italian, she also translated the writings of the antifascist politician and historian Gaetano Salvemini (1873–1957) into English. She is mentioned in Isabelle Richet, 'Marion Cave Roselli and the Transnational Women's Antifascist Networks', *Journal of Women's History*, 24 (2012), 117–39.

122 Perrett had taken a doctorate at Jena in 1902, his thesis being published as *The Story of King Lear: from Geoffrey of Monmouth to Shakespeare* (Berlin, 1904). Thereafter he spent some years as Lektor at Bonn before joining University College in 1907.

123 Rose (1894–1961) was educated at the Birmingham Hebrew School from where he entered the King Edward VI Grammar School, Birmingham. He went on to attend Birmingham and London Universities. During World War I, and until 1920, he served in the Royal Warwickshire Regiment, the Machine Gun Corps and then with the RAF. He was appointed

course, reminds us of another criticism of the Board of Studies: that it was terribly hierarchical.[124] First of all, one had to be a Recognised Teacher of the University to be admitted to membership, and until the 1970s 'Recognition' was not automatic on completing one's probation period of three years. One had to have a good publication record – when she was Chairman of the Board considering applications for recognition, Edna Purdie was heard to say, 'We'll have a few more thousand words out of him first!' Even when one was on the Board one was not necessarily trusted: George Wells told me in the 1970s that he had been on the Board for fourteen years before he was allowed to examine an Honours paper (before that he had had to be content to examine BA General and Subsidiary papers, of which, in those days, there were large numbers[125]). How all-powerful and overweening the professors

---

Lecturer at King's in 1920, under Robertson he obtained a London doctorate – possibly even the very first London doctorate in German – for his thesis on Goethe and Byron (1924), and became Reader at King's in 1927. He was appointed Sir Ernest Cassell Reader in German and Head of the Department of Modern Languages at the London School of Economics in 1935 (the Cassell Trust had given money to the LSE to have German taught to economists). In 1949 he was appointed to a Chair of German Language and Literature by the University, tenable at LSE. During World War II Rose was in the Intelligence Corps (1939–44) working on code-breaking at Bletchley Park. After 1933, he took a personal interest in the fate and welfare of German exiled intellectuals, and figures such as Franz Werfel and Stefan Zweig were frequent and welcome visitors to his house. He made his support public by being a member of the PEN-Club and joining in public condemnation of the Nazi regime with regard to the treatment of Jews, intellectuals and cultural life generally in Germany. He was involved in the 'German Library of Burned Books' scheme (1934, under the presidency of Heinrich Mann) whose British committee was headed by H. G. Wells. André Gide was among the honorary presidents. The core of Rose's research interests lay in the work of Goethe, Heine and Rilke, but he also worked on modern German lyric poetry and the Expressionists. As one of the growing band of Germanisten in British universities who were not German-born, he was an articulate and vigorous proponent of a new approach to German Studies. He believed that the connection between literature and life should never be forgotten, and pioneered the introduction of the psychoanalytical approach to the study of German literature, vigorously upholding his belief in its sociological implications. Like Jethro Bithell, he was regarded by some of his peer group as a popularizer. In his last years he had to contend with the onset of blindness, but did not allow this to interfere with his interests. He was active right up to the time of his death, having delivered a characteristically interesting and lively address at a farewell dinner given in his honour by the Board of Studies. He had a fall in Senate House following the dinner and died from his head injuries the next day. He had been due to be Visiting Professor at McGill University, Canada, in 1962.

124 The hierarchy stemmed from the University's distinction between 'Appointed Teachers' (Professors and Readers) and 'Recognised Teachers' (College-appointed Senior Lecturers and Lecturers who had achieved 'Recognition'; Assistant Lecturers did not qualify for membership of the Board). Status and social distinctions were rife: in the mid-1960s a humble research assistant to Brian Woledge, Fielden Professor of French at University College, was ordered always to travel first-class when on College business. And at King's there were quite distinct Senior Common Rooms for men and women until at least 1975.

125 The BA General degree involved studying three subjects to the same level, roughly equivalent to taking three subjects at the Subsidiary level. (The Subsidiary subject was

were still rankles with him: in his reply to a letter I had written to him to congratulate him on his ninetieth birthday, he wrote:

> Attitudes to heads of departments have undergone a remarkable change since the days of Purdie and Norman (and even Wilkinson). Then it was almost criminal to express any disagreement with the boss. Now the head is styled an insufferable tyrant if he (or she) fails to do what his junior colleagues tell him to do.[126]

Then, of course, there was the inner sanctum, the Higher Degrees Sub-committee, populated almost entirely by the professors. As well as handling various confidential matters, this Sub-committee controlled research in German across the University, approving or rejecting thesis titles, and appointing supervisors and examiners.

The Changing of the Guard in the 1930s

The 1930s saw the changing of the old guard, with a new generation of giants taking over, Leonard Willoughby succeeding Priebsch in 1931, Edna Purdie succeeding Robertson in 1933, and Frederick Norman succeeding Atkins in 1937. Willoughby, Purdie and Norman formed a powerful trio during the 1930s and beyond, and they had an impressive supporting cast of other scholars to assist them, including Arthur Hatto, W. F. Mainland,[127] D. F. S.

taken by candidates taking Single Honours degrees in another subject, e.g. Honours French with German Subsidiary.) Until the 1980s there were large numbers of candidates for the General degree and the Subsidiary Examination, including not only Internal Students (registered at the various Colleges but excluding University College which already had its own arrangements) but also very many External Students, presenting themselves for University of London degrees at various regional examination centres both in Britain and abroad. If memory serves aright, there were sometimes about three hundred General and Subsidiary candidates each year, but numbers declined rapidly with the introduction of more Combined Studies degrees in the early 1970s and the gradual demise of the External system following the enormous expansion of the Higher Education sector in Britain from the mid-1960s onwards.

126 G. A. Wells to the author, 4 June 2016. The 'days of Purdie, Norman (and even Wilkinson)' were the 1950s and 1960s. However great the power of these people, surely none of them could match the hubris of Professor Richard Heinzel, Director of the Germanistisches Seminar at Vienna, who shot himself in his office on 4 April 1905, leaving a note with strict instructions that his body remain there until his funeral – was the power of a professor in those days really so extensive, reaching from the beyond? For details of this amazing incident see Closs (ed.), *Robert Priebsch, Elias von Steinmeyer: Briefwechsel*, p. 145.

127 William Faulkner Mainland (1905–1982), Professor of German at Sheffield, 1953–70, was another distinguished pupil of Priebsch and Robertson. He taught at several London Colleges between 1928 and 1944. On him see Newton, *German Studies at the University of Sheffield*, pp. 82–86.

Scott,[128] Margaret Fitzgerald Richey, William Rose and others. The time when these three influential professors ruled the roost was perhaps the heyday of the Board – Arthur Hatto often referred to it, in his inimitable way, as 'the heroic age' of London Germanistik.

There was, however, one opportunity for the residual 'old guard' to flex its muscles for the last time: after the retirement of Priebsch and Robertson and especially before Purdie had been able to establish herself firmly in office, Atkins – having been in post for over thirty years and now decidedly the senior man – became undisputed Chairman of the Board of Studies and seized the opportunity to introduce an alternative syllabus alongside the one Priebsch and Robertson had carefully built up over the preceding three decades. With the support of Leonard Willoughby and William Rose (then Secretary of the Board), neither of whom took much interest in Medieval Studies, Atkins rushed a resolution through the Board of Studies in the summer of 1933 to provide for students to opt to take courses in philosophy or history in lieu of historical grammar and Old High German. Atkins ensured that the scheme was approved by 'Chairman's action' on behalf of the Academic Council, the chairman being his colleague Claude Jenkins, Professor of Ecclesiastical History at King's, during the summer vacation, and it was then presented at Senate, where Atkins was a very powerful member, and approved without anybody knowing very much about it. Very soon 'Syllabus II', as it was known, was in operation, and both at King's and even at University College students quickly opted to take it in preference to the heavily medieval-biased Syllabus I. Syllabus II was, however, not a success because the courses in philosophy and history were not controlled by the Germanists: the students' examination papers were marked by philosophers or historians, and if the philosophers or historians said the appropriate mark was gamma, then gamma it was, because the candidates were not really Honours students of philosophy or history and did not really know enough about the subject. This meant that the results of candidates taking Syllabus II were often depressed, so it was not very difficult to have Syllabus II abolished after a few years.

Within a few years of Willoughby, Purdie and Norman taking office, what, in Thomas Gray's phrase, had been their 'cool sequester'd vale of life' was disrupted dramatically with the outbreak of the Second World War. The effect of the war on the various Colleges is related in their individual histories and cannot be recapitulated here. Suffice it to say that staff from Senate House,

128 Douglas Frederick Schumacher Scott was appointed Lecturer at King's College in 1946, having taken a London MA under Leonard Willoughby, which he found to be more challenging a task than taking his Dr. phil. degree at Göttingen with a dissertation (under the name Douglas Frederick Schumacher) on *Der Volksaberglaube in den Waverley Novels* (Göttingen, 1935). His inaugural lecture as professor at Durham in November 1959 was entitled *Wilhelm von Humboldt and the Idea of a University.*

the headquarters of the University which had only been completed in 1936 (coinciding with its centenary), were transferred to Royal Holloway College; only the Library (thanks solely to the obstinacy of the aged Librarian, the Egyptologist Reginald Arthur Rye (1876–1945), who simply refused to budge) and the maintenance department remained in Bloomsbury. Apart from Birkbeck, all the other Colleges made arrangements to find alternative homes in other university towns – King's at Bristol, University College at Aberystwyth, Bedford College at Cambridge, Westfield College at Oxford, Goldsmiths' College at Nottingham, for instance. Only Birkbeck stayed wholly in central London, in its grotty surroundings at Breams Buildings in Fetter Lane, where its library, including its German collections, was totally destroyed by bombing on 11 May 1941.[129] By that date, seven thousand books transferred by King's College from the Strand to 'safety' in Bristol had already been similarly destroyed, and University College had also lost one hundred thousand volumes. The impact of such losses on individual subject areas such as German Studies can only be imagined. How those who experienced the devastation at first hand were affected we can now only speculate, but some sense of how stressful life was may be gleaned from this letter from Mary Wilkinson, newly appointed as Assistant Lecturer at University College, written from her temporary home in Epsom on 28 September 1940:

> My dear Professor Purdie,
>
> As you have probably heard, University College has been very badly damaged and we are going back to Aberystwyth. [...]
>
> 2 Gordon St. [where the German Department was housed] was wrecked by the same H[igh] E[xplosive] bomb which demolished the Great Hall of U.C, a week last Wednesday. My sister and I were very lucky indeed as we were sheltering in the trenches in Gordon Square. Next morning a policeman under pressure let us into the house and get some of our things which we carried away in our two suitcases and several blanket bundles. I got most of the books, some notes and some clothes, but the policeman was very nervous on account of the unsafe state of the house and three time bombs in the street, so he hurried us all the time and many things had to be left. I don't know how much more havoc the time bombs will cause. They hadn't exploded yesterday.
>
> Poor U.C. looked terrible in that early grey light but nothing to what it looked on Wednesday morning of this week when I went along. During Tuesday night incendiary bombs had been dropped and the big library and the arts libraries were burnt out. It made one feel dreadful inside. I don't know how much of value was destroyed – I wanted to go up and help with the salvage but Mr. Johnson would not let me. [...]

129 See E. H. Warmington, *A History of Birkbeck College University of London during the Second World War 1939–1945* (London: Birkbeck College, 1954), esp. pp. 15–23.

Figure 7: L. A. Willoughby.

> I have tried so hard to work on preparation for my lectures but it has been hopeless at the B[ritish] M[useum] lately. Every time the sirens go we have to leave all books + descend. Then last Monday a bomb fell and damaged the Reading Room so it hasn't been available. I don't know what the German library is like at Aberystwyth but I shall just have to manage as best I can. [...][130]

The first of the new professors to be appointed in the 1930s was Leonard Ashley Willoughby (1885–1977), Professor at University College from 1931 to 1950. He had been a student under Priebsch and Robertson from 1902 to 1906 – his reminiscences of that time are recorded in his papers preserved in the Institute's archive.[131] Just as Robertson had studied under giants like Zarncke and Sievers at Leipzig, so Willoughby had been taught by Joseph Seemüller (1855–1920), Jakob Minor (1855–1912) and Max

130 This letter is among the Purdie Papers at Royal Holloway, University of London.

131 See Clare George, '"Not just the product of personal and historical piety but still intellectually alive today." The Papers of Willoughby and Wilkinson', *Friends of Germanic Studies at IMLR Newsletter* 2015, 8–9 (p. 9). He took his MA under Priebsch in 1903 with a thesis entitled 'Zwei unbekannte Fassungen von Gedichten: über die Fünfzehn Zeichen und Das jüngste Gericht: Text und Untersuchungen'. On Willoughby see Martin Swales, 'Willoughby, Leonard Ashley', *ODNB*, http://www.oxforddnb.com/view/article/62526.

Hermann Jellinek (1868–1938) at Vienna. He also studied at Bonn, and spent two years as Lektor at Cologne, before being appointed Taylorian Lecturer in German at Oxford from 1910 to 1919. From 1919 to 1930 he had been at Sheffield, and had then held the Henry Simon Chair of German at Manchester from 1930 to 1931.[132] When appointed in 1931, he already had a reputation as a medievalist (his Vienna doctorate was on a medieval text concerning the Last Judgment, which, he was fond of observing, gave him a place both in this world and the next), but he is now remembered primarily, along with his pupil and colleague Elizabeth Mary Wilkinson (1909–2001), as a scholar of Weimar Classicism. One of his students at Sheffield recalled, 'Willoughby was a real star turn. He was a very good scholar. He had a very nice speaking voice, and he looked like Goethe, and he was a bit of an actor, and it was really quite a show'.[133] Among his many achievements would be to realize a proposal made by the Conference of University Teachers of German in Great Britain and Ireland (CUTG)[134] in 1935 to found the journal *German Life and Letters* in 1936 and the Institute of Germanic Studies in the 1940s. In the preface to the first issue of *German Life and Letters* Willoughby optimistically wrote: 'This Journal appears at an auspicious moment when, after years of tension, the relations between England and Germany are definitely improving'. Three years later he was compelled to bid farewell to his readers, noting 'The opinion of the late London correspondent of the *Völkischer Beobachter* that *German Life and Letters* was "a journal which no self-respecting German could read" we took as a proof that our contributors have maintained a balanced judgment amidst the welter of rival ideologies'.[135] The idea for an institute – modelled on the pattern of the Institute of Historical Research, founded in 1921 – seems to have been first aired in discussion of a paper headed

132 See Newton, *German Studies at the University of Sheffield*, pp. 71–77. Willoughby was only the first of several London Professors who had taught or had studied at Manchester: others were Ralph Tymms (Royal Holloway), Ronald Peacock (Bedford), Kenneth King (King's), Claus Bock (Westfield), and Martin Durrell (Royal Holloway). Jethro Bithell had also taught there from 1906 to 1910.

133 Cited by Newton, *German Studies at The University of Sheffield*, p. 76.

134 Founded in 1932, renamed as Association for German Studies in Great Britain and Ireland in 2009. The acronym CUTG was not devised by the organization itself. It was invented by CILT (the Centre for Information on Language Teaching and Research) around 1975 which observed that the Conference (as it was traditionally known to members) was the only subject association in the field of Modern Languages that was not identified by a handy acronym – unlike the MLA (The Modern Language Association), AUPF (The Association of University Professors of French), the ATG (The Association of Teachers of German), etc.

135 *German Life and Letters*, o.s. 4 (October 1939), 78. See Charmian Brinson, 'Sixty Years On: *German Life and Letters* and the National Socialists', *German Life and Letters*, n.s. 49 (1996), 479–87.

'Proposals for the Foundation of an Institute of Germanic Languages within the University of London laid before the meeting of the Board of Studies in German on July 23rd 1943 by Professor L. A. Willoughby'. This was a response to the Senate's invitation to Boards to give consideration to reconstruction of the University after the war whose tide had turned in favour of the Allies. Further discussion followed on 23 September 1943, and finally on 21 December 1943 the Board agreed to submit to the University a proposal for 'the establishment of an Institute of Germanic Languages and Literatures'. At this meeting thirteen members were present. These progenitors were, in addition to Leonard Willoughby and Edna Purdie (Chairman of the Board), Gertrude Craig Houston,[136] Wilhelmine Delp, Mary Gilbert, Arthur Hatto,[137] Reginald McClean, Isabella Massey, Karl-Werner Maurer, Margaret Richey, William Rose, Theodoor Weevers[138] and John Wilks.[139] Willoughby observed that since the federal nature of the

136 Gertrude Alice Craig Houston (*c.*1888?–1953), BA (Belfast), MA (London). I have been unable to ascertain her precise connection with the University of London but she was associated with William Rose and may thus have taught at the London School of Economics. In May 1930 she applied, unsuccessfully, for appointment as Head of German at the University of Sheffield (Newton, *German Studies at The University of Sheffield*, p. 77). She died in Oxford. Her article 'From The *Stundenbuch* of Rainer Maria Rilke' appeared in the very first issue of *German Life and Letters*, o.s. 1 (1936), 49–52. Her works include: *The Evolution of the Historical Drama in Germany during the First Half of the Nineteenth Century* (Belfast: W. Mullan & Son, 1920, repr. New York: Haskell House, 1972); *Rainer Maria Rilke. Aspects of his Mind and Poetry*, ed. by W. Rose and G. C. Houston, with an introduction by Stefan Zweig (London: Sidgwick & Jackson, 1938; repr. New York: Haskell House, 1973); *Rilke and Rodin* ([Oxford], 1938); *Goethe in Strassburg and Wetzlar: Being selections from books IX–XII of Dichtung und Wahrheit*, ed. by G. Craig Houston (Oxford: Blackwell, 1944); *Note on Some Problems of Rilke-Forschung* (Oxford: Oxonian Press, [1939]), based on an address given to the CUTG in London on 9 July 1939 (copy in the National Library of Scotland).

137 It is interesting that Hatto, then aged thirty-three, was able to attend despite serving at Bletchley Park at this time. All the other men were beyond military age: Willoughby (b. 1885), Maurer (b. 1905, but a German), McClean (b. 1899), Rose (b. 1894), Weevers (b. 1904).

138 Weevers (1904–1992) had studied at Groningen and Leiden, here under Albert Verwey. He came to London in 1931 and headed Dutch at Bedford College (in succession to Pieter Harting who was Reader in Dutch from 1924 to 1930), becoming Professor of Dutch in 1945 and remaining until his retirement in 1971. According to Warmington, *A History of Birkbeck College*, p. 115, Weevers held a joint Readership at Bedford College and University College and also a Lectureship in Dutch at Birkbeck College in 1942–43. 'There is no difference between a professor and his students', he used to say. 'Neither of them knows anything, but the professor knows where to find it' (Cited from an obituary by William Woods, http://neon.niederlandistik.fu-berlin.de/static/nem_geschiedenis/GB/woods_1992.pdf).

139 John Wilks, Librarian of University College, remained a member of the Board and of the Institute's Committee of Management, advising the Institute on library matters, until 1955; he was the author of *Bestrafte Untreue. Eine allegorische mittelhochdeutsche Minnerede*

University meant its constituent Colleges were all essentially doing the same thing, it would be advantageous to pool the existing considerable resources for the teaching of German:

> generally it would mean the elimination of the waste of effort by which so many lectures now duplicated could be given in some central building to the whole honours school of German. It would benefit the staff by relieving it of burdensome preparation on subjects with which it might not be immediately familiar and so enable it to specialise and become ever more expert on one particular branch of the subject. [...] Students would be taught by experts and would hear things not to be found in books [...].[140]

Willoughby argued:

> All this implies the provision of opportunity for the centralisation of teaching. The ideal way of attaining this would be through a separate Germanic Institute situated centrally to all the Colleges, preferably on the University site. The ideal would be a distinct building (or a floor of a building) which would provide lecture rooms, a seminar library, reading rooms, seminar rooms, staff rooms. Such an institution would provide a centre of attraction for all the Germanic Studies in the metropolis and a house of call for all foreign scholars passing through London. It is an ambitious and expensive project which may or may not be immediately realisable. But the Board feels very strongly that it is an ideal which can and should be realised in the course of the next decade after the war. Meanwhile a beginning might be made on more modest lines: a few rooms provided in a University building, comprising a seminar library, a lecture room, a staff common room, and one or two private rooms for interviewing students. These are the minimum requirements which could justify the use of the term Germanic Institute, and they seem to the Board realisable within a few years of the cessation of hostilities.

The acceptance by Senate of Willoughby's imaginative proposal for the founding of an Institute was, however, by no means a foregone conclusion as finances were tight in a capital city gradually rebuilding itself after the war and the demands on the University's budget were many. Yet eventually in 1950, coinciding with Willoughby's retirement from University College, the Institute did become a reality. Initially it was allocated two rooms at 26 Russell Square, then later it moved to occupy the whole of 29 Russell Square,

---

(London: University Press, 1923), a thesis written under the direction of Priebsch; *Catalogue of Works Dealing with the Study of Western Palæography in the Libraries of the University of London*, compiled by John Wilks and Arthur Douglas Lacey (London, 1921); and *The influence of R. W. Chambers on the Development of University Libraries* (London: H. K. Lewis, 1953).

140 'Proposals for the Foundation of An Institute of Germanic Languages within the University of London laid before the meeting of the Board of Studies in German on July 23rd 1943 by Professor L. A. Willoughby', p. 1.

its home until 2004.[141] Whilst centralization of teaching was never achieved, intercollegiate lectures did take place (though not at the Institute, and probably not in the form Willoughby envisaged) and Special Subjects were instituted which were often taught at the IGS. The provision of intercollegiate activities remained within the purview of the Board of Studies. Of particular importance was the scheme for Special University Lectures (a programme introduced by the University in the 1930s) under which the Board was able to issue an invitation to a distinguished scholar from abroad each year to give two or three lectures: already in 1933 the Board invited Leopold Jessner, former Generalintendant of the Staatliche Schauspielhäuser in Berlin, who in 1935 delivered three lectures on 'Die Bedeutung des Regisseurs für die deutsche Bühne im 20. Jahrhundert'. Later we invited Albrecht Schöne who spoke on 'Biegen und Brechen', Benno von Wiese, Friedrich Ohly who came during the miners' strike and had to lecture in the Chancellor's Hall by the light of a paraffin lamp during a power cut, and especially Wolfgang Mohr, who gave three enthralling lectures on Gottfried von Straßburg's *Tristan* to a huge audience of students in the Chancellor's Hall at Senate House.

Edna Purdie (1894–1968) had studied at King's College for Women in 1910, taking a First in German in 1913, then another in English and, simultaneously, an MA in German in 1916 under Priebsch and Robertson. After teaching at Liverpool (deputising for W. E. Collinson who was undertaking military service from 1917 to 1919) and Bangor (1921–33), where she taught both modern and medieval literature – she always believed that the modern tendency towards specialization restricts and impoverishes younger scholars –, she became the first woman Professor of German in London in 1933, succeeding her revered mentor Robertson at Bedford College.[142] As Peter Ganz remarked, within the established tradition of German Studies in London, 'Edna Purdie, who valued and upheld the idea of continuity and scholarship in academic life, took her place among predecessors and contemporaries like H. G. Atkins, J. G. Robertson, Robert Priebsch, L. A. Willoughby and F. Norman. She was proud to belong to a tradition and devoted her life to furthering it'.[143] The previous year she had

141 For a detailed account of the Institute's subsequent development see Anne Simon's contribution to the present volume.

142 Before this there had been women professors of German in Ireland: Mary Macken at University College Dublin, and Maria W. Swertz at University College Cork (both in post by 1914), the latter succeeded by Bride Danaher (later known as Bride Lindsay) in 1915.

143 P. F. Ganz, in *German Life and Letters*, n.s. 22, 4 (1968–69), 417–19. On Purdie see also König (ed.), *Internationales Germanistenlexikon 1800–1950*, II, 1441–42, and the appreciations by M. O'C. Walshe and Wilhelmine Delp on her retirement, in *German Life and Letters*, n.s. 16, 3–4 (1962–63), 161–63. Purdie was succeeded by Ronald Peacock (1907–1993; he retired in 1975) at Bedford College; on him see the obituary in *The Independent*, 9 June 1993. Some of Professor Purdie's papers, along with some of those of J. G. Robertson, are

Figure 8: Edna Purdie.

published what was probably her most important book: *Friedrich Hebbel: A Study of His Life and Work* (London: OUP, 1932); this had been preceded by an edition of *Von deutscher Art und Kunst* (Oxford: Clarendon, 1924) and *The Story of Judith in German and English Literature* (Paris: Honoré Champion, 1927) and was followed by an edition of Hebbel's *Herodes und Mariamne* (Oxford: Blackwell, 1944), a selection of Hebbel's poems (Oxford: Blackwell, 1953) and, after her retirement in 1962, by *Studies in German Literature of the Eighteenth Century* (London: Athlone, 1965), a collection of ten essays written between 1938 and 1963. Norman seems to have had a tense relationship with her – nothing gave him greater pleasure than to tease her by appointing a succession of her best students to be humble departmental secretaries at King's – but, on the other hand, there is evidence

preserved in the archive at Royal Holloway, University of London.

that he encouraged her to propose some of her Bedford German students for 'work of national importance' at Bletchley Park during the war. An important joint achievement of Willoughby and Purdie was their success in getting Dr Robert Pick (1885–1967) released from Dachau concentration camp. Pick, whom Willoughby had got to know in Vienna, had become Professor of English at the Handelsakademie in Vienna, and after the First World War he had made great efforts to encourage academic exchanges with British universities. His daughter had been a Lektorin under Purdie at Bedford College. Pick was arrested by the Nazis on 10 November 1938, but through the efforts of Norman, Purdie and Dame Lilian Penson, Vice-Chancellor of the University, he was released after three months and he and his wife were met by their saviours at Croydon airfield. Although he was briefly interned on the Isle of Man, he was appointed Lecturer at King's College in 1943, and when he retired in 1950 he became the first librarian of the Institute of Germanic Studies; he was an enormous help to Willoughby scavenging for suitable furniture and building up the library.[144]

Frederick Norman (1897–1968) was an extraordinary person.[145] For reasons best known to himself, the details he gave about himself in *Who's Who* are at variance with the facts. His original name was in fact Ferdinand Krott; his parents were a German couple who ran a laundry in Fulham. When his father died in 1906, his mother married Albert Edward Norman, but her children did not adopt their stepfather's surname until about 1918. Her unmarried brother, a fairly prosperous Hamburg businessman, arranged for his English nephew Ferdinand to be educated in Germany. After a private school in London he was enrolled in a school at Hamburg (allegedly, the famous Johanneum, founded in 1529 by the Reformer Johannes Bugenhagen, though Krott's enrolment there cannot now be verified). In Germany when war broke out in August 1914, when he was not yet quite seventeen, young Krott declined an 'invitation' to join the German army, so he was interned in a camp on the racecourse at Ruhleben, near Berlin, along with some four thousand merchant sailors, businessmen, students and hapless tourists after the German authorities decided that autumn to incarcerate all British males aged from seventeen to fifty-five in retaliation for measures taken against 'enemy aliens' in Britain.[146] As one of the very youngest internees, Krott was

144 Pick published *Schiller in England 1787–1960*, Publications of the Institute of Germanic Studies, 3 (London, 1961). On him see Willoughby's appreciation in *German Life and Letters*, n.s. 15 (1961–62), 1–3, and the obituary in *German Life and Letters*, n.s. 20 (1966–67), 242–43.

145 John L. Flood, 'Norman, Frederick', *ODNB*, http://www.oxforddnb.com/view/article/62277.

146 Other British Germanists interned at Ruhleben included David Evans (1887–1968, Professor of German at Aberystwyth 1936–52) and Maximilian Friedrich Liddell (1887–1968, from 1933 Lecturer in German and subsequently Professor at Trinity College Dublin), who took his doctorate at Birmingham in 1925 with a thesis on 'German Sea Poetry' and

Figure 9: Frederick Norman.

known as 'Bimbo' (from 'bambino'), a nickname that stuck. Of the thirty or so German class-mates who had read Homer with him at Hamburg in 1914, he was the only one to survive the war. Following his release in late November 1918, shortly after his twenty-first birthday, Frederick Norman (as he now called himself) studied German at University College London under Priebsch and Robertson. He was Priebsch's star pupil: even before he graduated, Priebsch persuaded the Provost of University College to appoint him as Assistant Lecturer in German from September 1922 on a salary of

---

was author of *Ferdinand Freiligrath and His Times* (London, 1930), *Irland* (Leipzig and Berlin, 1931), and editor of the poems of Freiligrath (Oxford: Blackwell, 1949). On the camp see John Davidson Ketchum, *Ruhleben: A Prison Camp Society* (Toronto: Toronto University Press; London: Oxford University Press, 1965); Matthew Stibbe, *British Civilian Internees in Germany. The Ruhleben Camp 1914–18* (Manchester: Manchester University Press, 2008). During the war Kuno Meyer, now Professor in Berlin, once appeared in the Ruhleben camp, along with the Irish nationalist George Chatterton-Hill (1883–1947), chairman of the Deutsch-Irische Gesellschaft. The pair lined up all the Irish internees and gave them a long lecture on the wicked British and urged them, as loyal Irishmen, to fight against the British and help the Germans liberate them. At the end of his peroration, Meyer encouraged them to sing the Irish national anthem – but at that date there was no Irish national anthem other than 'God Save the King', which they defiantly sang with gusto, thus putting a swift end to the proceedings.

Figure 10: Arthur Hatto.

£75 p.a. (In those days Finals were not taken until October; Norman took his BA in October 1922 and his MA with Distinction in 1925).[147] His great ambition was to succeed Priebsch at University College, so he was massively disappointed when Willoughby was appointed there in 1931 and he regarded his own eventual appointment as Professor at King's in 1937 as a nugatory consolation prize. Throughout the 1930s Norman held half a Readership at University College and half a Readership at King's, playing off one College against the other so that he achieved the then impressive combined salary of £600 per annum.[148] His appointment as full-time Professor rather than part-time Reader at King's in 1937 had one important side-effect: it meant that King's had no further need of Arthur Hatto who was an Assistant Lecturer. Fortunately for him, Norman was able to engineer Hatto's appointment as Head of the newly created Department of German at Queen Mary, a post he held until his retirement in 1977.

Norman and Hatto were barely settled into their new posts before they found themselves closely involved with military intelligence work at Bletchley

147 In 1927 Norman was also appointed part-time Lecturer and Head of Department at the University of Reading, for which he was paid £200 p.a., which prompted University College to increase his salary there to £200 also.

148 In 1907 the University of London stipulated that Professors had to be paid £600 p.a., Readers £300, and Recognised Teachers £150. In 1939 an Assistant Lecturer received £250 and a Lecturer's salary was £350, rising by biennial increments to £475, which was £25 below the minimum for a Reader.

Park. From the start Norman played a leading role in Hut 3 where his team sifted German army and air force decrypts for information which might indicate technological or scientific innovations, thus providing advance warning of the details of German secret weapons. Among the men with whom he worked at Bletchley were several German scholars, including a number of his own pupils, who later, partly thanks to his patronage – Norman always considered himself the key player in British German Studies –, obtained Chairs at universities around the country. Not for nothing did Peter Ganz (whose doctoral thesis had been supervised by Norman) call Bletchley Park 'that nursery of British academics'[149] and once remark on how ironic it was that German Studies at British universities were largely in the hands of the people with the greatest reason to hate Germany – people like Norman and, of course, colleagues of Jewish extraction who had fled the Nazis.[150] On 23 November 1943 Norman made a discovery of major significance: in elucidating an intercepted German radio message he brilliantly deduced that 'Heuschrecke', the German code name for an important reporting station, was a pun on the name of the small Baltic islet of Oie, near Greifswald, which provided vital information as to the whereabouts of the headquarters of a radar tracking detachment essential to the work of the experimental V1 and V2 rocket range at Peenemünde; indeed, Oie itself was a testing ground for the V2.[151] As the war progressed, Norman, a linguist with no science, became a key associate providing intelligence to a scientist with no German, R. V. Jones (1911–1997), Assistant Director of Intelligence (Science), in the Air Ministry. He kept in touch with Jones after the war and indeed, meeting in the Athenaeum in 1958, he floated with him the idea of making a small fortune by jointly writing a book revealing – notwithstanding the constraints of the Official Secrets Act (Norman always had a rebellious streak about him) – the nature of their wartime work.[152] Letters from

149 In his obituary for F. P. Pickering, in *The Times*, 1 May 1981; reprinted in Newton, *German Studies at the University of Sheffield*, p. 82. Germanists at Bletchley included: F. P. Pickering (1909–1981, Sheffield, Reading), A. T. Hatto (1910–2010, QMC, London), R. V. Tymms (1913–1987, Manchester, RHC, London), Dorothy Reich (née Knight, 1921–2001, King's and Bedford Colleges, London), Kenneth Brooke (1914–1984, Keele), William Rose (1894–1961, King's and LSE, London), Kenneth Charles King (1911–1970, Manchester, Nottingham, King's London), Trevor Jones (1908–1984, Cambridge), Ronald Gray (1919–2015, Cambridge). During the war, Ganz himself was employed at Trent Park in north London, listening clandestinely to the conversations of captured senior German officers.

150 These included Claus Bock (1926–2008), Ilse Graham (née Appelbaum) (1914–1988), Charlotte Jolles (1909–2003), Siegbert Prawer (1925–2012), Hans Reiss (b. 1922), Werner Schwarz (1905–1982), and Ganz (1920–2006) himself.

151 Christy Campbell, *Target London: Under Attack from the V-Weapons during WWII* (London: Little, Brown, 2012), pp. 15–16.

152 The story of the work carried out at Bletchley Park was only revealed to the public years later through books such as F. W. Winterbotham's *The Ultra Secret* (London: Weidenfeld and Nicolson, 1974) and Peter Calvocoressi's *Top Secret Ultra* (London: Cassell, 1980). The

Figure 11: Bletchley Park, where a number of Germanists served during the war. Standing in the back row are Kenneth Brooke (second from left) and Brinley Newton-John (fourth from the left).

Norman are among Jones's papers at Churchill College, Cambridge. Norman was a brilliant and energetic personality, an enthralling lecturer, a stimulating and witty conversationalist, a competent pianist, lover of classical music and a balletomane, and his erudition was such that he either fascinated or terrified his students. During the 1930s he ran a highly successful seminar at University College on comparative folklore in which many of his young postgraduates – among them Arthur Hatto, Kenneth King (an Oxford graduate) and Maurice Walshe – were involved, but the papers relating to this important enterprise were destroyed when the College was bombed during the 1940s. Norman's colleagues and students knew him for a hard, yet just taskmaster. He was above all an organizer rather than a writer:[153] his most substantial publication was *Henry Crabb Robinson and Goethe*. Crabb Robinson (1775–1867), who had studied at Jena, was a friend of Goethe, Schiller, Herder, Hegel, Wordsworth,

latter includes a photograph on the third page of plates between pp. 54 and 55 (captioned 'The Officers of 3A in 1943 or 1944'), showing amongst others, Kenneth Brooke (later Professor of German at Keele University), and Brinley Newton-John (Headmaster of what is now Hills Road Sixth Form College in Cambridge and later Deputy Vice-Chancellor at the University of Newcastle, New South Wales, and father of the pop singer Olivia Newton-John).

153 What Leonard Forster said of Trevor Jones, 'Sein umfassendes Wissen wurde direkt, ohne den Umweg über den Druck, in seiner Lehrtätigkeit verwertet' (*Die Zeit*, 23 November 1984), could just as well have been said of Norman.

Coleridge, Charles Lamb and William Blake, and having retired as a barrister in 1828 had bought a share in University College of which he remained a staunch supporter until his death in 1867.[154] Norman was very active in stimulating research activity in others, a large number of useful projects being successfully completed under his direction. For instance, he initiated a series of studies of individual manuscripts of the *Nibelungenlied* – including Rosemary Wallbank's 'The Nibelungen Manuscript B (St Gall). A Study of its Language' (MA thesis, King's College, 1954), George Gillespie's 'The Manuscript C of the Nibelungenlied (Hofbibliothek Donaueschingen, Lassberg no. 174): a Study of its Provenance, History and Language' (MA thesis, King's College, 1957), and Robert F. E. Watson's 'A Study of Manuscript D of the Nibelungenlied and Klage (Cgm 31)' (PhD thesis, King's College, 1958) (later summarized in Watson's article 'Manuscript D of the Nibelungenlied and Klage (Cgm 31)', *Euphorion*, 57 (1963), 272–91); George Gillespie went on to produce a PhD thesis on 'The Personal Names in German Heroic Literature: a Catalogue and Study of the German Vernacular Material' in 1963 (subsequently published as *A Catalogue of Persons Named in German Heroic Literature (700-1600)* (Oxford: Clarendon, 1973)), itself a worthy companion to 'A Catalogue of Names of Persons in the German Court Epics', an MA thesis submitted by another of Norman's students, Frank W. Chandler, in 1936.[155] From 1956 to 1965 Norman was director of the Institute of Germanic Studies (a part-time appointment which, as we have seen, he failed, to his chagrin, to have converted into a full-time paid post). Many honours came to him: he became a Fellow of University College (1936), OBE ('employed in a Department of the Foreign Office', *London Gazette*, 6 June 1947, p. 2585), FSA (1949), Fellow of King's College London (1954), was awarded the Gold Medal of the Goethe Institute (1964), and in 1965 the *Preis für Germanistik im Ausland* by the German Academy for Language and Literature, Darmstadt. Yet perhaps his proudest boast was to be the only professor with a private bathroom at College in London, a relic from the days when the premises occupied by the King's German Department had been a pub on the Strand. His ambidexterity enabled him to write different things with each hand on the blackboard simultaneously, and legend has it that he even marked two piles of School Certificate scripts at once in order to finance a ticket for a whole season of the Diaghilev ballet. He was a prolific reviewer – once anonymously reviewing in the *Times Literary Supplement* Walter Dornberger's *V2* (London, 1954; original title: *V2 – der*

154 Crabb Robinson's most significant achievement was the creation of the Flaxman Gallery at University College (Harte and North, *The World of University College London 1828–1978*, pp. 66–67).

155 This was later published as *A Catalogue of Names of Persons in the German Court Epics*, edited with an introduction and an appendix by Martin H. Jones (London: King's College London, Centre for Late Antique and Medieval Studies, 1992).

Schuss ins Weltall: Geschichte einer großen Erfindung (Esslingen, 1952)), the classic account of German secret weapons by one of the men whose activities Norman had for so long been tracking at Bletchley Park.

If Willoughby was instrumental in founding *German Life and Letters* and the Institute of Germanic Studies, Norman was – or at least claimed to have been – responsible for the founding of the Conference of University Teachers of German (CUTG) in 1932: he was its first secretary and his boss, Atkins, was the first chairman. Indeed, he always liked to think of himself as a real power in the land as far as German Studies were concerned. He believed that no one should be appointed to a Chair unless it was with his blessing. Kenneth Brooke once told me that after he (Brooke) had been appointed Professor at Keele he was cold-shouldered by Norman who had not been consulted; only after a long interval had elapsed, when Brooke was sitting one day somewhere near the back in the audience at a lecture in London, did he suddenly feel a hand on his shoulder: it was Norman telling him to move to a seat at the front. He knew then that he had been 'accepted' at last. Among the colleagues whose careers Norman actively promoted were Arthur Hatto, who was appointed at Queen Mary College, Maurice Walshe, whom he got appointed as Head of Modern Languages at Nottingham immediately after the war (Walshe succeeded Ernest Weekley (1865–1954), whose wife, Frieda von Richthofen, had run off with D. H. Lawrence in 1913), Kenneth King, who succeeded Walshe at Nottingham and was the first Professor of German there, George Gillespie (1917–2003), who taught at Cardiff from 1959 to 1984, and more recently Carl Lofmark (1936–1991), who was appointed to the Chair at Lampeter, thus creating a vacancy at King's College which I was fortunate enough to be appointed to fill in 1965.

One consequence of the dominating role played by Willoughby, Purdie and Norman and what one might call the Bletchley Park confraternity was that the position of British-born Germanists tended to be consolidated while those of German extraction tended to find career progression difficult until at least the 1970s. It is surely an exaggeration to claim, as Rodney Livingstone has done, that by the end of the 1960s German exiles had obtained 'the most important Chairs'.[156] At that time only Claus Bock (1926–2008, at Westfield College), Erich Heller (1911–1990, at Swansea), Siegbert Prawer (1925–2012, at Oxford) and Hans Reiss (b. 1922, at Bristol)[157] had achieved established chairs. Peter Stern (1920–1991) did not come to London until 1972. Werner Schwarz (1905–1982) was promoted to a personal chair at

156 Livingstone, 'The Contribution of German-speaking Jewish Refugees to German Studies in Britain', p. 143 and note 18.

157 Reiss taught at the LSE from 1946 to 1953 and at Queen Mary College from 1953 to 1958. He then became Professor at McGill University in Montreal, before succeeding August Closs at Bristol from 1965 to 1988.

University College London in 1963, and Peter Ganz (1920–2006, Oxford),[158] Ilse Graham (1914–1988, King's London) and Charlotte Jolles (1909–2003, Birkbeck, Prof. in 1974) achieved this distinction only during the 1970s. One who did not achieve this but became only Reader under Norman at King's was Mary Gilbert (1903–1976), whose mother was a Mendelssohn-Bartholdy and whose family owned Lessing's manuscript of *Nathan der Weise*.[159] Notwithstanding their merits as scholars, one gets the impression that these people, all refugees from Nazism, had a struggle against the powerful forces that the likes of Willoughby, Purdie and Norman represented who were concerned to emancipate British German Studies from decades of overbearing German Germanistik. This should not be interpreted to mean they were biased against scholars of German extraction, but they do seem to have tried to ensure that British scholars at last had a fair crack of the whip – one recalls Priebsch's grudging remark, 'Für einen Engländer hat übrigens Moore Smith seine Sache nicht schlecht gemacht'.[160] Willoughby, Purdie and Norman in fact devoted much effort to helping exiled scholars, but given the difficult conditions and limited resources in British universities in the 1930s and 1940s there was only so much they could do. People they did help included Erich Heller who taught at the LSE from 1943 to 1945 before going to Cambridge and later to the USA; Werner Milch (1903–1950) and Herbert Thoma (1899–1975, a relative of the Bavarian writer Ludwig Thoma),[161] who both had Lektorships at King's; the Hebbel, Kleist and Goethe scholar Albert Malte Wagner (1886–1962), who taught at Bedford College and the LSE, and Robert Pick, the first librarian of the Institute of Germanic Studies. Another who found refuge in London was Karl-Werner Maurer (1905–1995), who

158 Ganz was Assistant Lecturer in German at Royal Holloway from 1948–49, Lecturer at Westfield College from 1949 to 1960, before moving to Oxford, Wolfenbüttel, then back to Oxford.

159 Mary Enole Cecile Margarete Gilbert, Reader at King's College from 1953 to 1970, was the sister of the German-American historian Felix Gilbert (1905–1991). Their parents were the English ophthalmologist William Heinrich Gilbert (1860–1906) and Cécile Mendelssohn Bartholdy (1874–1923); the latter was a daughter of the chemist Paul Mendelssohn-Bartholdy (1841–1880) (second son of the composer, Felix) by his second wife, Enole Oppenheim (1855–1939).

160 Closs (ed.), *Robert Priebsch, Elias von Steinmeyer: Briefwechsel*, p. 66 (25 February 1899). George Charles Moore Smith (1858–1940) became Professor of English Language and Literature at the University of Sheffield.

161 On Thoma see the obituary by A. T. Hatto and K. Ostberg, 'Dr H. H. K. Thoma', *The Times*, 4 November 1975. He had been a student of 'giants' like Carl von Kraus (1868–1952) and Wilhelm Streitberg (1856–1925), and was Assistent to Hermann Paul (1846–1921) at Munich. He came to London as a refugee in 1939 and was invited by Frederick Norman to continue the work of Robert Priebsch on German manuscripts in England. He was appointed Lektor at King's in 1947, becoming Lecturer in 1948 and Senior Lecturer in 1959 before his retirement in 1967.

had taken a doctorate at Tübingen under Karl Bohnenberger and Hermann Schneider; he was appointed Lektor at University College in 1931, where, dismayed over the turn of events in Germany, he stayed until 1951 when he emigrated to Canada to become Professor at Manitoba.

The Later Twentieth Century and the End of the Board of Studies

The long period of domination of London German Studies by Willoughby, Purdie and Norman ended with their retirements in 1950, 1962 and 1965 respectively. However, their influence remained marked for another decade or so, their legacy operating through their somewhat younger colleagues, notably Elizabeth Mary Wilkinson at University College, Arthur Hatto at Queen Mary, and, to a lesser extent, Kenneth King, Norman's successor at King's, but very soon this generation, too, had gone: King died in 1970, Wilkinson retired in 1976 and Hatto in 1977. The period between the end of the Second World War and the mid-1970s also saw considerable strengthening of the teaching staff, through the recruitment of distinguished scholars from outside London – Ralph Tymms, Ronald Peacock, Siegbert Prawer, and later Peter Stern, William Yuill, Roy Wisbey, for instance –, supported also by a considerable expansion in the number of junior staff.[162]

There was expansion, too, in terms of the number of Departments of German in the University: new Departments had been created at Westfield College in 1947 and at Goldsmiths' College in 1970. On these, I offer just a few brief notes.

One of the earliest teachers of German at Westfield College was Werner Rüdenberg, export merchant and Sinologist, who was born in Hanover in November 1881. He spent sixteen years in Shanghai spread over a thirty-year period. He compiled a Chinese–German dictionary, first published in 1924, with a second edition in 1936. He arrived in Britain in 1938 and taught for a few months at the School of Oriental Studies, whilst working on an English–Chinese dictionary (Shanghai dialect). In 1940 he was interned on the Isle of Man. Later he taught German at Westfield College and continued his merchant activities with China. He died in or around 1955. His papers are held by the Wiener Library. When a proper German Department was established at Westfield College, the first Head of German was Dr Mary Beare (1897–1985), who was Reader from 1947 until she retired in 1964. Born at Ballymoney, Northern Ireland, she graduated at Queen's University Belfast in 1924 and took a doctorate at Bonn in 1927 with a thesis on *Die Theorie der Komödie von Gottsched bis Jean Paul* (Bonn: Rhenania-Verlag [1927]). She was Fellow and Director of Studies in Modern Languages at Newnham College, Cambridge,

162 For a fairly comprehensive list of staff around 1970 see note 17 above.

from 1936 to 1947. She served as Vice-Principal of Westfield College from 1948 to 1951. Her publications included: *The German Popular Play Atis, and the Venetian Opera: a Study of the Conversion of Operas into Popular Plays, 1675–1722* (Cambridge: CUP, 1938), and *Hans Sachs: Selections* (Durham, 1983). In preparation of the latter she had travelled in inhospitable parts of East Germany during the darkest days of the Cold War. When Dr Beare retired from Westfield College, she was succeeded by Siegbert Prawer (1925–2012) as the first Professor of German there (he left in 1969 when he was elected Taylor Professor of German at Oxford). He, in turn, was succeeded by Claus Victor Bock and then, in 1984, by Marianne Wynn (1921–2009).

At Goldsmiths' College, which progressed from being an 'Institution having Recognised Teachers' to become a full 'School of the University', German was initially offered as a minor subject. Head of Department from 1970 to 1987 was Edward Batley. In 1987 he was appointed Head of the newly formed Department of European Languages. His publications include *A Preface to the Magic Flute* (London: Dobson, 1969) and *Catalyst of Enlightenment: Gotthold Ephraim Lessing* (Bern: Peter Lang, 1990).

*

The chief focus of this account has been on the first 150 years of German Studies in London, from 1826 to about 1976. Since then, a further forty years have elapsed, during which arrangements for the teaching of German within the University have changed considerably. The recent upheavals are, perhaps, still too fresh in most of our memories to require or merit detailed recording – one is reminded of F. E. Sandbach's assertion that 'ein Schriftsteller muß fünfzig Jahre tot sein, ehe man seine Bedeutung erkennen kann';[163] what may be true of writers may possibly be equally true of scholars.

Warning signs that change was coming could be detected at least as far back as the later 1960s. The so-called Saunders Report (1966–67) recommended that the University be reorganized with increased devolution of responsibilities from the centre to the constituent Colleges.[164] Germanists at University College seceded from the federal University's examination system, developing their own curriculum and examinations, while still maintaining their links with what was going on in other Departments through their continued membership

163 Francis Edward Sandbach (1874–1946), Professor of German in the University of Birmingham, cited by Keith Spalding, *33 – alles umsteigen. Eine Autobiographie* (Lübeck: Edition Outline, 1992), p. 162. The Birmingham department consisted of Fiedler and Sandbach until Fiedler left in 1907, to be replaced by Karl Wichmann (who married Fiedler's daughter, Minna Elise Fiedler).

164 Sir Owen Saunders (1904–1993), who chaired the enquiry into reorganization of the University, became Vice-Chancellor in 1967.

of the Board of Studies and participating in the work of the Board of Staff Examiners for German, the latter partly through a continuing sense of collegial teamwork and partly no doubt because marking federal (as opposed to College) examination papers earned them modest additional remuneration – 7*s*. 6*d*. per script at one time). The 1970s and 1980s saw a number of developments such as the introduction of various MA courses taught, mostly at the Institute of Germanic Studies, on an intercollegiate basis, the introduction of an extended essay that might be offered in lieu of one of the so-called 'content papers' at the BA Examination, and also the revival of a range of 'special subjects', likewise taught on an intercollegiate basis. At least in part, these initiatives were deliberately designed by the Board of Studies to strengthen the continuing presence of German in the federal University as a whole. But the arrival of the Thatcher government in 1979 presaged other far-reaching changes.[165] There was much talk of reorganization and of redundancies. An early loss was the decision of Dr David McLintock (1930–2003), Reader at Royal Holloway College, who had an outstanding reputation as a philologist, to take early retirement in 1982 and to set up a translation agency; while this project did not flourish well, he made a highly successful career for himself as a literary translator, translating not only Heinrich Böll but notably several novels by Thomas Bernhard whose work he in effect introduced to English readers. He was twice awarded the Schlegel-Tieck Prize for translation (for Böll's *Women in a River Landscape* (1990) and for Bernhard's *Extinction* in 1996).[166] As the 1980s progressed the threat of mergers of Departments and closures of Colleges became a stark reality: some departments of Westfield College moved to the Queen Mary site at Mile End, though the German Department remained at Hampstead until the early 1990s, and Bedford College merged with Royal Holloway College to become Royal Holloway and Bedford New College in 1985.[167] The Department

165 In the early 1980s, faced with rising costs and funding cuts of 20%, the University's Committee on Academic Organisation (chaired by Sir Peter Swinnerton-Dyer) concluded that sites must close, and it looked in particular at the University's smaller multi-faculty Schools, including Bedford, Royal Holloway and Westfield. There followed a series of Subject Area Review Committees, special Working Parties, and a tangle of bilateral negotiations between Schools. Directed now by an enlarged Senate, the University's cost-cutting exercise was driven primarily by the interests of its larger institutions and its experimental scientists. Boards of Studies sought to mitigate the academic effects by advising on staff redeployment. The role of Deans of Faculties was crucial, most notably perhaps that of Professor William Yuill of the German Department at Bedford College.

166 Other London Germanists winning this prize include the poet Christopher Middleton (Lecturer in German at King's College and long-serving co-editor of *German Life and Letters*, until, in 1966, he took up an appointment in Texas) for Gert Hofmann's *The Spectacle at the Tower* (1986), William Yuill for Ulrich im Hof's *The Making of Europe: The Enlightenment* (1995), and Joyce Crick for Sigmund Freud's *The Interpretation of Dreams* (2000).

167 On the background to this merger and the difficulties it entailed, see John Prebble, *Struggle and Achievement: Royal Holloway University of London 1980-2002* (Egham: Royal Holloway and Bedford New College, 2005).

of Dutch moved from Bedford to University College. Some of the German staff were reassigned to different Colleges, thus Patricia Howe moved first to Westfield College and later to Queen Mary, while Silvia Ranawake moved from Bedford to Queen Mary, and William Yuill, Kurt Ostberg,[168] Bruce Watson and Margot Zutschi moved from Bedford to Royal Holloway. From Westfield, William Jones moved to Royal Holloway, Jeremy Adler to Queen Mary, while John White had already moved to King's, where he had been appointed Reader in 1977. A further upheaval was the reduction of German at Goldsmiths' in the early 1990s which, amongst other things, sparked off an international campaign to secure – in vain as it turned out – the position of the distinguished medievalist Cyril Edwards (b. 1947).

Space has not permitted individual reflections on all the remarkable personalities that helped shaped the subject over the years; others may be able to supply further telling details. Teachers at University College have included Leonard Forster, Werner Schwarz, Mary Wilkinson, Brian Rowley, Geoffrey Butler, Joyce Crick, Irene Frowen, Irving Dworetzky, Bill Larrett, Kenneth Northcott, Timothy McFarland, Christopher Smith, Peter Stern, Adrian Stevens, Alec Stillmark, Martin Swales, Fred Wagner; at King's Kenneth King, Ilse Graham (who in the mid-1960s was hauled up before the Principal of King's for the misdemeanour of being the first female member of staff to wear trousers), Mary Gilbert, Richard Beckley, Michael Beddow, the poet Christopher Middleton (1926–2015), Herbert Thoma, Derek Glass, Robin Harrison, Martin Jones, Dietmar Rösler, John White; at Bedford College Ronald Peacock, William Yuill,[169] Hugh Sacker, Maurice Walshe, Margaret Atkinson, David Mowatt, Dorothy Reich, Kurt Ostberg, Silvia Ranawake, John Sandford, Stewart Spencer, Bruce Watson, David Wells;[170] at Westfield College Peter Ganz, Siegbert Prawer, Claus Bock, Marianne Wynn, Jeremy Adler, Mary Beare, Bill Jones, Alan Marshall, Marie-Luise Waldeck; at Queen Mary Arthur Hatto, Frank Fowler, Rosemary Combridge, Mary Alexander,

168 Kurt Ostberg had a most interesting career. Born to Jewish parents in Berlin in 1919, he was sent to Bryanston School in England at the age of fourteen. In 1937 he started studying for an External degree of the University of London. In 1940 he was immediately interned as an 'enemy alien', deported to Australia, returned to Britain in 1941, and was released a year later. From 1947 to 1949 he worked as a miner in Co. Durham, then for the BBC as a foreign language monitor. In the late 1950s he took an MA under Frederick Norman, and his PhD under Herbert Thoma. He taught at Bedford College from 1956 as Lecturer, from 1972 as Reader. He died in 2010.

169 A nice story about Bill Yuill (1921–1997) concerns his inaugural lecture at Bedford College in 1975 where he spoke of Robertson's mantle having fallen on him almost literally, as it was indeed Robertson's gown, green and shiny with age, that he wore on that occasion. Subsequently, this was worn by William Jervis Jones who, when he retired in 2001, handed it on to Robert Vilain (later Professor at Bristol).

170 David Wells later became Professor of German at Queen's University, Belfast, and in 1986 returned to London where he became Professor at Birkbeck College.

Corbet Stewart; at Birkbeck Reginald J. McClean, William Robson-Scott, George Wells, Charlotte Jolles, Paul Salmon, Philip Brady, Sylvia Harris, Lothar Huber; at Royal Holloway Margaret Richey, Irene Morris (who had some wonderful stories about life there during the war), Ralph Tymms, Marion Gibbs, Máire Davies, David McLintock, Peter Prochnik, Ann White; at Goldsmiths' Edward Batley, Robert Aylett, David Jenkinson, Andreas Kramer, Frank Krause, Hanne Castein, Cyril Edwards; at the LSE Brigitte Hay, Norman Denison and William Rose; at Imperial College Charmian Brinson.[171] I hope I have not forgotten anyone, and of course various of us and them taught at more than one College, doing what Paul Salmon used to call 'the Cook's tour' – I myself, for instance, taught at various times at seven different Colleges: King's, Queen Mary, Goldsmiths, LSE, Birkbeck, University College, Westfield, as well as teaching students from Royal Holloway and examining for many years at Imperial.

*

Although the Colleges of the University have long since gone their separate ways and the Boards of Studies that held the disciplines together were abolished in the mid-1990s, and even though the German Departments at University College, King's, Queen Mary, Birkbeck, and Royal Holloway seem to be thriving (albeit under new guises such as 'Department of Cultures and Languages', 'School of Modern Languages, Literatures and Cultures'), it is not impossible that, given the parlous standing of languages in the British educational system overall, some consolidation may become desirable. Thus perhaps before long we may see the Board of Studies reinvented.

171 Details of the teaching and research interests and the publications of most of these colleagues may be found in successive editions of the DAAD Handbook of Germanists in Great Britain and Ireland, issued (under various titles) in 1973, 1984 (published 1985), 1988, 1992/93, and 1997/98.

Bibliography

This bibliography restricts itself largely to secondary literature. For publications by many of the historical figures discussed see the footnotes.

Alter, Peter and Rudolf Muhs (eds), *Exilanten und andere Deutsche in Fontanes London*, Stuttgarter Arbeiten zur Germanistik, 331 (Stuttgart: Heinz; London: IGS, 1996) [= Festschrift for Charlotte Jolles on her 85th birthday]

Andrews, John S., 'Jethro Bithell (1878–1962)', *The University of Leeds Review*, 5 (1962), 146–53 (with portrait)

— *Inventory of the Correspondence and Other Material bequeathed to the University of Leeds by Jethro Bithell (1878–1962)* (Leeds: Brotherton Library, University of Leeds, 1962; revised edn 1967) [Some 600 items of correspondence; see the review by L. W. Forster in *German Life and Letters*, n.s. 16 (1963), 136–67]

Ashton, Rosemary, *Little Germany: Exile and Asylum in Victorian England* (Oxford: OUP, 1986)

— 'Gottfried Kinkel and University College London', in *Exilanten und andere Deutsche in Fontanes London*, ed. by Peter Alter and Rudolf Muhs, Stuttgarter Arbeiten zur Germanistik, 331 (Stuttgart: Heinz; London: IGS, 1996), pp. 23–40

— 'Germans in Bloomsbury', http://www.ucl.ac.uk/bloomsbury-project/articles/events/conference2009/ashton.pdf [accessed 6 April 2016]

Bentley, Linna, *Educating Women: A Pictorial History of Bedford College, University of London, 1849–1985* (St Albans: Alma, 1991)

Bock, Claus Victor, *Untergetaucht unter Freunden. Ein Bericht 1942–1945 Amsterdam* (Amsterdam: Castrvm Peregrini, 1985)

Brenn, Wolfgang, 'British "Germanistik" and the Problem of National Socialism', *German Life and Letters*, n.s. 42 (1988–89), 145–67

Brinson, Charmian, 'Sixty Years On: *German Life and Letters* and the National Socialists', *German Life and Letters*, n.s. 49 (1996), 479–87

Chambers, R.W., *Philologists at University College* (London: University of London Press, 1927)

Closs, August (ed.), *Robert Priebsch, Elias von Steinmeyer: Briefwechsel* (Berlin: Erich Schmidt, 1979)

Dymond, Dorothy (ed.), *The Forge. The History of Goldsmiths' College, 1905–1955* (London: Methuen, 1955)

Firth, A. E., *Goldsmiths' College: A Centenary Account* (London: Athlone Press, 1991)

Flood, John L., 'Bernays, Adolphus', *ODNB*, http://www.oxforddnb.com/view/article/61615

— 'Hatto, Arthur Thomas', *ODNB*, http://www.oxforddnb.com/view/article/103459

— 'Norman, Frederick', *ODNB*, http://www.oxforddnb.com/view/article/62277

— 'Priebsch, Robert', *ODNB*, http://www.oxforddnb.com/view/article/98340

— 'Robertson, John George', *ODNB*, http://www.oxforddnb.com/view/article/61619

— '"Verwandlung des Fremden in ein Eignes." Exilgermanisten an der Universität London', unpublished manuscript, 24 pp. (1993)

— '"A Man of Singularly Wide Experience of Affairs". Eugene Oswald as Writer and Journalist', in *Exilanten und andere Deutsche in Fontanes London*, ed. by Peter Alter and Rudolf Muhs, Stuttgarter Arbeiten zur Germanistik, 331 (Stuttgart: Heinz; London: IGS, 1996), pp. 77–100

— 'Ginger beer and sugared cauliflower: Adolphus Bernays and language teaching in nineteenth-century London', in *Vermittlungen. German Studies at the Turn of the Century. Deutschlandstudien an der Jahrhundertwende. Festschrift für Nigel B. R. Reeves*, ed. by Rüdiger Görner and Helen Kelly-Holmes (Munich: iudicium 1999), pp. 101–15

— 'The London Branch of the Allgemeiner Deutscher Sprachverein', in *'Proper Words in Proper Places'. Studies in Lexicology and Lexicography in honour of William Jervis Jones*, ed. by Máire C. Davies, John L. Flood and David N. Yeandle (Stuttgart: Heinz; London: IGS, 2001), pp. 230–53

— 'German Studies', in *A Century of British Medieval Studies*, ed. by Alan Deyermond, British Academy Centenary Monographs (Oxford: Oxford University Press and London: The British Academy, 2007), pp. 427–59

— 'Arthur Thomas Hatto 1910-2010', *Proceedings of the British Academy*, 172: Biographical Memoirs of Fellows, X (Oxford: Oxford University Press for the British Academy, 2011), pp. 173–98

Flood, John L. and Martin Swales, 'Die Förderung der Auslandsgermanistik: Großbritannien als Beispiel', in *Spuren in die Zukunft. Der Deutsche Akademische Austauschdienst 1925–2000*. Bd. 1: *Der DAAD in der Zeit*, ed. by Peter Alter (Bonn: Deutscher Akademischer Austauschdienst, 2000), pp. 152–63

Glass, Derek, 'From Moravia to the Strand: The Career of Karl Adolf Buchheim', in *Exilanten und andere Deutsche in Fontanes London*, ed. by Peter Alter and Rudolf Muhs, Stuttgarter Arbeiten zur Germanistik, 331 (Stuttgart: Heinz; London: IGS, 1996), pp. 41–76

Gooch, G. P., 'John George Robertson, 1867–1933', *Proceedings of the British Academy*, 19 (1933), 360–80

Guthrie, John, 'How German began in Cambridge', a talk given on 13 June 2015 (unpublished MS) [mostly about Karl Breul]

Harte, Negley and John North, *The World of University College London 1828–1978* (London: University College, 1978)

Hearnshaw, F. J. C., *The Centenary History of King's College, London, 1828–1928* (London: Harrap, 1929)

Herzig, Martin, *"Ich hab's gewagt!" Das Leben des Ludwig von Mühlenfels (1793–1861)* (Berlin: Nora, 2009)

— 'Ludwig von Mühlenfels (1793–1861): Vom Lützower Jäger, Burschenschafter und verfolgten Demagogen zum liberalen 1848er Reichskommissar', in *Akteure eines Umbruchs. Männer und Frauen der Revolution von 1848*, III, ed. by Walter Schmidt (Berlin: Fides, 2010), pp. 463–506

Howe, Patricia, 'German', in *Bedford College, University of London: Memories of 150 Years*, ed. by J. Mordaunt Crook (London: Royal Holloway and Bedford New College, 2001), pp. 181–200

Huelin, Gordon, *King's College London 1828–1978* (London: University of London King's College, 1978)

Husbands, Christopher T. , 'German academics in British universities during the First World War: the case of Karl Wichmann', *German Life and Letters*, 60 (2007), 493-517

— *German-/Austrian-origin professors of German in British universities during the First World War: the lessons of four case studies* (2013) (unpublished), http://eprints.lse.ac.uk/49797/1/-Husbands_German_Austrian_origin_2013.pdf [accessed 24 May 2016]

Kenyon Jones, Christine, *King's College London: In the Service of Society* (London: King's College London, 2004)

König, Christoph (ed.), *Internationales Germanistenlexikon 1800-1950*, 3 vols (Berlin: de Gruyter, 2003)

Livingstone, Rodney, 'The Contribution of German-speaking Jewish Refugees to German Studies in Britain', in *Second Chance. Two Centuries of German-speaking Jews in the United Kingdom*, ed. by Werner E. Mosse (Tübingen: J. C. B. Mohr (Paul Siebeck), 1991), pp. 137–52

McLelland, Nicola, *German through English Eyes. A History of Language Teaching and Learning in Britain 1500–2000* (Wiesbaden: Harrassowitz, 2015)

Miller, Edward, *Prince of Librarians: The Life & Times of Antonio Panizzi of the British Museum* (London: André Deutsch, 1967)

Mordaunt Crook, J. (ed.), *Bedford College, University of London: Memories of 150 Years* (London: Royal Holloway and Bedford New College, 2001)

Moss, G. P. and M. V. Saville, *From Palace to College – An Illustrated Account of Queen Mary College (University of London)* (London: The College, 1985)

Newton, Gerald, *German Studies at the University of Sheffield. An Historical Perspective, 1880–1988, together with a graduate list, 1910–1988* (Sheffield: University of Sheffield, 1988)

The Political and Occasional Poems of Winthrop Mackworth Praed, ed. by Sir George Young (London: Ward, Lock & Co., 1888)

Proescholdt, C. W., 'The Introduction of German Language Teaching into England', *German Life and Letters*, n.s. 44 (1990–91), 93–102

Raraty, M. M., 'The Chair of German at Trinity College Dublin 1775–1886', *Hermathena. A Dublin University Review*, 102 (1986), 53–72

Sagarra, Eda and Peter Skrine, *The Department of German at the Victoria University of Manchester, A Brief History 1895–1996* (Manchester: University of Manchester, 1996)

Semmelroth, Kurt, *Die Gründung der Universität London und ihre historischen Voraussetzungen, unter besonderer Berücksichtigung des deutschen Einflusses* (doctoral thesis, University of Münster, 1937)

Sondheimer, Janet, *Castle Adamant in Hampstead: a History of Westfield College 1882–1982* (London: Westfield College, University of London, 1983)

Swales, Martin, 'Wilkinson, Mary Elizabeth', *ODNB*, http://www.oxforddnb.com/view/article/75274

— 'Willoughby, Leonard Ashley', *ODNB*, http://www.oxforddnb.com/view/article/62526

Thompson, F. M. L. (ed.), *The University of London and the World of Learning, 1836–1986* (London: Hambledon Press, 1990)

Tuke, Margaret, *A History of Bedford College for Women 1849–1937* (London: Oxford University Press, 1939)

Wakely, Richard, 'Modern Language Studies at Scottish Universities: The Early Days', in *France and Germany in Scotland: Studies in Language and Culture. Papers from the Centenary Celebrations of the Departments of French and German at the University of Edinburgh 1994–1995*, ed. by Richard Wakely and Philip E. Bennett (Edinburgh: The Department of French, University of Edinburgh, 1996), pp. 1–21

Wallace, Stuart, *War and the Image of Germany. British Academics 1914–1918* (Edinburgh: John Donald, 1988)

Warmington, E. H., *A History of Birkbeck College University of London during the Second World War 1939–1945* (London: Birkbeck College, 1954)

Waterhouse, Gilbert, *The War and the Study of German. A Public Lecture delivered in Trinity College, Dublin, on Tuesday, May 29th, 1917* (Dublin: Hodges, Figges and Co., 1917)

Appendix

University of London Board of Studies in Germanic Languages and Literatures[172]

Chair

J. G. Robertson (1922–31)
H. G. Atkins (1932–36)
L. A. Willoughby (1937–42)
E. Purdie (1943–49)
F. Norman (1950–54)
R. J. McClean (1955–57)
R. V. Tymms (1958–60)
A. T. Hatto (1961–63)
W. D. Robson-Scott (1964–67)
K. C. King (1968–70)
C. V. Bock (1971–73)
F. M. Fowler (1974–75)
R. A. Wisbey (1976–77)
J. P. Stern (1978–79)
W. E. Yuill (1980)
D. R. McLintock (1981–82)
F. M. Fowler (1982–84)
J. J. White (1985–86)
M. W. Swales (1986–87)
W. J. Jones (1988)
M. Durrell (1989)
E. M. Batley (1990–92)
D. A. Wells (1993–95)[173]

Secretary

I. M. Massey (1922–31)
W. Rose (1932–36)
H. S. M. Stuart (1937–38)
W. F. Mainland (1938–39)
A. T. Hatto (1939– ?)
E. M. Wilkinson (1949–51)
C. P. Magill (1952)
M. E. C. M. Gilbert (1953–55)
M. E. Atkinson (1955–59)
W. D. Robson-Scott (1959–62)
P. B. Salmon (1963–66)
G. A. Wells (1966–68)
F. M. Fowler (1969–70)
J. L. Flood (1971–75)
W. J. Jones (1975–77)
M. H. Jones (1977–79)
J. D. Adler (1979–81)

Administrative Secretary

J. Lancaster [UoL] (1981–91)
J. Maynard [UoL] (1991–95)

172 The list is incomplete, since some of the relevant records in the University Archives are lacking.

173 The last meeting of the Board of Studies was held on 8 March 1995.

‘Sehr schön, Piglet?’ ‘Ja, Pooh.’

A History of the Institute of Germanic Studies, University of London

Anne Simon

Father Tony MacDonald and Professor Volker Honemann
In memoriam

And for all staff of the Institute of Germanic Studies, past and present, in gratitude for their extraordinary commitment, their generous vision, their oft-unsung hard work and for giving German Studies such a remarkable institution

Acknowledgements

In writing this History of the Institute of Germanic Studies I have received invaluable help from a number of people, whose generosity in giving up their time to read drafts, perspicacity in spotting errors and kindness in sharing their knowledge and memories have greatly enriched and improved this account. To the following, therefore, I owe a considerable debt of gratitude: Ms Karin Hellmer; Professor Rüdiger Görner; Professor Martin Swales; Professor Roy Wisbey and Dr Godela Weiss-Sussex. Professor John Flood, Ms Jane Lewin and Mr Edward Batley in particular went to great lengths to provide me with detailed information (and anecdotes!) not contained in the IGS Archives (now housed in the Library of Senate House, University of London): to them I am especially grateful, since their collective knowledge of the Institute's history and development is unparalleled and has made this a more informative study. Jane Lewin also came up with the inspired suggestion for the title, gave sage advice and helped with illustrations. My thanks go to Dr Heide Kunzelmann for information on the Ingeborg Bachmann Centre; to Tansy Barton, Charles Harrowell, Anne McLoughlin and Richard Temple of Senate House Library for their help in locating and retrieving archival material; to Dr Séan Williams for reading a late draft of the history and making a number of helpful comments; and to Dr Clare George, Miller Archivist at the Institute, for her guidance through the minefield that is copyright, for valuable information on the Martin and Hannah Norbert Miller Trust and on Exile collections in the Germanic Studies Library and for help with illustrative material. My thanks also to SAS Publications, especially Emily Morrell, for their collegiality and hard work on this volume. Finally, I would like to thank Jane Lewin and Clare George most warmly for helping to make my time at the Institute so very enriching and enjoyable.

'Sehr schön, Piglet?' 'Ja, Pooh.'[1]
A History of the Institute of Germanic Studies, University of London

In his review for *German Life and Letters*, 20 (1966) of *Essays in German Literature* (1965), Dr Clair Baier[2] cites Frederick Norman's preface to that volume: 'It was pure chance, though a fortunate one, that three of the essays in this volume concern "folly", and thus folly may be considered as giving a somewhat spurious cohesion to this collection'. He continues:

> We must see Professor Norman's impish style as he writes these words in his Preface. But we see, too, a sincere desire, which must be supported, to realize the unity of our discipline. Far too often, we might unfortunately say 'usually', it is the case that we scarcely know (one wonders whether one dare add 'or are interested in') the full field of German studies, beyond the nodding acquaintance which we obtained as undergraduates. Immediately we gain our first degree we put on our blinkers and from then on the normal thing is to intensify interest in a part of our subject and seldom, if ever, to cover the whole range once again.

Regrettably, Dr Baier's remarks are even more apposite today, not least since the last thirty-odd years have seen the syllabus in German departments up and down the country shrink alarmingly, with the virtual disappearance of Medieval Studies and the Early Modern period (even from departments like Durham, Exeter, Bristol and Stirling which used to be renowned for them) and the widespread reduction of German Studies to the twentieth century, in some departments to the post-war period alone. The persistent disregard by successive governments – no matter what colour – of the vital importance of Modern Languages for the scholarly, cultural and economic life of the United Kingdom, the equally persistent underfunding of Higher Education, the advent of school league tables in 1992,[3] Britain's inability to forget the Second World War, the general British reluctance to learn foreign languages – these and other factors have contributed to the decline of German-teaching in schools and hence the

1 For an explanation, see p. 102.

2 Dr Clair Baier was Head of the Department of German at Hull in the 1950s and 1960s and author of *Deutschland und die Deutschen* (1952).

3 German is considered a 'hard' subject and is consequently less and less taught in schools worried that it may affect their ranking in the league tables.

study of German at university.[4] Against this background, the very foundation of the Institute of Germanic Studies at the University of London so soon after the war, its untiring commitment to supporting and furthering German Studies in this country, its various publication series, its success in establishing scholarly links to Germanists across the world and in raising the international profile of German Studies in the UK and Ireland – all these achievements are truly remarkable and are due in no small part to the sterling work on the part of the Institute's (Honorary) Directors and Deputy Directors, to whom German Studies in these Isles owe an enormous debt. Moreover, Germanists in the UK and from across the globe would doubtless agree that many a visitor to the IGS would have been lost, and events hosted there less successful and productive, without the wisdom, experience, helpfulness and professionalism of its main pillars, Karin Hellmer and Jane Lewin, who, together with the Deputy Director Professor John Flood (in office 1979–2002), contributed enormously to the Institute's success and prestige. What follows is an account of the foundation and subsequent history of the Institute. It is necessarily uneven, even patchy in places, as such is the nature of archival material. However, it is hoped that even an imperfect history is better than no history at all; and, above all, that the IGS, which in 2004 was merged with the younger Institute of Romance Studies to form the Institute of Germanic & Romance Studies, itself renamed the Institute of Modern Languages Research in 2013, may be permitted to continue its proud tradition – in however transmuted a form – and to flourish and excel. Anything else would be folly indeed.[5]

4 It is difficult precisely to quantify what effect the Second World War had on the teaching of German in the British Isles. Just how difficult is made clear by Nicola McLelland, who notes that 'the raw numbers of pupils taking German at age 16 increased more than sevenfold between 1938 and 1985, and the number taking it at age 18 even more, by nearly ninefold' (Nicola McLelland, *German Through English Eyes: A History of Language Teaching and Learning in Britain 1500–2000* (Wiesbaden: Harrassowitz, 2015), p. 157. However, she then points out that 'the number of entries for German at age 16 as a proportion of all subject entries [for O-level] declined steadily (from 1.9% in 1938, to 1.2% in 1985)' (p. 157). In 1938 there were 9,935 entrants for German at School Certificate (school-leaving exams taken at age 16 between 1918 and 1951); whereas the year 1965 saw 33,723 entrants for O-level and CSE German combined (p. 159). Entrants for German A-level numbered 899 in 1938 and 7,107 in 1965 (p. 160). However, there are no figures for the immediate post-war period. McLelland does, however, draw attention to the fact that after World War II 'key developments in language teaching gave fresh impetus to the teaching and learning of German' (p. 155). These included adapting for schools the teaching methods used on American Armed Services personnel during the war; language laboratories and other new technology (tape recorders, film, radio and television, especially the BBC school broadcasts and language courses); and new branches of linguistics and their application to language teaching and learning (pp. 155–57). In Chapter 6 McLelland undertakes a fascinating analysis of what textbooks taught about the history and culture of Germany (and, to a lesser extent, of Austria and Switzerland) between 1900 and 2000.

5 Indeed, the Institutes in general have long been regarded as the 'jewel in the crown' of the University of London, as vital for their contribution to knowledge.

Foundation and Early Years

The Institute of Germanic Languages and Literatures at the University of London[1] was founded in 1950, although the idea for an Institute was older than that: as the Minutes of the Board of Studies in Germanic Languages and Literatures show, it was first mooted in 1943 at a meeting of the Board in the midst of war-damaged London, where the Blitz had started on 7 September 1940. Despite the war the University of London had continued to function: when war had broken out in September 1939, it had had 14,000 registered students. The Colleges and their students had been evacuated out of London to other parts of the UK: for example, King's to Bristol University; Bedford College to Cambridge; parts of Imperial to Swansea; German at University College to Aberystwyth. The exception was Birkbeck, which had stayed in London and suffered a direct hit to its library in 1941. Senate House, the foundation stone for which had been laid by King George V on 26 June 1933, had been completed in 1937, although parts had been occupied by the central University administration from August 1936, when between 17 and 21 August the University had moved from South Kensington to Bloomsbury. In 1939, Senate House had been taken over by the Ministry of Information, its roof becoming a valuable observation point for the Royal Observer Corps (at 209 feet, the tower of Senate House was the highest secular building in London at the time). However, as John Flood points out, by 1943 the war was gradually turning in the Allies' favour:[2] the Battle of Stalingrad (23 August

1 The University of London, founded by Royal Charter on 28 November 1836, is the third oldest university in England. The two founding Colleges of the University, UCL (founded 1826) and King's College London (founded 1829), both pre-date the University, as do many of the University's constituent institutions. For example, St Bartholomew's Hospital Medical School (now part of Queen Mary College) and St Thomas's Hospital Medical School (now part of King's College London) both have twelfth-century origins. The University of London was initially established to act as an examining body for its Colleges and other 'approved institutions'. It acted solely in this capacity until 1858. The University awarded its first degrees in 1839 to twenty-nine students. Today roughly 143,000 students studying at its seventeen Colleges and ten institutes in and around London and 50,000 studying through its distance learning programmes in 180 countries receive University of London degrees each year.

2 An important source of information for this history is: John Flood, 'The Institute of Germanic Studies and its Library. A brief account of their origin and their first forty years. With an appendix: The incunabula in the Priebsch-Closs Collection of the University of London Institute of Germanic Studies', in *London German Studies IV*, ed. by R. A. Wisbey, Publications of the Institute of Germanic Studies, 52 (London: Institute of Germanic Studies, 1992), pp. 269–83. Further sources include: L. A. Willoughby, '*Wine that maketh glad . . .*'. *The Interplay of Reality and Symbol in Goethe's Life and Work*, The First Bithell Memorial Lecture (London: Institute of Germanic Studies London, 1976); University of London Calendars; the Archive of the Institute of Germanic Studies; the University of

1942–2 February 1943) had been won; the U-boat threat in the Atlantic had been repulsed (in June 1942 German U-boats had retreated from their American coastal positions; and although the Battle of the Atlantic lasted the entire war, it was at its height from mid-1940 to the end of 1943); on 13 May 1943 the German Afrika Korps and Italian troops in North Africa surrendered to Allied forces; 16 May saw the Dam-Buster Raids by RAF 617 Squadron on three German dams, the Sorpe, Möhne and Eder; Allied troops invaded the Italian mainland on 3 September 1943 and Italy not only surrendered on 28 September but declared war on Germany on 13 October.

Thus by 1944 the Colleges were beginning to return to London and exams were again taking place in the capital. The Principal of the University reported that these had been carried out 'without casualties, other than those normally caused by these exacting but essential tests'. Similarly, Senate had begun thinking about the post-war rebuilding of the University and invited colleagues to consider what might be done after the war. One initiative had, however, already been suggested: the Minutes of Board of Studies in Germanic Languages and Literatures for 23 September 1943 state: 'The Board considered at some length a statement by Professor Leonard Willoughby (UCL) on the problems of teaching resources and syllabus and examination requirements in the future'.[3] Subsequently, the Minutes of the Board for 21 December 1943 (at which meeting thirteen members were present) outline details of a potential solution, namely, Professor Willoughby's proposal for the 'establishment of an Institute of Germanic Languages and Literatures'.[4] Since the federal nature of the University meant its constituent Colleges were all essentially doing the same thing:

> [t]he advantages of pooling the existing considerable resources for the teaching of German are apparent; generally it would mean the elimination of the waste of effort by which so many lectures now duplicated could be given in some central building to the whole honours school of German. It would benefit the staff by relieving it of burdensome preparation on subjects with which it might not be immediately familiar and so enable it to specialise and become ever more expert on one particular branch of the subject. [...]

London website; and the Administrator to the Institute, Jane Lewin (especially for the biographies of those who endowed named funds and prizes).

3 It must be remembered that in order to attend the Board its members had to travel into London from the various parts of the country to which their Colleges had been evacuated. For a fuller account of the Board and its members, see John Flood's essay 'Taught by Giants' in this volume.

4 The thirteen members were: Gertrude Craig Houston, Wilhelmine Delp, Mary Gilbert, Arthur Hatto, Reginald McClean, Isabella Massey, Karl-Werner Maurer, Edna Purdie (Chairman of the Board), Margaret Richey, William Rose, Theodoor Weevers, John Wilks and Leonard Willoughby.

> Students would be taught by experts and would hear things not to be found in books [...].[5]

Using Professor Willoughby's own wording, the Minutes continue:

> All this implies the provision of opportunity for the centralisation of teaching. The ideal way of attaining this would be through a separate Germanic Institute situated centrally to all the colleges, preferably on the University site. The ideal would be a distinct building (or a floor of a building) which would provide lecture rooms, a seminar library, reading rooms, seminar rooms, staff rooms. Such an institution would provide a centre of attraction for all the Germanic Studies in the metropolis and a house of call for all foreign scholars passing through London. It is an ambitious and expensive project which may or may not be immediately realisable. But the Board feels very strongly that it is an ideal which can and should be realised in the course of the next decade after the war. Meanwhile a beginning might be made on more modest lines: a few rooms provided in a University building, comprising a seminar library, a lecture room, a staff common room, and one or two private rooms for interviewing students. These are the minimum requirements which could justify the use of the term Germanic Institute, and they seem to the Board realisable within a few years of the cessation of hostilities.[6]

The acceptance by Senate of Professor Willoughby's proposal for the founding of an Institute was, however, by no means a foregone conclusion as funding was tight in a capital city gradually rebuilding itself after the devastation of the war and the demands on the University's budgets were many and various. For example, the Principal's Report in the University Calendar 1950–51 mentions the air raid damage still being repaired, for example, at Bedford College and the London School of Hygiene and Tropical Medicine, although war-time damage to Senate House had been almost completely repaired (pp. 120–22). At that time there were forty institutions within the University with demands on the capital allocation from the Treasury. Many of the concerns then plaguing the University in particular and Higher Education in general remain depressingly familiar. The Principal's Report from the University Calendar 1948–49 records a prime concern as being 'the new school examination the Ministry of Education is introducing in 1951 to replace School Certificate and Higher School Certificate' – in other words, the new General Certificate of Education. One issue was the extent

5 'Proposals for the Foundation of An Institute of Germanic Languages within the University of London laid before the meeting of the Board of Studies in German on July 23rd 1943 by Professor L. A. Willoughby', p. 1. The model was the Institute of Historical Research, founded in 1921.

6 Whilst the centralization of teaching was never achieved, intercollegiate lectures did eventually take place and Special Subjects were instituted which were often taught at the IGS.

to which it could be accepted as granting exemption from the University's matriculation requirements. Another was:

> devising the best arrangements for giving financial assistance from public funds to enable properly qualified students to come to university [...]. In view, however, of the rising cost of a university education and of the changing social and economic conditions in this country, the number of students who can find from private sources the money for a university education is rapidly decreasing (pp. 115–16).

The Principal's Report in the University Calendar of 1950–51 (dated 31 March 1950) opens with a reference to the 'economic crisis' currently gripping the country:[7]

> On the present occasion universities are more vulnerable than ever before in view of the great increase in the proportion of their recurrent income derived from the Treasury and of their almost complete reliance on that source for the capital to carry out the expansion programme which had been undertaken at the request of the Government (p. 119).

On 26 October 1949 there had been an announcement in the House of Commons by the Chancellor of the Exchequer (Sir Stafford Cripps) of 'a "retardation" of the building programme of universities by £1,000,000 a year'. No major building programme put forward by the University since April 1949 had been licensed (with one unspecified exception). The situation was exacerbated by the large amount spent on construction for the Festival of Britain (pp. 119–20).[8]

Nonetheless, Professor Willoughby's proposal apparently passed through Senate without a problem, partly due to energetic support by Professor Frederick Norman:[9] a note from the first Deputy Director of the Institute,

7 It is easy to forget the grim economic state in which Britain found itself after World War II. The Treasury was close to bankruptcy; the ports and industrial fabric of the country had been badly damaged; cities required rebuilding and with them affordable accommodation for those who had lost their homes in bombing raids; food rationing continued until 1954; and the country was reliant on loans from the USA, including $3.75 billion (equivalent to $57 billion in 2015) through the Anglo-American Loan Agreement in 1946 (finally paid off in 2006). Canada lent an additional $1.19 billion (in American dollars); and further funds (not requiring repayment) came from the Marshall Plan between 1948 and 1950.

8 The Festival of Britain was held throughout the United Kingdom in the summer of 1951. Organized by the British Government, it was intended to infuse the nation with optimism; to foster recovery in the bleak aftermath of the Second World War; and to promote the British contribution to Science, Technology, Industrial Design, Architecture and the Arts. The focus of, and lasting testimony to, the Festival was the South Bank complex on the River Thames in London.

9 For a detailed biography of Professor Norman, see 'Taught by Giants', pp. 62 ff., and John Flood's entry on Frederick Norman in the *Oxford Dictionary of National Biography*.

Maurice O'Connell Walshe, dated 1 July 1974 and written in response to a request for information by Eric John Morrall (Durham), mentions that he had asked Professor Elizabeth Mary Wilkinson about the founding of the Institute. She had replied that the idea had first come from Professor Willoughby, but '[w]hen Prof. Norman returned from War service in 1946, he persuaded Senate to provide the necessary funds. The credit for the actual establishment of the Institute therefore belongs jointly to Professors Willoughby and Norman'.[10] Similarly, in a letter dated 29 April 1970 from Professor Wilkinson to Professor William D. Robson-Scott[11] about honouring Professor Willoughby on his eighty-fifth birthday (4 June 1970), she writes:

> This [the IGS] was entirely Professor Willoughby's dream child during our evacuation to Aberystwyth; and I well remember his reading out his original memorandum to Mrs. Willoughby and myself before leaving for one of the meetings of the Board of Studies in London. He would be the first to say – and has expressed it in print – that it was due to the energy and influence of Professor Norman on the Academic Council and the Senate that it got off the ground after the War. But it was also due to his own energy and drive as first Hon. Director, together with Dr Pick as first Secretary (he would also

10 Both extracts are reproduced with the kind permission of University College London. According to the obituary by R. H. Stephenson, 'Professor Elizabeth M. Wilkinson [1909–2001] was one of the greatest, and – across the whole spectrum of the humanities – one of the most highly regarded, scholars of German culture the United Kingdom has produced, in particular because of her illuminating work, both historical and theoretical, on German Classicism, which did much to bring home its living significance. All who knew her were impressed by the depth and breadth of mind that she brought to bear on her work. She is fondly remembered as a teacher of genius who combined in a uniquely charismatic way sheer intellectual excitement, tender (and patient) regard for the development of individual students, and a passionate – sometimes fierce – dedication to the resolution of first-order problems' (http://britishacademy.universitypressscholarship.com/view/10.5871/bacad/9780197263020.001.0001/upso-9780197263020-chapter-22) [accessed 23 August 2016]. The respect and affection in which Professor Wilkinson was held by her students is illustrated by a letter dated 11 September 1969 from Arthur Groos (Emeritus Avalon Foundation Professor of the Humanities at Cornell University): 'Now that my term as a graduate student is almost finished, let me also take the opportunity to thank you for your stimulus and inspiration, both in person and in your writings. [...] I am proud to be your student, however short of your standards I may still be. [...] P.S. Mrs Jolles says that you are planning to return to Ithaca, next year, and I hope it will be possible for you to make a trip to the West coast. If an extreme inducement is necessary, I will even promise to teach you to ride a surfboard'. When at Cornell, where she had been one of that university's first distinguished Andrew Dickson White Professors at Large in 1965, Professor Wilkinson and her then-student Art Groos had gone swimming in a farm pond, hence the offer of surfing lessons! The letter is quoted with the kind permission of Professor Art Groos, who also provided additional details.

11 William Douglas Robson-Scott had been Head of German at Birkbeck College, from which he retired in 1968, dying in Florence on 12 June 1980, aged seventy-eight. Between 1968 and 1973 he was also Honorary Director of the Institute of Germanic Studies. The Institute's Robson-Scott Travelling Scholarship was established in his memory.

Figure 12: Mary Elizabeth Wilkinson and C.P. Magill. Photograph taken at the presentation of Tradition and Creation – Essays in Honour of Elizabeth Mary Wilkinson *to the dedicatee in the IGS in 1978.*

have been 85 this year) that it became more than an empty house. They did everything themselves, down to buying the furniture and the books. Above all, through their unrivalled knowledge of, and personal acquaintance with, an immense number of Germanists on the Continent, in the Commonwealth, and in America, they made it a place to which scholars came whenever they were in London.[12]

12 Leonard Willoughby (1885–1977), Chair of German at UCL and a code-breaker during World War I, seems to have been particularly active in rebuilding and promoting good Anglo-German relations, as may be deduced from the typescript of the Bithell Memorial Lecture delivered by Professor W. H. Bruford on 8 November 1979. Professor Bruford's personal reminiscences include the following: 'At our first post-war Conference of University Teachers of German at Oxford in September, 1945, Dr Closs and I had opened a discussion on the renewal of contacts with Germany, and not unnaturally found many of our colleagues not yet ready to welcome the help of native German assistants as before the War, but there were many well-qualified German refugees to fill the gap. [...] At the next year's conference at Sheffield, arrangements were made, at the suggestion of Leonard Willoughby, for a Goethe conference of

The acceptance by Senate of the proposal raised the issue of accommodation for the Institute; and the University Calendar 1949–50 reports that a 'scheme of management was approved by the Senate in May 1948, and temporary premises will be available at 26 Russell Square, W.C.1, as soon as the necessary repairs and alterations have been effected' (p. 373). In fact, the first premises of the Institute were a mere two rooms in an empty, dirty 26 Russell Square, into which it moved in 1950. Furniture to fit the house was bought at auctions; a letter dated 22 May 1950 discusses the acquisition of second-hand book shelves from the Institute of Historical Research; the Director, Leonard Willoughby, and first Secretary-Librarian, Robert Pick,[13] often had

Germanists in London in 1949 to which six of our German colleagues would be invited as our guests. A fund was raised by subscription to cover their expenses. The conference took place early in August at Westfield College and was a great success. I remember meeting at it for the first time the bearers of such familiar names as Beutler, Alewyn, Günther Müller and Trunz, and reporting with some trepidation on recent Goethe literature, our Committee having thought that few scholars in Germany would yet have as full access to recent publications as we had ourselves' (pp. 34–36). That Willoughby's generous efforts to reach out to colleagues in Germany were appreciated and reciprocated by them is shown in a letter dated 10 August 1946 from the German author and publicist (and Nazi-sympathizer) Hans Grimm (1875–1959): 'The volume of the English Goethe Society Publications has also arrived and was especially welcome to me, a proof that in England as well as in Germany there are people who earnestly strive to keep the lamp of European civilisation burning in spite of all political propaganda and camouflage. To counterbalance that propaganda and camouflage I have for the last eight years never once finished a day, including the days & nights with bombs, without reading 3–5 pages of English books not excepting those of Kipling who is an old favourite of mine from my Africa days and including that exceptionally good political book of Carr The Twenty Years Crisis [*sic*]'. (The extract is published with the kind permission of Professor Tiemo Grimm.) Similarly, a letter from the German jurist and writer Hans Friedrich Blunck (1888–1961) dated 30 December 1952 and thanking Willoughby for the review of Blunck's memoirs *Unwegsame Zeiten* (1952) remarks: 'Es ist die erste grosse Besprechung aus England, dass sie gerade aus Ihrer Feder stammt, ist für mich unschätzbar und hat mir eine rechte Festfreude gebracht. [...] Wir wollen versuchen, neu zu erbauen, was damals zerbrochen ist, und ich glaube, Ihr Artikel ist ein sehr heller und sehr edler Stein'. (The extract is published with the kind permission of Herr Blunck's niece.) Between 1933 and 1935 Blunck had been first President of the Reichsschrifttumskammer; in 1936 he had founded the Stiftung Deutsches Auslandswerk with the aim of spreading a positive picture of the Third Reich abroad; and had joined the NSDAP in 1937. However, he had spoken out against persecution of Jews who had served in the German army in World War I.

13 Robert Pick (b. 1885) had been Professor of English at the Wiener Handelsakademie and had actively promoted Anglo-German relations. In the 1930s his daughter had been appointed *Lektorin* at Bedford College. In November 1938 Robert Pick had been arrested by the Gestapo and sent to Dachau; he was, however, released after three months, partly due to the intervention by Professor Edna Purdie, Chairman of the German Board of Studies and Professor and Head of German at Bedford from 1933 to 1962. The duties of the first Secretary-Librarian seem to have been wide-ranging and not always terribly glamorous; but Robert Pick's contribution to the success of the Institute and building-up of its Library was duly acknowledged: in a letter dated 9 January 1962 written by Robert Pick from hospital, where he was recovering from a heart attack, to the editors of and contributors to

to 'clean the pieces we bought as well as the wall against which they were to stand'.[14] Willoughby continues:

> We had to beg, borrow – or purloin – such books as the University grant could not run to. We had to use our minds to improvise the cataloguing and the accounts. And our hands to shift, arrange, and adjust. It was all great fun, and very hard work, this gradual em-body-ing of an idea (p. 5).[15]

A letter dated 10 October 1950 records that the Regulations for Admission to the Institute of Germanic Languages & Literatures had been approved by the Committee of Management on 18 July 1950 and were to go to Senate on 18 October 1950. Admission was to be granted to:

> Senior scholars in the field of Germanic Languages and Literatures, from other Universities and University Colleges in this country, from Colonial University Colleges and from Universities in other countries, who make application for admission to the Institute as occasion arises.

In the University Calendar 1950–51 the Institute is listed amongst the University Institutions:

> The objects of the Institute are 'to promote the advancement of the study of Germanic Languages and Literatures, to provide opportunities for contacts between scholars in the Germanic field, both within the University and from other centres of learning at home and abroad; and to arrange facilities for advanced study and research in the relevant subjects' (p. 408).[16]

German Life and Letters, he thanks them for his Festschrift, a special edition of *German Life and Letters* which Leonard Forster had taken to him in hospital.

14 Willoughby, '*Wine that maketh glad . . .*', p. 5.

15 Although Professor Willoughby had retired from the Chair of German at University College London in 1950 (to be succeeded by Leonard Forster), he remained Honorary Director of the Institute, which duly honoured his hard work and dedication. A letter dated 30 April 1970 from Professor Robson-Scott to Dr Geoffrey Templeman (who himself became Vice-Chancellor at Kent and Chairman of the IGS Committee of Management) records the former's letter from, and subsequent informal conversation with, Professor Wilkinson about honouring Professor Willoughby on the occasion of his eighty-fifth birthday. They had agreed that 'an appropriate way of marking the event might be to name the Main Library the "Willoughby Room" on the analogy of the Robertson-Priebsch Rooms on the ground floor. We would also, of course, place a photograph of Professor Willoughby in the Main Library'. Professor Robson-Scott requests that the proposal be put to the Management Committee at their next meeting (unless Professor Willoughby were present). His proposal was duly accepted. Dr Templeman, Dr J. R. (Hamish) Stewart (after whom Stewart House, a wing of Senate House, is named) and others, as Chairmen of the IGS Committee of Management, made a vital contribution to the survival of the IGS at various points. One such was the year 1985 to 1986, when the future of all the University of London Institutes was under serious review and Dr Stewart's knowledge of the University (he had been Principal from 1978 to 1983) and tactical advice proved invaluable.

16 This wording is taken over from the previous year's Calendar.

The Principal's Report records that:

> the Institute of Germanic Studies should soon commence operations in the upper part of 26 Russell Square. Professor L. A. Willoughby, who retires at the end of this session from the Chair of German at University College, will be the first Director (p. 129).

A little further on the Report remarks:

> One interesting result of the inspection of the Theological Schools, which was undertaken in 1947, is that a recommendation of the Inspectors for a system of central lectures on certain theological subjects will be brought into operation next session at Senate House. This development will augment the facilities for intercollegiate work which are already so well established in subjects such as History, Law and Germanic Languages and Literature, and marks yet another step in the proper utilisation of our teaching resources on a university basis (pp. 131–32).[17]

Finally, the Principal's Report in the University Calendar 1951–52 mentions the Institute of Germanic Languages and Literatures at 26 Russell Square as 'functioning as centre[s] of teaching and research' (p. 133).[18]

The establishment of the Institute met with warm support: for example, a letter from the Professor of German at Bristol, August Closs, dated 9 December 1950, described the foundation of the Institute as splendid news. W. L. Wardale of the German Department at Edinburgh University wrote to Professor Willoughby asking for information on the new Institute so he might include it in that term's issue of their Linguistic Society's paper *The Bridge*. He felt that Honours students in particular should know something about the Institute. Approbation also came from further afield: the Bundespressedienst of the Bundeskanzleramt, Vienna, wrote on 31 January 1951 expressing interest in the Institute and offering support. T. E. Carter at Canterbury University College, Christchurch, New Zealand, in a letter dated 12 March 1951, wrote the following to Dr Pick, Secretary-Librarian of the Institute:

> I have taken it upon myself as the only person teaching German here to thank you for your circular letter informing us of the opening of the Institute of Germanic Languages and Literatures. In our isolation here we shall be doubly

17 Under the heading of 'Student Activities' the Calendar notes: 'Parties of German students working in harvest camps have been entertained, and an expression of deep gratitude from the Ministry of Agriculture and Fisheries for the work of the Union in this respect has been received' (p. 153). Thus five years after the end of the war exchange between the UK and Germany was already taking place.

18 The other Institute referred to is the Institute of Commonwealth Studies at 27 Russell Square. The Institute of Germanic Languages and Literatures (as it was then known) initially cost the University around £3,000 p. a., including *c.*£1,000 for salaries.

Figure 13: Robert Pick.

> grateful to see the yearly bulletins of the Institute's activities, & we wish you every success.[19]

Richard Samuel, School of Germanic Languages, University of Melbourne, wrote in much the same vein on 8 March 1951:

> We are very interested in them [the activities of the newly founded Institute] and glad to know about the Institute for our post-graduates going to England as it will mean a great stimulus for them. Copies of the bulletin will be much appreciated by the Department. A note about the Institute will appear in the 1950 Proceedings of the Australian Institute (due to appear in about a fortnight's time) and in the News Letter of the Modern Language Teachers of Victoria.[20]

Similarly, on 3 February 1951 Professor T. A. Rompelman, University of Groningen, wrote:

> I can assure you that we take a keen interest in your institute and its activities in the future and should be, therefore, pleased to receive copies of its bulletins. We are very much obliged to you for your kind invitation to see you, your staff and your institute, and, no doubt, the members of staff of our section

19 T. E. Carter subsequently visited the Institute in person on 14 January 1957.

20 This extract is cited with the kind permission of the University of Melbourne.

(Germanic Philology and German Language and Literatures) and also our post-graduate students, who might, in the future, visit your town, will avail themselves of your offer with pleasure.

Wilmarth H. Starr, Head of the Department of Modern Languages and Classics, University of Maine, between 1937 and 1960, went even further in a letter dated 29 January 1951: 'In these troublous times it is always heartening to take note of new evidence of the vitality and growth of our heritage of permanent values'.[21] Approval, albeit of a somewhat equivocal kind, even came from East Germany: a letter from the Germanisches Institut, Friedrich-Schiller-Universität Jena, dated 22 January 1951, to Robert Pick, comments:

> Wir danken Ihnen für Ihre kürzliche Mitteilung und hoffen, daß das neue Deutsche Institut der Universität London dazu beitragen wird, der englischen Germanistik eine wissenschaftliche Grundlage zu geben. In diesen Bemühungen werden wir Sie selbstverständlich unterstützen und hoffen gleichzeitig, daß Sie die Möglichkeit haben, den jüngsten Zuwachs Ihrer Universität in den Dienst des so sehr gefährdeten Friedens zu stellen.

However, perhaps most moving is the response from Professor Hans Neumann, Direktor des Seminars für deutsche Philologie at Göttingen, in a letter to Dr Pick dated 21 December 1950:

> Ich danke Ihnen für die liebenswürdige Benachrichtigung über die Begründung des neuen Instituts für germanische Sprachen und Literaturen an der Universität London. Wir Göttinger Germanisten sind sehr erfreut darüber, dass eine solche Zentralstelle für das Studium des Deutschen eröffnet worden ist und begrüssen es besonders, dass die Bibliothek Priebsch auf diese Weise der Germanistik wieder zugänglich gemacht wird. Sicherlich wird das neue Institut die Zusammenarbeit unter den Germanisten der ganzen Welt energisch fördern und die persönliche Verbindung zwischen den Kollegen aller Länder zu verbessern in der Lage sein.

Professor Neumann invites Leonard Willoughby and Robert Pick to visit Göttingen, adding 'und eins seiner [Professor Willoughby's] mir damals [twenty years previously] überreichten Bücher gehört zu den wenigen geretteten Bänden meiner im Kriege verloren gegangenen Bibliothek'. He concludes, 'Wir sind gern bereit, die Arbeiten Ihres Instituts nach Kräften zu unterstützen und bitten um geeignete Vorschläge, wie wir Ihren Bemühungen dienlich werden können'.[22]

21 The Korean War had started on 25 June 1950 with the invasion of South Korea by North Korea; on 5 July 1950 the American Task Force Smith attacked the North Koreans at Osan; the Armistice Agreement was signed on 27 July 1953.

22 Both extracts are cited with the kind permission of the University of Göttingen. Indeed, the IGS is still very warmly regarded in Germany: it was a chance, highly appreciative remark

Establishing the Institute in 26 Russell Square did not, however, herald plain sailing and initial plans had to be revised due to lack of funds.[23] The building itself threw up a variety of problems, some a result of the war: a letter dated 26 July 1951 from K. Marr-Johnson of Clutton's (a firm of Chartered Surveyors and Land Agents) to Robert Pick states: 'In addition, most of the floors [of 26 Russell Square] appear to be of an experimental nature and were, I believe, laid by the Ministry of Works in conjunction with the Building Research Station at Watford. In some cases they are of different heights . . .'. Further, on 5 October 1951 K. Marr-Johnson writes to Robert Pick:

> Included in Messrs Holloway's tender is an amount of £1934 for works which I consider to be repair of war damage. I understand from the War Damage Commission that the war damage claim is not now open, but in view of the substantial amount of this figure I am again taking up the matter with the War Damage Commission in an endeavour to re-open the claim.

More alarmingly, a letter dated 12 November 1952 from Clutton's to Robert Pick regarding the 'Dangerous Structure Notice' recently served on 26 Russell Square stated that shoring-up work needed to be carried out at once. Such were the hazards of devotion to the Institute's cause![24]

Soon a move to a new building at 29 Russell Square was being contemplated, although this house, too, required work to render it properly usable:[25] a letter dated 4 January 1952 from the Secretary to the Senate, J. Hood Philips, to Robert Pick regarding the emergency repairs needed to the roof and stairwell of 29 Russell Square gave their estimated cost as £825. Court authorized the expenditure on 16 January 1952.[26] On 29 May 1952 Hood Phillips wrote to the Director of the Institute of Germanic Languages and Literatures that before the building could be taken over £2,850 worth of work needed to be done, this over and above the £4,890's worth of work already carried out on 29 Russell Square. Fortunately, the University continued its support of the Institute and the expenditure was authorized by Court on 11 June 1952. As with its initial establishment in 26 Russell Square, the Institute had to scrounge and barter. An unsigned letter to Professor Edna Purdie, dated 28 May 1952, states:

---

by Professor Volker Honemann (Münster) about the foundation of the Institute so soon after WWII that sparked my interest in the topic.

23 Financially straitened times affected the University of London as well: a letter dated 25 October 1951 from the Secretary to the Senate, J. Hood Philips, to the Director of the Institute, mentions the University's building allocation for 1951–52 was only half that for 1950–51.

24 This correspondence is quoted with the kind permission of Cluttons LLP. Cluttons assume no responsibility for disclosure to third parties.

25 For the history of 29 Russell Square, see Appendix 4.

26 Clutton's wrote on 7 April 1952 to say the Institute's fire insurance cover was to be raised from £16,535 to £24,000.

> Thank you very much for your letter of May 22nd. I fully share your view that we should get all the essential equipment before the end of the financial year. Indeed I would have written about it before, but for the fact that I am still negotiating with Birkbeck College for some of the equipment they left in 29 Russell Square. We have already bought some good steel shelving which will come in very useful when placed in one of the basement rooms. I should also like to buy two gas stoves, (one for the kitchen, the other for the caretaker's flat) if we can get them at a reasonable price. The other items they left there would be of no use to us, except for the refrigerator. I seem to remember that you were in favour of getting it last year. I am having it tested, and if it is in good working order, and if Birkbeck College do not charge too much, I think we should get it. It cost £90 five years ago, and I think we could pay for it up to half that amount. Considering that the smallest type of refrigerator now costs about £50, I think it would be a sound investment.[27]

The letter goes on to discuss ordering furniture for the lecture room on the ground floor. On 20 January 1953 Clutton's wrote to Robert Pick to inform him that the works of adaptation had been completed on 31 December 1952; and that occupation of 29 Russell Square was 'deemed to have commenced on 7 January'. Rent on the building amounted to £425 per annum (exclusive of rates) and remained at this sum for decades. Thus in January 1953 the Institute moved to 29 Russell Square. An undated typed sheet records the estimates for the reconstruction and adaptation of 29 Russell Square, declaring a quotation of £4,890 (from Holloway Brothers) 'reasonable'. The quotation covered re-wiring; decoration throughout; the re-boarding of floors in Rooms 4, 6, 7, 9 and the Caretaker's living room. However, problems with the building continued: on 24 September 1953 Robert Pick wrote to Clutton's regarding the impossibility of opening some of the windows since the external repainting of building; in April 1955 correspondence dealt with roof repairs at a cost of £13 9s 8d; on 2 May 1955 Robert Pick wrote to Clutton's regarding blocked drains; and on 20 December 1955 he wrote again regarding a crack in the staircase wall and another item which had caused considerable consternation: a letter dated 13 October 1955 to Mr Hood Phillips records 'a catastrophe of considerable magnitude', namely, a defective gas boiler flue which necessitated major repair work (five to six weeks) at great expense and would cause disruption because of holes being banged in walls etc. The problem had probably been caused when work was done on 28 Russell Square. As it was, '[b]lack fumes were issuing in three or four rooms which have a party wall with number 28'. Fortunately, the Institute proved equal to this challenge as well and went on to thrive, its vision unclouded.

27 Birkbeck College had occupied 29 Russell Square in the late 1940s.

Figure 14: Exterior of 29 Russell Square.

The Institute of Germanic Languages and Literatures: Consolidation at the Centre

The progress and vision of the Institute can be seen in its various policy documents, beginning with the *Development Policy for the Quinquennium 1957–1962*:[1]

> During the present quinquennium the Institute has consolidated its position as a centre of communication between scholars from all parts working in the field of Germanic Languages and Literatures; the library has been greatly strengthened, especially in certain branches (18th- and 19th-century authors, extinct periodicals, lexicography, Festschriften), and is becoming increasingly recognised as an important research library. It is obvious that provision should be made during the next quinquennium for further development along these lines and for maintaining the steady expansion of the library as a whole.

Noting the desire to expand the Institute's activities were funding to be available, the report records the *Union Catalogue of Periodicals* compiled by the IGS,[2] remarking that it would be:

> a great advantage if this catalogue could be followed by one listing the holdings in Transactions and special sets; further developments (such as catalogues referring to selected authors or topics) might then be undertaken in due course. [...] even now many enquiries of this nature are addressed to it and answered.

Beyond its very useful bibliographical activities, the Institute sought to 'encourage not only the verbal communication of research findings [at colloquia and seminars] but also their communication in print'. To this end, the establishment of a fund for the 'publication of suitable addresses and articles' constituted 'one of the most desirable developments in the immediate future'. It was also felt that 'a series sponsored by the Institute would help in some measure to ease the present difficulty of publishing scholarly work in the Germanic field in this country'. Finally, it was thought that the establishment of a Senior Research Fellowship attached to the Institute and awarded annually would 'stimulate original work in subjects particularly appropriate to the Institute'. The Fellowship was to approximate the initial salary of a Lecturer, i.e., about £800 per annum.

1 Quinquennial funding from the University Grants Committee continued until about 1982, after which funding was allocated on an annual basis. Five-year funding enabled sensible medium-term planning.

2 See section on 'Publications'.

In *The First Ten Years* (15 January 1960), his report to the Honorary Director of the Institute,[3] Robert Pick finds some cause for satisfaction amidst the gloom: although the Institute had been operating with extremely limited resources, since in its early years the grant had been little more than half what it was in 1960 and the money had been spent mainly on building a *Präsenzbibliothek* from scratch, increased grants had then made it possible to augment the Library holdings more than initially expected. Despite operating with only a skeleton staff (up until 1952 only the Secretary-Librarian and Library Assistant; between 1952 and 1956 there had been three people on the staff; after 1956 there had been only short periods when more than four staff were employed), the Institute had still established itself as *the* centre of German Studies in the UK and was also known to and visited by scholars from abroad. The first entries in the Visitors' Book are by a Dr Manfred Schlenke, Historisches Seminar, Universität Marburg, and Irmtraut Schlenke on 23 July 1956; the Austrian author Heimito von Doderer on 30 January 1957; and the eminent Germanists Benno von Wiese and Fritz Martini on 17 July 1959. By the end of 1960 the Institute had welcomed visitors from Marburg, Rotterdam, Mainz, Mannheim, Heidelberg, Vienna, Greifswald, Basle, Clinton N.J., Melbourne, Sweden, Berlin, Jena, Yale, Göttingen, the University of Alberta (Edmonton), Chicago, Otago University (Dunedin), Clark University (Worcester, Massachusetts), the South African College (Cape Town), the Austrian Bundesministerium für Unterricht, the German Embassy, Williamsport (Pennsylvania), Munich, Stuttgart, Harvard, Bonn, Victoria University (Wellington, New Zealand), the University of Wrocław (formerly Breslau), Toronto, Tokyo and the University of Western Australia (Perth). Subsequent years also saw visitors from across the globe: the Visitors' Book beginning on 24 November 1983 records scholars from France, Germany, Mexico, Holland, Israel, Portugal, the USA (including Alaska), Austria, Hungary, Australia, Canada, Japan, Hong Kong, Italy, Belgium, Russia, Sweden, Bulgaria, Stockholm, New Zealand, Taiwan and Greece. These visitors were no less august than earlier ones: the GDR author Stefan Heym; on 8 April 1970 Johann Wolfgang von Goethe, then at King's College London (!);[4] and – most excitingly – on 6 October 1988 Pooh and Piglet (address: Big Tree, 100 Aker Wood, Pine Forest). Under 'Remarks' we find the ultimate accolade: 'Sehr schön, Piglet?'. 'Ja, Pooh'.

Not only had the Institute succeeded in its stated aim of serving as a focal point for scholars from abroad, it had also been active in realizing its

3 The Honorary Director of the Institute was a rotating office, held by one or other of the Professors of German at the University of London, usually for three years and carrying an honorarium. The arrangement was only abolished with the appointment of a part-time Director in 1998.

4 Obviously such was the reputation of the Institute that Goethe had descended from Mount Parnassus to see it for himself.

development plan, publishing a *Union List of Periodicals* in 1956; and Robert Pick put forward a proposal for the Institute to establish a scholarly journal, as 'Germanisten have far too few opportunities in this country, and have to go to the United States or to Germany to see their work in print'. He also suggested that the Institute should be made the centre of information about impending visits from scholars abroad and addressed the desirability of improved relations with the representatives of foreign countries. However, Robert Pick did express disappointment on a number of issues, first regarding the expansion of the *Analytical Index of Festschriften* to include material in other University of London libraries: the index had come to a standstill in spring 1959 due to lack of staff (as had other projects). Second, he raised the problem of lack of space for the Library, an issue which continued to preoccupy the Institute throughout its tenancy of 29 Russell Square and has only been exacerbated by the move to Senate House. Third, he points out that a jewel in the Library's holdings, the Priebsch-Closs Collection (which contains several hundred plays by little-known authors of the eighteenth and nineteenth centuries), remained unexploited.[5]

These issues, arising mainly from lack of sufficient staff and funding, continued to plague the Library: in a report of 7 March 1965 for the Director, the Librarian Lindsay Newman outlines the following problems: a) an acute lack of shelf space; b) an inadequate catalogue; c) the stock remaining largely unclassified; d) a backlog of donations and bequests not even sorted; e) the main library being insufficiently quiet; f) the care of books largely unconsidered; g) an insufficient stock of general reference books. Further, Mrs Newman points out that users were becoming discouraged as books were constantly being moved due to lack of space and therefore became hard to find. At that time the Library staff consisted of one librarian with a degree in German; one trainee librarian with a degree in German; and occasional assistance from an untrained postgraduate. The posts of Librarian and Secretary were not separated until January 1965.

However, one activity the Institute did start was *Research in Germanic Studies*, published annually from 1968 to 1996–97. This survey of all the research being undertaken by scholars of German in Great Britain and Ireland was initially a project of the Conference of University Teachers of German in Great Britain and Ireland (the predecessor to the Association for German Studies). Annual lists were produced by one of the two Joint Honorary Secretaries, a considerable burden. In 1967 Siegbert Prawer (then Honorary Director of the Institute) suggested the Institute take over responsibility. Initially the Conference paid £30 per annum for the work! *Research in Germanic Studies* also included MA and doctoral dissertations.

5 More will be said about the Priebsch-Closs Collection in the History of the IGS Library. For a full account of the Collection see the essay by John L. Flood in this volume.

The last volume is the thickest, testifying to the strength, breadth and richness of German Studies at that time. Examples selected at random from the first (1969) and last (1996–97) volumes include:

1969

Frank Shaw, 'Ovid und die "Kaiserchronik"' (*Zeitschrift für deutsche Philologie*); D. Brüggemann, *Die sächsische Komödie – Studien zu ihrem Sprachstil* (Böhlau); Brian Keith-Smith, 'Hugo von Hofmannsthal's "Drei kleine Lieder" – a note on their genius and present form as a trilogy' (*ASNS*); A. W. Stanforth, *The German Linguistic Atlas*; H. B. Nisbet, *Herder and Science* (MHRA). Dissertations include: K. A. G. Mills, 'The Theme of Isolation in German Drama from Grillparzer to Hebbel' (Cambridge); D. Waters, 'Semantic Function as Influenced by International Organization'; P. Belling, 'The Pronoun in Old Frisian'; C. K. Millward, 'Aspects of the Apocalyptic Literature of the Teutonic Order'; and C. J. Smith, 'Goethe's Book Reviews after 1804 and Their Significance for His Literary Theory and Practice'.

1996–97

Theses in Progress show a marked shift from the earlier period to the twentieth century, especially post-war, and include: K. Gebel, 'Identity-generating Potential of Indigenous Bilingualism with Special Reference to the Promotion of Gaelic in Scotland and Sorbian in Germany'; G. Horan, 'Diversity and Development in the Language of National Socialism'; A. J. Williams, 'Tricksters and Pranksters in Medieval and Renaissance French and German Literature'; J. A. Tiplady, 'Time in Middle High German Narrative Literature, with Special Reference to Wolfram von Eschenbach's *Parzival*'; S. Allan, 'A Comparative Study of Byron's *Don Juan* and Goethe's *West-östlicher Divan*'; S. Hart, 'The Jewish *Kaffeehausliteraten* of Twentieth-century Vienna'; and G. Pye, 'Comedy and Contemporary German Drama'. Work due to be published in 1997 (which included much more on language generally) lists: G. Shaw, *Deutsch für Juristen*; M. Chinca, 'Knowledge and Practice in the Early German Love-Lyric' (*FMLS*); A. Volfing, *Heinrich von Mügeln: 'Der meide kranz': a Commentary*; M. R. Minden, *The German Bildungsroman: Incest and Inheritance*; H. Chambers, *The Changing Image of Theodor Fontane*; J. M. Ritchie, *German Exiles: British Perspectives*; J. M. Tudor, 'How Many Cultures Make a Sub-Culture? Turkish Migrant Literature in Germany and Other (post-Colonial) Stories', in: *Unity and Difference in European Culture(s)*; and G. L. B. Paul, 'Schwierigkeiten mit der Dialektik in Christa Wolf's *Medea, Stimmen*' (*GLL*).

Despite, then, the constraints imposed by lack of funding and space, the Institute of Germanic Languages and Literatures had succeeded in establishing itself as a central force in Germanic Studies; and continued to flourish and fulfil its stated aim of functioning as the centre of Germanic Studies in the UK and further afield: for example, the *IGS Development Policy 1972/77*, in its review of the years 1967–72, remarks that the Institute had become:

> a research centre of ever increasing value, and a meeting place for scholars in the Germanic field in the University of London and elsewhere in the UK.[6] It also plays an important role as a centre for postgraduate students of Germanic languages and literatures in the University of London and elsewhere, to whom the Library is an invaluable asset in the prosecution of their studies.

The report goes on to note that 'the Institute is now well established as the principal centre of communication, and information, in the UK for scholars from all over the world'. It was also in 1972 that the decision was made to add symposia of one or two days' duration to the Institute's events; and to try to further contacts with Dutch and Scandinavian.[7]

There had been, however, one small change: Minute 529 of a meeting of the Committee of Management on 28 November 1962 records that, due to the long and cumbersome nature of the Institute's name, it had been agreed to alter it to the simpler 'Institute of Germanic Studies'. This change was approved by Senate on 27 March 1963; and it was under this name that the Institute was known until its merger with the Institute of Romance Studies in 2004 to form the Institute of Germanic & Romance Studies. The *IGS Development Policy 1972/77* refers also another of the Institute's roles, namely, as a support (through its library provision) and central venue for postgraduate teaching. The MA

6 The term 'Germanic' seems to have been interpreted quite generously: a letter to the Editor of *The Times* from M. O'C. Walshe, Deputy Director of the IGS, dated 2 December 1969, addresses the use of adverbs in English: 'Sir, // Another transatlantic locution which has recently come to plague us is hopefully, used in the sense of "I hope" or "it is to be hoped". Its origin would seem to be clear: Americans of German origin hit upon it when struggling to find an equivalent for the German hoffentlich. Why we should imitate this rather primitive mistake I don't know. // Hopefully, then, this locution will prove not to be viable. But I am unhopeful about it. Such being the case, I can only sign myself, Sir, // Yours hopelessly, M. O'C. Walshe, Deputy Director'.

7 Dutch and Scandinavian have been less represented in the Institute Library, mainly for financial reasons: a letter from Professor Frederick Norman to Mrs Newman about the Library remarks that since Scandinavian Studies were strong at University College London and Dutch at Bedford, the Institute would not compete as it could not afford to build up comparable libraries. However, from the start the Committee of Management of the Institute included all Professors of Germanic languages (excluding English) *ex officio* in its membership. They always received papers and regularly attended meetings of the Committee.

Figure 15: MA seminar in the Willoughby Room (Lecturer: Dr Andreas Kramer [Goldsmiths']). Among the students on the far right: Margaret T. Gajewski who was to continue to complete a doctorate at the Institute.

courses themselves were run by the Board of Studies. In 1967–68 and 1968–69 the Institute housed postgraduate seminars which included twenty-six hours on Meister Eckhart; in 1969–70 eighteen. Further, it was expected that '[a]t least one substantial publication will result from the Meister Eckhart study'.[8] From about 1970 onwards several MA options were on offer: Twentieth-Century Studies; Rilke; George; Hofmannsthal; the Literature of the Conversion of the Germanic Peoples (taught only two or three times); the Medieval Courtly Romance; Heroic Poetry (never actually taught!); the German Novel between the Wars; ten hours of Gothic and twenty-six hours of Old Saxon (possibly taught as part of the course 'The Conversion of the Germanic Peoples'); and Tradition and Innovation in Modern German Literature (taught every year for twenty-five years).[9]

Other aspects of the Institute's activities are also highlighted: a list of Theses in Progress at British Universities, which was published annually and

8 These seminars were run in conjunction with Maurice O'C. Walshe's project to translate Meister Eckhart's sermons – presumably the 'substantial publication'. His *Meister Eckhart: Sermons & Treatises* was published in three volumes in 1987; in 2010 a revised, single-volume (third) edition was published under the title *The Complete Mystical Works of Meister Eckhart*.

9 Details of the various options were listed in the 'Red Book', the *Regulations for Internal Students of the University of London*, published annually until the 1990s.

offered for sale; the Bulletin of Work in Progress, which was not a public document but intended as confidential information for members of the CUTG, which sponsored both lists;[10] the catalogue of Festschriften was being pursued with Paul Raabe and the Herzog August Bibliothek, Wolfenbüttel; and a Union List of Periodicals Dealing with Germanic Languages and Literatures had been compiled (published in 1956). Moreover, the Institute provided editorial accommodation and facilities for *German Life and Letters*, which – as the *Quinquennium 1977/82 Development Policy* notes for the period 1972/77 – met there regularly. In fact, the founder of the Institute, Professor Willoughby, had also founded *German Life and Letters* 'precisely with the object of providing a forum for reflecting the momentous political and cultural changes then taking place in the country which – whatever our academic predilections – must be the focus of our study'.[11] Its first issue appeared in October 1936; publication was suspended in 1939 and resumed in 1947. The Institute also provided a home for the English Goethe Society, which regularly held its meetings there and had placed its library on deposit at the Institute. In its review of the period 1972 to 1977, the *Policy* further records that membership of the Institute had increased since in 1977 there were 550 members (compared to 355 in 1966/67). In April 1975 there had been as many as 680, which had included sixty-four full-time teachers in Departments of Germanic Languages and Literatures in the University; and 124 postgraduates pursuing postgraduate studies in such departments. The report continues:

> In the U.K., the Institute is recognised as a centre of communication and information. An important function is the regular reading of papers (usually three or four per term) by scholars of repute from this country and abroad, followed by discussion. The series of post-graduate seminars at the Institute has been developed and expanded.

Intercollegiate MA seminars continued to be held at the Institute.

A decade later, the *Institute of Germanic Studies Thirty-fifth Annual Report. 1st August 1984 – 31st July 1985* records that the Institute:

> is in good heart, and the gloomy financial prospects for research in the humanities have in no way affected the manifold activities which justify the Institute's existence and which its staff are determined to continue undiminished. [...] Taken together, these activities [research, symposia, seminars, undergraduate colloquia, publications] confirm the Institute's unique role as the focus for German Studies in Great Britain, a role which is

10 Eventually both were combined into *Research in Germanic Studies*, a title coined by Professor John Flood when Secretary of the CUTG.

11 Minutes of the Board of Studies in Germanic Languages and Literatures, 21 December 1943, p. 8.

Figure 16: Professor William Douglas Robson-Scott.

recognised in universities outside London as well as among our Continental colleagues (p. 1).

It also notes the establishment of the William Robson-Scott Travelling Scholarship. William Robson-Scott had been Honorary Director of the Institute from 1968 to 1973 and the Scholarship, which enables a postgraduate from a British university to travel to the German-speaking countries, the Netherlands or Scandinavia for the purposes of research, was funded by his bequest.[12] Five options of the intercollegiate MA in German had been taught at the IGS and three undergraduate symposia had taken place on Heinrich von Kleist, Bertolt Brecht, and German Comedy. Three BA Special Subject

12 William Douglas Robson-Scott had been appointed Honorary Director of the Institute of Germanic Studies after his retirement and during his five years in office had contributed vigorously, constructively and loyally to the Institute's wide range of activities. His scholarly interests were unusually wide-ranging: English, German and Dutch literature and the visual arts. With his wife Elaine, he translated the correspondence between Sigmund Freud and Arnold Zweig (1970) and Freud and Lou Andreas-Salomé (1972); academic publications included *German Travellers in England 1400–1800* (1953; based on his Vienna doctoral thesis awarded *c.*1938) and *The Younger Goethe and the Visual Arts* (1981).

options were taught there as well: 'Wolfram von Eschenbach';[13] the 'Tristan Legend in Medieval Germany and its Reception by Thomas Mann and Richard Wagner'; and 'Heinrich Heine'. Over three hundred more volumes had been acquired by the Library than in the previous year (1983–84), over a quarter of them in the form of gifts and exchanges. Finally, the Institute had attracted visitors from Cairo, Rome, Pittsburgh and Santa Barbara; and had hosted major names from the German and English literary world: in November 1984 Günter Grass had been present at a research symposium in honour of Uwe Johnson, who had died that year. Michael Hamburger and Alan Sillitoe had also participated (Minutes, p. 7).

At the end of the 1980s the standing and excellence of the Institute of Germanic Studies were even explicitly recognized by its own institution: the first issue of the *Friends of the Institute Newsletter* (1987–88) includes a report by the Honorary Director Roy Wisbey to the effect that, during 1986, the Institute had emerged strengthened from two searching appraisals of its role, its academic standing and its contribution to scholarship.[14] In particular it had been included by the University Grants Committee in a group of London postgraduate institutes the activities of which, it was recommended, 'should continue to be protected as far as practicable' and which were to be given 'level funding in terms of the forecast level of general inflation specifically in order to protect present levels of activity at centres of outstanding excellence with a clear national role'. The report continues: 'A major new venture of particular interest has been the institution of a

13 The acquisition of editions of Wolfram's works and secondary literature on Wolfram had been a Library priority from the beginning. The IGS's own archive contains a file of Wolfram Correspondence between such distinguished medievalists as Walter Johannes Schröder, Sidney M. Johnson (Kansas), Arthur Hatto, Marianne Wynn, Roy Wisbey, Peter Ganz, Maurice O'C. Walshe, a Mr/Dr(?) Van Rest (whom it has not proved possible to identify) and, from 23 October 1961, Dr Gottfried Weber. Together they constituted a Medieval Study Group, which had been proposed in 1959 but had come to nothing until 1961. The Minutes of their meetings discuss the compilation of a bibliography and commentary on Wolfram von Eschenbach. On 14 November 1961 the group decided to start with a *Willehalm* commentary as one on *Parzival* already existed. From the Minutes it is clear they engaged in very detailed discussion on individual points of text, such as the architecture of the banqueting hall in *Willehalm*; or the precise meaning of words like 'amer', 'sünden' and so forth. The various books in *Willehalm* were divided up between the individual members of the group. Considerable correspondence between different members of the group continues until the end of 1962; then all is silence.

14 The *Friends' Newsletter* for 1989 notes that statistics compiled for the University's Grants' Committee Research Selectivity Exercise record the following activity at the IGS in the previous five years: twenty-one research symposia involving 272 speakers, 189 from the UK and eighty-three from twelve overseas countries; and sixty-eight guest lecturers, forty-three of them from overseas. The same *Newsletter* records that at a ceremony in London on 23 February 1989 Professor Wisbey was awarded the Großes Ehrenzeichen für Verdienste um die Republik Österreich for his work as Honorary Director of the IGS.

national forum for postgraduate students from all universities to meet and discuss their research. The first such colloquium took place at the Institute in February 1987'.

Changing Times: 1995–2004

The following decade brought a change in status for the IGS: on 1 August 1994 it formally joined the eight other Senate Institutes of the University of London to form the new University of London Institute of Advanced Study (ULIAS),[1] officially launched by Sir Anthony Kenny, Chairman of the British Library Board, in March 1995. Inevitably, the status of the Institute was affected by changes within the structure of the University of London, such as the gradual disintegration of the federal system, and within Higher Education generally. The then Honorary Director, Mr Edward Batley, writes:[2]

> Overall management of the Institute was by [...] the Board of Directors, to which Hon. Directors were also responsible. The SAS [...] changed the title and the new terms of governance [...]. Because the various Schools of the University were flexing their muscles ever more firmly, growing more and more competitive in terms of recruitment, scholarship and funding, carrying out advanced, specialised, minority functions (quite understandably given the parameters being set nationally by HFC and Research Reviews, Teaching Reviews, Funding Formulae and FTEs), which simply undermined the federal, shared and joint co-operative tradition of the University generally and the Institute in particular, the IGS did what it could in an attempt to sustain and reinforce that tradition. The undergraduate federal lectures on Thursday, usually attended by over a hundred students and organised by the Federal Board of Germanic Studies, had died the death already. The Federal Board itself soon followed suit. For their part, the German Departments in the Schools began to offer their own MAs in German and understandably became concerned about their 'free' contribution of teaching, supervision and examining to the federal MA in German (taught at the Institute), the most popular option of which was on Modern German Literature (not the exact title).[3] At one stage it achieved a recruitment figure of 27 students in one year [...].

1 Now the School of Advanced Study or SAS. The other Institutes were: the Institute of Advanced Legal Studies, the Institute of Classical Studies, the Institute of Commonwealth Studies, the Institute of Historical Research, the Institute of Latin American Studies, the Institute of Romance Studies, the Institute of United States Studies and the Warburg Institute. In 1982 Sir Peter Swinnerton-Dyer, a mathematician and Vice-Chancellor of the University of Cambridge, published the *Swinnerton-Dyer Report* on the academic organization of the University of London. This initiated the wholesale reorganization of the federal university, notably the merger of Colleges (e.g. Royal Holloway with Bedford College; Queen Mary with Westfield). Now Bedford and Westfield no longer exist even in name.

2 I am greatly indebted to Mr Edward Batley for much of the information in this section.

3 Actually, 'Tradition and Innovation in Twentieth-Century German Literature'.

The Institute attempted to counteract the dilution of the federal structure and to maintain the coherence of German Studies within the University of London by putting a number of measures into place. Traditionally, students taking the Federal MA in German registered at the University of London College of their choice and this College collected their fees. However, this practice failed to recompense the other Colleges for the teaching provided by their staff on the MA or the Institute for its contribution. To redress the balance and prevent other University of London Colleges from forbidding their staff to teach on the federal MA, the then Honorary Director, Edward Batley, devised a complex scheme for reimbursing individual departments for the teaching provided by their staff: the fees collected were put into a metaphorical pot, the number of hours' input by academic staff from the various Colleges was calculated and the income was redistributed accordingly. In this way the Colleges and the IGS received remuneration commensurate with their input. The calculations were done by the Institute and signed off by whoever was in charge of the MA at that point. Senate House then redistributed the funds.[4] Two further measures were put in place: first, an Academic Committee of the Institute was established to oversee its academic affairs; it included the Honorary and Deputy Directors as well as two representatives from each German Department. Second, postgraduate research students were registered at the Institute for an MPhil or PhD and the number of potential supervisors thereby increased.[5] In all these initiatives the Friends of the Institute provided invaluable support and funding.[6] Much thought was devoted in this chillier academic climate to the profile of the Institute and 'brain-storming' sessions tackled the following issues: ways in which the focus of the Institute mission could be sharpened; how its mission and objectives could be made more appealing and exciting, especially to potential sponsors; how the mission might more clearly reflect

4 This happened for the last time in 2005, after which the federal MA in German was abandoned and the IGRS launched its own MA/MRes.

5 The Institute was at this time (1996–97), as always, aware of the increasing demands on its teaching, Library, conference and general space. Needs included teaching rooms for University Special Subjects and MA Options; meeting rooms for lectures, international symposia, conferences; rooms for meetings of MA and MPhil/PhD Examiners, the Board, the Academic Committee (and sub-committees thereof); a meeting room for the editors of *German Life and Letters* and other literary and philological societies such as the English Goethe Society, the Research Centre for German & Austrian Exile Studies etc.. As well as a central computing room for students and staff in the SAS, it was suggested that at least twenty computers would be needed in the Institute library (with CD Rom facilities, etc.) as well as demarcated work positions for readers. While these desiderata point to the need for a larger home for the Institute, they also make clear the range of its activities.

6 The Friends of the Institute were founded in 1986, at the proposal of Professor John Flood, to promote activities which were beyond the means of the Institute's budget. For more information see the section on the Friends of the Institute of Germanic Studies.

the interdisciplinarity and modernity of German Studies; how the 'corporate image' of the Institute might be 'smartened up' and made more welcoming to younger scholars; and how the Institute might raise awareness of the central role played in Europe by Germany, as well as the importance of Austria and Switzerland, and convert this awareness into increased financial support for the work of the Institute. In other words, in a Higher Education system increasingly determined by market forces and commercial considerations, the Institute was forced to develop and market a new brand for itself.

Implementation of the aims thus identified included the appointment in 1996 of a part-time Development Officer (supported by the Initiatives Fund of the School of Advanced Study) for the new Research Centre for German & Austrian Exile Studies at the IGS (see below); and ultimately of a Director of the Institute. Moreover, possibilities for generating external income were explored, such as research grants, sponsorship (for example, from German banks) and even some sort of tie with the Department of Trade and Industry and similar agencies for whom (above all) economic links with Germany were important. In the *Strategic Plan 1998–2003*, included in the Honorary Director's Report of 21 October 1998, it is noted that the University had increased the core grant to the Institute; that the increase was to be used to enable the appointment of a Director at 0.5; and that the managers of the Bithell Bequest had agreed to supplement the increase in core grant.[7] Interviews for the part-time Directorship had been held on 14 October 1998. In the meantime, the excessive demands on the administrative staff continued and it is a tribute to their commitment and loyalty that the Institute continued to function without the strains being noticed by the wider Germanist community.

As the Institute moved towards its jubilee in 2000, it was keenly aware of the changing political and academic context within which it operated, as the (draft) Mission Statement for 1998–2003 indicates:

> 1.2.2 Changes have occurred in recent years which necessitated a revision of the Institute's role as it moves towards its jubilee in 2000 and into the next century. The four most important of these are: (i) a broader understanding of what is meant by the cultures of the German-speaking countries; (ii) the impact on German Studies, nationally and internationally, of the unification of Germany in 1990 and of the stronger relations between the German-speaking communities of Europe and the European Union.

Thus the Institute was well positioned to take advantage of the new trend towards interdisciplinarity and aware of the necessity to do so. However, its

7 Jethro Bithell had been Head of the Department of German at Birkbeck College, London, between 1910 and 1938; he and his wife Alice Emily Bithell had left their entire estate to the Institute. For more information see the section on Benefactors and Bequests.

original brief to promote German (Austrian/Swiss) culture in its broadest sense remained at the heart of Institute activities; and the mid-1990s had even seen the proposal that a new research centre be founded, the Research Centre for the Study of German Language and Literature, with the aim of countering the outdated clichés about Germany propagated by the British press by raising public awareness of Germany's remarkable cultural and humanitarian traditions. Enhancing the Institute's research environment and attracting young researchers, fellows and postgraduate students remained another key objective.

Leaping into the new millennium, we find the *IGS Annual Report 2001–2002* recording the outstanding achievement of a 5* in the previous Research Assessment Exercise (p. 1).[8] The Institute's well-established Thursday-evening lecture series, for that session on 'Politics in Literature', had resulted in stimulating cross-disciplinary debate and included papers ranging from Kleist's political stance to Jean Améry's novelistic prose to features of New Right culture and its intellectual traditions since the 1920s. Three international conferences had taken place: on the German-Jewish writer and journalist Georg Hermann (the 'Jewish Fontane': he wrote on late-nineteenth-century Berlin); on 'Vienna Meets Berlin' (culture in the metropolis between the wars, part of the London-wide festival 'Vienna – Berlin – London, The Trails of Creativity 1918–1938'); and on 'Seelenarbeit an Deutschland' (the motif of German (self-)consciousness in Martin Walser's work) (p. 9). The Friends' Lecture for that year had been given by Professor R. S. Furness (St Andrews) on 'The lewd magnolias of Tavistock Square and other botanical freaks: an extravaganza'.[9] At the end of the academic session the IGS boasted 1,319 members in total (p. 8).

However, all good things – it seems – must pass (or, at least, bow in the face of perceived financial necessity) and in 2004 the Institute of Germanic

8 The Institute had also achieved the then-top ratings of 5* in the RAE in 1996 and 5 in 1992. For readers fortunate enough never to have encountered the RAE, it began in 1986 and is undertaken approximately every five or six years on behalf of the four UK Higher Education Funding Councils with the aim of evaluating the quality of research undertaken by British institutions of Higher Education. RAE submissions from each subject area (or Unit of Assessment) are ranked by a subject-specialist peer review panel; the rankings are then used to decide the amount of quality-weighted research funding (QR) each subject in each university receives from its respective funding council. Some Units of Assessment receive no funding at all if the submitted research is not deemed to be of high enough quality. RAEs have taken place in 1986, 1989, 1992, 1996; 2001 and 2008 (the IGS was not permitted to submit in 2008 as this would have been seen as conflicting with its role and funding as a facilitator of research nationally); and their results are used by organs such as the *Times Higher Education Supplement* to construct university league tables. The results of the successor exercise, rechristened the REF (Research Excellence Framework) and sharpened by the addition of compulsory Impact case studies, were published in December 2014.

9 See the section on the Friends of the Institute of Germanic Studies.

Figure 17: Five Directors and One Caretaker. From left to right: John Flood, Martin Swales, L. J. Watts, Roy Wisbey, Edward Batley, Rüdiger Görner.

Studies and the Institute of Romance Studies (founded 1989) merged under the umbrella of the School of Advanced Study. In the *Friends Newsletter 2004*, Professor Rüdiger Görner (Queen Mary & Westfield), sums up the achievements of the previous fifty-four years:[10]

> Es heißt Abschied nehmen von einigem. Abschied von einem Kleinod in der Welt der Germanistik. Zahllose Kolleginnen und Kollegen aus aller Herren und Frauen Länder haben auf die Nachricht, daß das Institute of Germanic Studies seine Autonomie im Rahmen der School of Advanced Study verlieren werde, mit Unverständnis, nicht selten mit Bestürzung reagiert.[11]
>
> Natürlich gibt es wie überall materielle Zugzwänge in den Geisteswissenschaften, in der sogenannten Auslandsgermanistik zumal. Und sie haben bekanntlich längst Vorrang vor intellektuell-akademischen Erwägungen erlangt. Doch wenn ein international renommiertes germanistisches Forschungsinstitut, das bei allen Research Assessments

10 Apparently one reason given for the moving of the IGS into Senate House was the cost of maintaining 29 Russell Square, even though a Structural Engineer's Report on the building from April 1998 concludes, 'This property appears to be in very good structural order for its age. No significant structural defects were observed'.

11 Years earlier Professor John Flood had initiated the appointment of Corresponding Fellows of the Institute, selected from amongst eminent colleagues in Germanic Studies in foreign institutions. The purpose of the Corresponding Fellows was to act as a powerful voice from abroad whenever the continued existence of the Institute was under threat.

Spitzenwerte erzielen konnte und dem das Higher Education Funding Council of England noch vor wenigen Jahren ein imposantes Zeugnis ausgestellt hat, wenn eine solche Institution zur Fusion freigegeben wird mit einem Partner, dessen akademisches Profil von allen geisteswissenschaftlichen Instituten der School of Advanced Study zumindest bislang am wenigsten zu dem unseren gepaßt hat, dann herrscht unweigerlich akuter Erklärungsnotstand, der sich noch steigert, wenn man die Art und Umstände dieser Zusammenlegung bedenkt ... [...]

[...] Man weiß es – andernorts womöglich genauer (und mehr zu schätzen) als in Malet Street –: eine einzigartige Bibliothek, eine ausgeglichene Bilanz, zwei neue (inzwischen aufs Vielversprechendste besetzte) akademische Stellen im Lecturer-Rang, das Ingeborg Bachmann Centre for Austrian Literature, Doktorandenstellen (Dank der *Friends*!), diverse Fonds, deren Verwendung, dafür ist inzwischen hinreichend Sorge getragen, auf den Bereich der Förderung im Bereich der Germanistik beschränkt bleiben wird. Hinzu kommt ein immenses Vertrauenskapital unserer Friends [...] sowie der langen Reihe der Corresponding Fellows aus der Welt der internationalen Germanistik.[12]

12 Ironically, in a 'Memorandum on the Future of the Institute from the Deputy Director to Professor Stern' (8.2.82) a similar merger had almost been foreseen, although under different auspices and in a different form from the Institute of Germanic & Romance Studies. In the wake of the CAOIII (Committee on Academic Organisation) and SARC (Subject Area Review Committee) Report on Languages a suggestion was made at the meeting with the Chairman of the FGPC (Finance and General Purposes Committee) on 2 February 1982 that the IGS consider closer integration with the University Library. In fact, the IGS was being 'threatened' with the 'spectre of a merger with the University Library'. The CAO on SARC Languages recommended that the IGS continue in existence, but the following question was raised: 'Should we not tell the FGPC that we wholeheartedly support the CAO and SARC proposals for the establishment of an Institute of Romance Languages and Literatures and recommend that the University make available premises large enough to accommodate the Romance Institute, the Germanic Institute, and the (relatively small) French and German sections of the University Library? London could then have a centre for advanced work in modern languages (comparable in some ways with the Taylorian at Oxford), a research institute with a substantial library serviced by staff seconded from the University Library'. According to Mr Edward Batley, several reasons were given for the eventual move of the IGS into Senate House: '(i) the reason advanced by the Dean of SAS and the University Administration that the 9 Institutes of SAS should be brought under the same roof, partly to take up the space otherwise in danger of not being used, and partly to allow a "rationalisation" of the administrative costs of running individual institutes (i.e. a common secretariat); (ii) the literally miles of extra shelving needed by the Institute Library, not only in the future, but almost immediately. Bill [William Abbey, Institute Librarian] made his point to me most effectively; (iii) 29 Russell Square had no foundations. Cracks below stairs had appeared in the walls and their movement was being monitored. The potential cost to the University of repairing such a structural problem would be considerable, not to name the interim cost to the Institute of putting the building out of use for some time, and the potential damage to its holdings'. The building at 29 Russell Square is now occupied by the Wiener Library.

For many who have known and loved the IGS over decades, its amalgamation with the IRS to form the IGRS and its move in October 2005 from 29 Russell Square into Stewart House, a wing of Senate House, could and can only be registered as an immense loss. The house in Russell Square, although inconvenient in some ways (and prone to admit rainwater by the bucket as the caretaker and the librarian knew to their cost), had a particularly gracious Georgian ambience and beauty that were truly remarkable and served to foster both intellectual exchange and the sense of belonging to a united community with a common purpose: the exploration, support and dissemination of a rich, exciting language and culture. Senate House cannot match that. However, it should be noted that the Germanic section of the IGRS was nothing if not resilient. It adapted well to the more modern seminar and teaching rooms (some of them really quite handsome) that are available; and it sustained and strengthened its lively and diverse programme of lectures, seminars and colloquia. The English Goethe Society continues to hold its meetings there; and, more recently, the annual Heads of German meeting (or HOGmeet, which brings together Heads of German from all over the UK and Irish Republic) has used the Institute as its venue. Moreover, although the Institute library has significantly less space than previously, it is housed in the splendid Middlesex North Reading Room in Senate House Library. Subsequent to the merger, the Germanic section of the IGRS lost none of its wish or flair for 'outreach', a most notable recent example being a programme entitled 'Shakespeare – a German Writer?', masterminded by Professor Martin Swales and Dr Godela Weiss-Sussex (IGRS). This consisted of readings from Shakespeare in both German (by Sebastian Koch, well known for his superb performance in the film *Das Leben der Anderen*) and English (by Philip Cumbus, a most gifted young actor from the Globe Theatre Company). The readings were linked by a historical and interpretative commentary provided by Martin Swales. In all, three performances were given: one at the Globe Theatre in London in October 2010; then two at the International Shakespeare Festival held at the Globe Theatre in Neuss, near Düsseldorf, in July 2011.[13] In June 2014 this engagement with Shakespeare and his (European) legacy was taken up by the conference 'Adapting, Performing and Reviewing Shakespearean Comedy in a European Context', which addressed such questions as what happens to Shakespeare's texts in translation and how an audience's background shapes their understanding of the plays and their performance. Other examples of inspired outreach were the Bithell Memorial Lectures[14] in November 2010, when the journalist and broadcaster Matt Frei spoke on 'Berlin. A Clash of Cultures'; and in October

13 For a full account, see the *Friends Newsletter* 2010.

14 The first Bithell Memorial Lecture was held in 1975. See the section on Benefactors and Bequests..

2015, which took the form of a conversation between the renowned author A. S. Byatt, Professor Martin Swales (UCL) and Dr Godela Weiss-Sussex which explored the connections between English and German culture in A. S. Byatt's recent work, especially *The Children's Book* (2009).[15]

15 Podcast available at http://www.sas.ac.uk/videos-and-podcasts/culture-language-and-literature/english-and-german-cultural-encounters-byatt-con [accessed 4 July 2016]; also published in the Institute's 'Bithell Memorial Lectures' series (December 2016).

Institute Events

The events and exhibitions held at the Institute of Germanic Studies since its inception in 1950, as well as the volumes published in its various series, are testimony to both the strength, vitality and range of German Studies in Great Britain and Ireland and the impact of the Institute's activities at home and abroad. Many of the events and exhibitions celebrated key cultural events or figures, brought together people from different areas and provoked considerable interest, including abroad, as the following selection demonstrates.

Gerhart Hauptmann Exhibition

The Hauptmann Exhibition (15 November–14 December 1962) was intended to mark the centenary of the author's birth (15 November 1862). A preview evening was held on 14 November 1962 and the exhibition opened in the presence of the German Ambassador. The first entries in the Visitors' Book for the exhibition were the German Cultural Attaché Dr Brigitte Lohmeyer; R. Sickingen from the Austrian Institute; and representatives of Südwestfunk. The exhibition included material borrowed from the Schiller-Nationalmuseum Marbach, the Goethe Institute Munich and private individuals in Oxford and London; and was subsidized by the government of the Bundesrepublik Deutschland to the tune of £266.13s.10d. A small catalogue was prepared by Dr H. F. Garten (London: University of London, Institute of Germanic Languages and Literatures, 1962).[1] It contained

1 H. F. Garten (1904–1975; originally: Hugo Friedrich Königsgarten) was born into a Jewish family in Brünn, Moravia, Austria. He was educated at a Gymnasium in Berlin, then at the Universities of Jena (1923), Vienna (1923–24), Berlin (1924–26) and Heidelberg, where he obtained his doctorate in 1930. Between 1928 and 1933 he was a freelance writer in Berlin; in 1933 he moved to Vienna and in 1938 to London. He was a teacher at New College School, Oxford, between 1940 and 1945 and a member of the staff of *Die Zeitung*, London, from 1941 to 1944. He took his DPhil at Oxford in 1944; taught Modern Languages at Westminster School from 1946 to 1965; and was Lecturer at the Universities of Surrey and London from 1965 onwards. During his later years and after his retirement (*c.* 1968) he was often called in to help teach at King's College London. Dr Garten was a member of the International PEN Club, the English Goethe Society and the Gerhart Hauptmann-Gesellschaft; and the author of *Modern German Drama* (London: Methuen, 1959; 2nd edn, 1964) and editor of Friedrich Dürrenmatt, *Romulus der Grosse* (London: Methuen, 1962). His papers are now in the Germanic Archives in the library of the University of London and include copies of letters from the Expressionist playwright Georg Kaiser (1878–1945) and his wife Margareta; typescripts of work by Kaiser; periodicals, programmes and photographs relating to the productions of plays by Kaiser; and letters from Stefan Zweig, Fritz von Unruh, Jakob Wassermann, Karlwien Wassermann, Robert Neumann, Friedrich Gundolf and Alfred Weber.

a biographical note (including the fact that a DLitt h.c. was conferred on Hauptmann by Oxford in 1905); then I) a list of first editions of his works; II) Manuscripts and letters (including letters to Otto Brahm (co-founder of the Freie Bühne), Arthur Schnitzler, his publisher H. Fischer, his Oxford friend Professor H. G. Fiedler and Sir Max and Lady Beerbohm; pages from manuscripts of *Fuhrmann Henschel*; from a draft of the novel *Der Narr in Christo Emanuel Quint*; from the typescript of *Vor Sonnenuntergang* etc.); III) Portraits and photographs (including photos of Hauptmann and his two wives; and a drawing and a caricature of him by Sir Max Beerbohm); IV) Illustrations and stage photos (including a woodcut entitled *Die Weber* by Otto Schubert; an etching entitled *Der Weberzug* by Käthe Kollwitz; a photo of a performance of *Einsame Menschen* at the Arts Theatre, London, October 1961; etchings and lithographs illustrating Hauptmann's works; photos of various performances and actors); V) Hauptmann and England (including translations of his works: *Before Dawn* (1908, first English translation), *Lonely Lives* (London 1898, first English translation), *The Weavers* (London 1899, first English translation), *The Dramatic Works* (an English edition of his collected plays up to 1925); studies in English on his plays; and a Latin oration (with German translation) delivered on 30 May 1905 when the degree of DLitt h.c. was conferred on Hauptmann by Oxford; VI) Miscellaneous (including an appreciation by Eugene O'Neill in honour of Hauptmann's seventieth birthday). A copy of the accounts shows that total expenditure on the exhibition amounted to £242 (including £40 for food and wine from Senate House).

The exhibition attracted some laudatory attention in the German-language press: the *Allgemeine Zeitung* (Mainz, Wiesbaden, Darmstadt); the Hermes Zeitungsausschnittbüro Bonn, which mentions that *The Times* had devoted four columns to Hauptmann, calling him 'den letzten deutschen Autor, dessen Werk ganz Deutschland gehört' and noting that *Vor Sonnenaufgang* pre-empted *Look Back in Anger* by sixty years; the *Rhein-Neckar-Zeitung* (Heidelberg); the *Wetzlarer Neue Zeitung*; the *Frankfurter Allgemeine*; the *Mannheimer Morgen*; *Der neue Tag* (Weiden); the *Braunschweiger Zeitung*; *Neues Österreich* (Vienna); *Neue Zürcher Zeitung*; the *Süddeutsche Zeitung*, in which Professor Frederick Norman is mentioned as 'der unermüdliche Förderer deutscher Dichtung in London' and praised for his 'viel erfolgreiche Liebesmüh' expended on the exhibition; *Der Allgäuer* (Kempten); and the *Deutsche Zeitung*, Köln, in which a review by Gideon Freund concludes: 'Alles in allem eine aufschlußreiche Ausstellung, mit viel Mühe zusammengetragen und angeordnet. Das Londoner Universitätsinstitut der Germanistik hat gute Arbeit geleistet'. *Der Kurier* (Berlin) proclaims:

> Höhepunkt jedoch [of the events in England marking the centenary of Hauptmann's birth] ist eine Gerhart-Hauptmann-Ausstellung der Universität

> London, die vom 'Institute of Germanic Languages and Literatures' organisiert wurde und einen Monat lang in den schönen altertümlichen Räumen dieses Instituts am eleganten Russell Square zu sehen sein wird. Die 141 Ausstellungsstücke sind mit besonderer Sorgfalt und Sachkenntnis zusammengetragen und sind vor allem von großer Verschiedenheit. [...] Die Gerhart-Hauptmann-Ausstellung in London ist eine der interessantesten deutsch-englischen Kulturveranstaltungen des letzten Jahrzehnts.

However, the Hauptmann Exhibition also became embroiled in controversy. On 15 November 1962 *The Daily Telegraph* published a small review by Peterborough of the exhibition under the headline 'National Socialists Only':

> The Ambassador [Dr Etzdorf] carefully toured the exhibits, which do not evade the fact that Hauptmann, born 100 years ago to-day [*sic*], was in the words of an obituary on display 'subservient in his attitude to the Nazi regime'.
>
> Perhaps the saddest comment on the once radical writer's declining years is a playbill poster from Vienna indicating that certain evenings in the theatre would be restricted to National Socialist members.
>
> Near by [*sic*] is a 1942 programme from Newcastle-on-Tyne for his play, 'The Beaver Coat.' 'In the event of an air raid,' says a note before the cast list, 'you will be informed from the stage.'

The review prompted an acrimonious exchange of letters and phone calls between *The Daily Telegraph* and an incensed Frederick Norman, who also fired off a letter of apology to the German Cultural Attaché Dr Brigitte Lohmeyer, a prominent supporter of German Studies, asking her to pass on his apologies to the German Ambassador. In his letter to the *Telegraph*, Frederick Norman points out:

> No writer can be held responsible for the audiences theatres choose to admit, and the quotation from the Times obituary – written with little understanding and less knowledge – displayed at the Exhibition, merely gives the obituarist's opinions. Hauptmann was widely blamed by refugees and others for not leaving Germany in 1933, as Thomas Mann did (who happened to be in Switzerland, anyway, when Hitler took over). Hauptmann was then 71, he was deeply attached to his native Silesian soil, and with short interruptions that is where he stayed. It would be difficult to prove that he was a Nazi, and the friendly letters preserved – and published – of Thomas Mann to Hauptmann would not support such a view.

Further, Professor Norman criticized the manner in which the review referred to the German Ambassador. The *Telegraph*'s Managing Editor, Colin R. Coote, replied, defending the paper and claiming that many visitors to the Exhibition thought it did leave the impression that Hauptmann was a supporter of the Nazi regime. Finally, a letter to Peterborough from the then

Secretary-Librarian to the Institute, [Dr] K[enneth] G[raham] Knight, of 21 November 1962 foreshadows the concerns of the Leveson Inquiry regarding the accuracy of reporting by the national press:[2]

> In drawing Mr Day Lewis' [author of the review but not Peterborough himself] attention to the programme of the People's Theatre, Newcastle upon Tyne, and the theatre-bill of the Vienna Burgtheater I was trying to show that Hauptmann was still being performed in Britain and Germany during the War. I was at pains to point out that the advance notice in small type on the Burgtheater poster, announcing a performance for members of 'Kraft durch Freude', did not refer to a play by Hauptmann. On Monday I looked at the theatre bill again more closely and discovered that the play in question was Twelfth Night. Even Shakespeare was performed for 'National Socialists Only'.

Other exhibitions caused less furore, such as those on Hugo von Hofmannsthal from 7 February to 3 March 1961; on Thomas Mann in 1964; on Martin Luther in 1983; and on the Brothers Grimm in 1986.[3]

Hugo von Hofmannsthal Exhibition

Many of the exhibits for the Hugo von Hofmannsthal exhibition were lent by the poet's son, Raimund von Hofmannsthal, who worked for an American magazine group in London. The opening lecture was attended by ninety-seven people. Cuttings in the IGS archives include one from *Die Presse* (11 March 1961), which calls the exhibition 'ungemein interessant[e]':

> Sie bietet auch für den Österreicher viele neue faszinierende Einblicke in das Schaffen Hofmannsthals [...]. [...] Man fühlt hier [in the manuscripts in Hofmannsthal's own hand] mit großem Heimweh den Hauch einer Welt, die geschlossen, in sich beruhend und doch ganz ins Weite gespannt ist.

A broadcast was recorded at the opening of the exhibition on 6 February 1961 and transmitted on the Austrian programme of the BBC on the evening of 8 February. As well as a BBC interviewer, the participants included Dr Ritschl (Direktor des österreichischen Kulturinstituts), Professor Norman, Herr Direktor Hadamovsky[4] and Michael Hamburger.

2 The Leveson Inquiry into the practices of the press was initiated by Prime Minister David Cameron in July 2011 in response to allegations of phone-hacking by the *News of the World*. Its report, *Culture, Practices and Ethics of the Press*, was published on 29 November 2012.

3 This was organized by Professor John Flood in the University of London Library to mark the bicentenary of their births (Jacob Grimm 1785; Wilhelm Grimm 1786); it used material from that library and from the Institute's own substantial collections.

4 Possibly (no details are given) Franz Hadamovsky, until 1966 Direktor der Theatersammlung at the Österreichische Nationalbibliothek, Vienna.

Figure 18: Hugo von Hofmannsthal Exhibition.

Thomas Mann Exhibition

Another very successful exhibition was that on Thomas Mann mounted in the foyer of the Royal Festival Hall, although arranged by the IGS. It opened on 31 January 1964 and attracted attention from *The Guardian*, which published a review on 4 February 1964:

'All so Germanic'

> The shade of a great German writer and seer looms up at those who perambulate the foyer of the Royal Festival Hall this week in the intervals of hearing great German music played by a great German orchestra. Blown-up photographs of Thomas Mann, his family, his manuscripts, his American passport, the Buddha on his desk and the denunciation his uncle inserted in the Lübeck papers on first reading 'Buddenbrooks,' tell the story of a life dedicated to art and enlightenment with a thoroughness hard to conceive here. Yet in his pictures as in his work Mann is not just grave; [*sic*] at the corners of his mouth there plays an ambiguous smile.
>
> Mann under the palms at Pacific Palisades, Mann the intellectual burgher meeting Claudel[5] the quintessential French peasant – these are some of the

5 Possibly Paul Claudel (6 August 1868–23 February 1955), a French poet, dramatist, diplomat and the younger brother of the sculptor Camille Claudel.

UNIVERSITY OF LONDON

SPECIAL UNIVERSITY LECTURES IN
GERMANIC LANGUAGES

A LECTURE
(IN ENGLISH)
ON

THE PHILOSOPHY OF FRIEDRICH NIETZSCHE IN THE LIGHT OF OUR EXPERIENCE

WILL BE GIVEN AT

The University of London: The Senate House
(entrance from Russell Square or Malet Street, W.C.1)

BY

THOMAS MANN

at 5.15 p.m. on

TUESDAY, 20th MAY, 1947

The Lecture is addressed to students of the University and to others interested in the subject

ADMISSION FREE, WITHOUT TICKET

JAMES HENDERSON,
Academic Registrar

THE CHISWICK PRESS, N.11

Figure 19: Poster advertising a public lecture on Nietzsche by Thomas Mann in Senate House in 1947.

memorable scenes in the exhibition (organised by the German [now: Goethe] Institute and the Institute of Germanic Studies at London University). Best of all is a shot of Mann, his wife and his brother-in-law at a degree ceremony at Berkeley – three learned, devoted, life-tested old Germans under the California sun.

Martin Luther Exhibition

The Luther exhibition was devised to supplement the exhibition material on Luther sent to the IGS by the GDR to mark the quincentenary of the reformer's birth. The material assembled by Dr John Flood at the IGS illustrated a) Luther's place in the history of Bible translation in Germany; b) the reception of Luther's ideas and works in England; c) King Henry VIII and Luther; d) Bible translation in England. It was drawn from collections at London University Library, Lambeth Palace, the Institute of Historical

Figure 20: Official opening of the exhibition 'Martin Luther 1483–1546' in the Chancellor's Hall, Senate House, on 29 June 1983. From left to right: Douglas J. Foskett, Goldsmiths' Librarian; Professor Randolph Quirk, Vice-Chancellor of the University of London; Minister Heinz Knobbe, GDR Embassy; Herr Georg Menzel, GDR Embassy; Herr Rainer Dobbelstein, FRG Embassy.

Research, the British Library, Cambridge University Library and the Institute itself. From the catalogue we see that the exhibition was mounted in the Chancellor's Hall, Senate House, from 30 June to 12 July 1983. It was officially opened on 29 June 1983 by Minister Heinz Knobbe from the Embassy of the Deutsche Demokratische Republik in London, who was welcomed by the Vice-Chancellor, Professor Randolph Quirk. The North Korean Cultural Counsellor was also present, as was a representative from the Embassy of the Bundesrepublik Deutschland.

Goethe Exhibition

In fact, the Institute, especially under Deputy Director Dr (later: Professor) John Flood, was anxious to be on good terms with all four German-speaking countries. Concerned that the Institute be seen as politically neutral, from about 1981 onwards Dr Flood made a deliberate attempt to cultivate relations with the East Germans by establishing a series of symposia, lectures and events involving them. He had already established good relations in the 1970s by assisting them in organizing book exhibitions in the UK, for example, at King's College London in 1979.[6] This policy bore public fruit when, in 1982, the East German Ambassador, as well as the Ambassadors of the Federal Republic of Germany and of Austria and the Cultural Attaché of Switzerland attended the dinner celebrating the 150th anniversary of Goethe's death and the fiftieth anniversary of the CUTG, but one manifestation of the GDR's willingness to collaborate.[7] The Ambassador's attendance is recorded in a photo and press cutting from the *Redbridge Guardian*, 9 April 1982, which notes that the Ambassadors of East and West Germany and Austria attended a dinner at Queen Mary College Halls of Residence, South Woodford, to mark the 150th anniversary of Goethe's death (22 March 1832). The dinner, arranged by the Conference of University Teachers of German and the English Goethe Society, coincided with the three-day conference organized by the latter. As mentioned, the dinner also marked the fiftieth anniversary of the first meeting of the CUTG. Over one hundred guests and members attended. The photo shows Dr Bernhard Stillfried (Director of the Austrian Cultural Institute), Professor K. G. Knight (Leeds; Chairman of CUTG), Sir James Menter (Principal, QMC) and Dr Reginald Thomas (Austrian Ambassador).

Indeed, Dr Flood and the Institute were the initiative behind all the events to celebrate the Goethe anniversary. Dr Flood set up and chaired an organizing committee (including the Institute, the BBC, the Goethe Institute, the English Goethe Society and the British Library); devised the programme, including the exhibition (which boasted an eye-catching poster showing a slender female arm lovingly draped around the shoulders of a bust of Goethe that was displayed in the Underground); the lectures (later published as a book, *Goethe Revisited*); the programmes on the BBC. It was also Dr Flood who wrote to the Palace to ask Prince Philip to contribute the preface to the exhibition catalogue. A copy of the catalogue, sumptuously bound, was subsequently presented to the Duke for the Royal Library. The richness and variety of events are a tribute to Dr Flood's vision, energy and organizational skills. For example, in conjunction with the anniversary of Goethe's death a

6 In 1981 Dr Flood received an official invitation to the Jahresversammlung (AGM) of the Goethe-Gesellschaft in Weimar; and in 1988 his efforts to establish good relations with the GDR were recognized when it awarded him the Grimm-Preis.

7 The Institute was always under pressure from the University to raise money for its activities and the University was also keen for it to approach the West Germans for financial support, which from time to time was, indeed, forthcoming (e.g., for symposia), sometimes through the Embassy, sometimes through the Goethe Institute. The Austrians regularly supported events and also the Institute library. The Swiss occasionally helped, generally through Pro Helvetia. The GDR, on the other hand, had no distinct cultural presence.

recital of Schumann Lieder based on texts by Goethe and Kerner was given at the Wigmore Hall by Doris Soffel and Aribert Reimann on Sunday, 18 April 1982. Another celebratory recital had already taken place at the Wigmore Hall on 21 March 1982 entitled 'A portrait in song of a father of the Lied'. Indeed, in one way or another Goethe was celebrated throughout the UK, even in the British media. A long article on Goethe was published in the *Observer Review* on 21 March 1982; in the same month *The Reader's Digest* carried an article by Ernest Hauser entitled 'The Giant Who Was Goethe' (pp. 113–18). The *Radio Times* published a long article on Goethe and *Faust* and even produced a poster to advertise Goethe celebrations, whilst the BBC broadcast a number of programmes about Goethe or actual performances of his works:

- 21 March on Radio 3: Goethe's *Faust* Part I from an abridged translation by Louis MacNeice and E. L. Stahl; 28 March on Radio 3: Goethe's *Faust* Part II. Simon Callow starred as Faust, Ronald Pickup as Mephistopheles, Angharad Rees as Gretchen and Maureen O'Brien as Helen. Both the translation and production of *Faust* were critically reviewed in the *Observer* and the *Telegraph*
- 28 March on Radio 3: talk by Frank Lamport entitled 'Papageno in Weimar' on Goethe's fascination with *The Magic Flute* and attempt to write a sequel
- 4 April on Radio 3: *The Passion of Young Werther* (abridged and adapted for radio; three voices)
- 5 April: Book of the Week on Radio 4 was *Elective Affinities* (abridged!)
- 8 April: Broadcast of 'Goethe: the German Miracle', the talk on Luther, Goethe and Bismarck first broadcast on the Third Programme (now Radio 3) by Thomas Mann on 22 May 1949
- 15 April on Radio 3: *Ironhand* (after *Götz von Berlichingen*). David Suchet starred as Ironhand, John Woodvine as Weislingen, Patrick Troughton as Selbitz and Anna Massey as Adelheid
- 18 April on Radio 3: *Torquato Tasso*. Michael Pennington starred as Tasso; David Suchet as Antonio; David Buck as Prince Alfonso, Eileen Atkins as the Princess and Rosalind Shanks as Leonora
- 20 April: *The Young Goethe in Love*, a broadcast of the musical settings to some of his poems
- 24 April: 'The Devil You Don't Know. Goethe, Jung, Faust and Alchemy', a talk by Stephen Abrams

Radio 3 also broadcast three half-hour readings of Goethe's poetry in English and German, translated and presented by Michael Hamburger. Moreover, a programme on 'Goethe and Love' was compiled and presented by Professor Elizabeth Mary Wilkinson, Emeritus Professor of German at UCL. A letter to the *Radio Times* of 1–7 May 1982 from a listener in Bradford-on-Avon complained about Goethe's being broadcast in English, especially in the case of *Werther*, as 'the English language is simply incapable of handling the emotional power of the *Sturm und Drang* movement'. The reply by Ian McIntyre, then Controller of Radio 3, says the BBC had actually considered broadcasting Goethe's plays and poems in German but had decided this would prove too daunting for a general audience.

Another event aimed at a wider audience was the exhibition staged, at the Institute's initiative, by the Goethe Institute. The brochure for the Goethe Anniversary lists the exhibition patrons, its organizers (Professor Brian A. Rowley, University of East Anglia, who also wrote the catalogue; Clifford Simmons and the Goethe Institute, London) and events taking place across the country. The Goethe Society exhibition went to London, Oxford, Leeds, York, Manchester, Glasgow and Norwich. Patrons included not just the Ambassador of the Federal Republic of Germany, Lord Inglewood (President of the Anglo-German Society) and Dr Klaus von Bismarck (President of the Goethe Institute, Munich), but also Lord (Laurence) Olivier, Sir Owen Chadwick FBA (President of the British Academy), Sir Peter Hall (Director of the National Theatre), Professor Elizabeth Mary Wilkinson FBA (President of the English Goethe Society), Professor W. H. Bruford (Past President of the EGS), Sir Randolph Quirk FBA (Vice-Chancellor of the University of London), Professor M. W. Thompson DSc (Vice-Chancellor of the University of East Anglia) and Ian McIntyre MA, Controller of BBC Radio 3 – names which indicate both Goethe's broad appeal and a widespread awareness of his considerable importance for European culture generally. The catalogue included a foreword by HRH the Duke of Edinburgh:

> The names of many of the famous men of history are well known to millions of people but that is no guarantee that the reasons for their fame are equally well known.
>
> The 150th anniversary of Goethe's death provides an opportunity to add substance to his memory by drawing attention to the many sides of his creative genius. Author, playwright, poet, philosopher and statesman, his influence on his contemporaries and on men of letters throughout the world ever since is incalculable.
>
> I hope this special exhibition will encourage many more people in this country to discover for themselves the reasons for Goethe's great and lasting fame.

The IGS lent titles from its holdings for the London exhibition (they were asked for seventeen) but did not wish them to be part of the travelling exhibition because they might be absent from the Institute for nine to ten months, just at the time when IGS readers would be most interested in seeing them. In addition, a number of titles were rare and valuable. For example, a first edition of the *West-östlicher Divan* (1819) had recently (1979) fetched £350 at auction; and the IGS were being asked by the Goethe Institute to lend theirs. The extremely rare *Sechzehn Tafeln zur Farbenlehre* (1810),[8] although a 'slim brochure', was then (25 February 1982) valued at £2,300. The total sum for which exhibits lent by the IGS were to be insured was £6,950. The IGS were also asked for Sir Walter Scott's translation of *Götz von Berlichingen* (1799); various editions and translations of *Werther* (1775, 1825; a French translation from 1776; an English translation from 1779; and others); *Wilhelm Meisters Lehrjahre* in the translation by Thomas Carlyle (Edinburgh: Oliver & Boyd; London: G. & W. B. Whittaker, 1824) and other works.

The anniversary of Goethe's death also saw the screening of film versions of his work: *Die Wahlverwandtschaften*, *Die Leiden des Jungen Werthers*, *Iphigenie auf Tauris*, *Clavigo*, *Faust*, *Die Neuen Leiden des Jungen W.*, *Lotte in Weimar*, *Jules et Jim*. On the academic side, lectures were given in Glasgow, Lancaster, Manchester, London and Cambridge, some to be published in a volume edited by Professor Wilkinson;[9] and the English Goethe Society sponsored a competition for the best translation of three Goethe poems: 'Prometheus', 'Natur und Kunst' and 'An vollen Büschelzweigen'. For its part, the IGS mounted an exhibition entitled 'Faust on the German Stage', prepared by Bill Abbey and Alicia Moule, which ran from 22 March throughout the summer. Moreover, university students of German also made valiant contributions to the Goethe celebrations: students at Southampton University staged *Urfaust*; and in February 1982 a theatre group at King's College London performed *Egmont* in German in the New Theatre KCL.[10] The Deputy Director of the IGS, John Flood, wrote an article entitled 'King's College London's brave attempt, as part of the first Student German Drama Festival, at *Egmont*'.[11] He notes that its 'producer is Rory Bremner, a second-year German student'. Did the universal genius that was Goethe help the universal satirist that is Rory Bremner to launch his stage and screen career?

8 Its catalogue card has following entry: *Erklärung der zu Goethe's Farbenlehre gehörigen Tafeln* [no title page], pp. 24 + 16 Tafeln + Anzeige; ([Tübingen: Cotta]? n.d.).

9 The volume, entitled *Goethe Revisited*, appeared in 1983 in the USA and 1984 in Great Britain, published jointly by the IGS (Publications of the Institute of Germanic Studies, 30) and John Calder, who had attended some meetings of the organizing committee.

10 Its first night was 17 February.

11 *Treffpunkt* (March 1982), pp. 24–26 (p. 25). *Treffpunkt* was the Journal of the Association of Teachers of German, the German Section of the Modern Language Association.

Other Events

Other events organized by the IGS over the years include the following papers and symposia. While the selection is random and many others could have just as easily been mentioned, these once again demonstrate the richness of the Institute's cultural offering and its international profile:[12]

- **Exhibitions**: Karl Wolfskehl (27 November–11 December 1969)
- **Colloquia**: the Anglo-German Medieval Colloquium at Cumberland Lodge, Windsor Great Park (22–26 March 1976), organized by Maurice O'C. Walshe, John Flood and David Wells, included a reception at the IGS on 24 March preceded by a specially arranged visit to the British Museum to inspect items of medieval and Early Modern German interest in the collections of the British Library (housed in the Museum until 1997)
- **Lectures by distinguished speakers**: a) Manès Sperber (Paris) (13 May 1976); b) 'Ursachen und Folgen der deutschen Ostpolitik in der Zeit des Kalten Krieges' (14 November 1996), the Bithell Memorial Lecture given in German, in the Beveridge Hall in Senate House, by former Bundespräsident Dr Richard von Weizsäcker at the invitation of the IGS; the lecture discussed Willy Brandt and Germany's *Ostpolitik* during the Cold War; c) Professor Bernhard Fabian (Münster) spoke on his work for the *Handbuch der historischen Buchbestände in Deutschland* and other volumes in the project (30 April 1998); d) Professor Adolf Muschg (Zurich) lectured on 'Das Verhältnis Autor-Literaturwissenschaftler' (28 April 1983); e) Professor Martin Durrell (Manchester) spoke on 'Germany and German: Language, State and People' (Keith Spalding Lecture, 7 May 1998);[13] and Alison Marten (Kassel) lectured on 'Narratives of Mobility: German Travel Writing on England, 1780–1830' (Keith Spalding Lecture, 5 October 2006)
- **Readings**: Christa Wolf (18 May 1978); Max Frisch's reading of a selection from his works (21 February 1983); the first ever public reading from his autobiography *Mein Leben* by Marcel Reich-Ranicki (the 1999 Bithell Memorial Lecture); a reading of his own poetry by Alfred Brendel as part of the celebrations for the fiftieth anniversary of the Institute in 2000
- **Symposia and Research Fora**: *Robert Musil* (November 1980);

12 The IGS Annual Reports all contain a full list of events in the previous academic year.

13 Keith Spalding was Professor of German and Teutonic Philology at Bangor; he endowed an annual lecture on an Anglo-German topic. For more information on the Keith Spalding Bequest see the section on Benefactors and Bequests.

Gegenwartsprobleme der DDR-Literatur (April 1981);[14] *Minnesang in Österreich* (April 1982); *Adelbert Stifter* (May 1983); *Franz Kafka* (October 1983); *Modern Swiss Literature: Unity and Diversity* (March 1984);[15] Karl Kraus (March 1984); *Chrétien de Troyes and Medieval German Literature* (April 1988); *Das Theater der DDR* (December 1988); *Translation in Transition. The Case of Sigmund Freud and James and Alex Strachey* (April 1989); *Anglo-German Literary Relations* (September 1989); *Mozart* (1991); *'Hitler's Gift to Britain'. Second International Symposium on German and Austrian Exiles in Great Britain* (September 1996); *Changing Conceptions of German Studies* (March 1996); *Heine und die Weltliteratur* (April 1997); *Murder in Bloomsbury: The Detective Story* (June 1996; in conjunction with the Institute of Romance Studies); *Rainer Maria Rilke* (December 1996); *Theodor Herzl* (April 1996); *German Language Education: Building and Interface* (May 1998); *European Theatre. Justice and Morality* (June 1998), co-organized with the Centre for English Studies, Institute of Romance Studies, Royal Holloway and held in collaboration with the Austrian Cultural Institute and the French Embassy[16] with financial support from the Embassy of the Bundesrepublik Deutschland and the Goethe Institute; *Wolfram's 'Willehalm'* (April 1998); *The New Media, Television and Film in German Studies* (February 1999); *Friedrich Schiller. Poetry, Drama, Ideas* (January 2005; to mark the bi-centenary of Schiller's death); *Thomas Mann. A Classic Writer in a Postmodern Climate?* (March 2005); *The Regional Literature of the Austrian Federal States* (February 2004), organized by the

14 This was the first of Dr Flood's collaborative ventures with the GDR and was attended by the East German author Hermann Kant (1926–2016), possibly best known for his novel *Die Aula* (1965). Kant was president of the Schriftstellerverband and without his blessing no further visits of GDR writers and scholars to the Institute would have been possible.

15 As with many symposia at the IGS, the proceedings were subsequently co-published by the IGS, in this case in collaboration with Oswald Wolff, London, under the same title, *Modern Swiss Literature: Unity and Diversity* (1985).

16 The conference volume that subsequently appeared is not normally listed under Institute publications: *Morality and Justice: The Challenge of European Theatre*, ed. by Edward Batley and David Bradby, *European Studies: A Journal of European Culture, History and Politics*, 17 (Amsterdam, New York: Rodopi, 2001). The wide-ranging conference covered such topics as Popular Theatre, Carnival and Comedy; Theatre of Ideas – Morality, Sexuality and Politics; Audience Response and Reception Aesthetics; Theatre, Censorship and Law; Issues of Race, Culture, Religion and Nation. Another volume not listed as an Institute publication is *The Romantic Period in Germany*, ed. by Siegbert Prawer (London: Weidenfeld & Nicholson, 1970), a collection of essays originally given as papers at the Institute in the 1960s.

Figure 21: A seventy-fifth-birthday portrait of Claus Victor Bock taken in Amsterdam.

Ingeborg Bachmann Centre at the Institute;[17] *The Unconscious in Nineteenth-Century German Thought* (September 2006); *Hubert Fichte. Texte und Kontexte* (December 2006); and a symposium in memory of Claus Victor Bock, Honorary Director of the IGS for eight years (1973–81) and responsible for establishing a number of its core events and series. It was Professor Bock who supervised the Bithell Bequest and came up with ideas for its use, such as the Bithell Memorial Lectures, Bithell Prizes and the Bithell Series of Dissertations. He was also responsible for the addition of the twentieth-century Room, named the Bithell Room, in the basement of 29 Russell Square, negotiating this with Senate House. He had also wanted to use some of the Bithell Bequest to build an annex to the rear of the Institute, but his idea was rejected by the University of London

- **Workshops**: *Auf Deutsch. Lyrik in London / Poetry in German by Writers in and Around London* (20 October 1995; 7 June 1996; 13 June 1997; 29 May 1998); workshop in commemoration of Frank Fowler: *On Page and Stage: German Drama of the Late Eighteenth and Early Nineteenth Centuries* (organized with the English Goethe Society, 13 October 2006)

Events hosted by the Institute might also include the unexpected: in a letter of 20 February 1951 from Arthur Hatto to Leonard Willoughby, Professor Hatto – after suggesting medieval purchases for the Library – mentions a paper he will be giving at the Institute on 28 February:

> Will it be all right if I talk for just under an hour on 28th? I have a little surprise at the end that will take about 15 mins. J.A.S. Watson, an undergraduate of ours at Q.M.C reading for German Hons. will sing some mediaeval Tagelieder, and perhaps our Miss Wnek, a Pole, will sing a Wendish one, with

17 For more information, see 'Research Centres'.

Figure 22: Formal portrait of Siegbert Prawer taken on his election as a Fellow of the British Academy in 1981.

> your permission. May they sup for their singing – that is, may I bring them along to tea, though they are undergraduates? I'm sure you will think they deserve it when you've heard them. (Mr Watson is the best tenor in college at the moment.)[18]

Unfortunately, it was also the case that expected events failed to take place. The IGS archives contain correspondence between Siegbert Prawer (28 October 1968) and William Robson-Scott (Honorary Director of IGS) concerning the latter's invitation to the GDR author Günter Kunert to give a talk at the IGS (at the instigation of Michael Hamburger).[19] William Robson-Scott had written to Günter Kunert inviting him also to join Siegbert Prawer's *Doktorandenseminar* on modern poetry on 9 December 1968. Although

18 This extract is cited with the kind permission of Queen Mary College London.

19 Günter Kunert (b. 6 March 1929) is an originally East German writer who was permitted to leave the GDR for West Germany in March 1979, having protested against the dissident singer-songwriter Wolf Biermann being deprived of his GDR citizenship whilst on an officially sanctioned tour of West Germany in 1976.

Figure 23: Professor John Flood in his office.

the author was keen to come, his reply (15 November 1968) mentions the difficulty of acquiring an entry visa to the UK from the British Embassy in Berlin in such a short space of time; however, he could only be given a Pass by the Alliierter Kontrollrat if he had a visa, as British authorities did not recognize the GDR passport. Thus he asks William Robson-Scott to keep the invitation open so that he (Kunert) might come a little later. Eventually, it was arranged that Günter Kunert would give a lecture at the IGS on 16 October 1969. However, the author had to cancel at the last minute, sending a telegram to that effect on 6 October. In a subsequent letter (9 October 1969) to William Robson-Scott he says that at the last minute the GDR had withdrawn permission for his wife to accompany him, adding, '[I]ch bin zu eng mit meiner Frau verbunden, als daß ich nun allein hätte reisen können. [...] vielleicht kommt doch einmal eine Zeit, da menschlichere Entscheidungen getroffen werden'.[20] Another prospective guest, Elias Canetti, winner of the Nobel Prize for Literature in 1981, was forced to decline an invitation from John Flood to deliver the 1983 Bithell Memorial Lecture on the grounds of ill health.

20 This extract is cited with the kind permission of Günter Kunert.

Institute Publications

The Institute further promoted work in Germanic Languages and Literatures in the UK through its various publication series, including the 'Publications of the Institute of Germanic Studies' (launched in 1956), the sub-series 'London German Studies', the 'Bithell Series of Dissertations', *Theses in Progress* and *Research in Germanic Studies.* These publications demonstrate the range and depth of German scholarship in the UK and the central role played by the Institute in fostering and promoting it, as many arose out of events at the Institute. The first, deceptively modest publication was the *Union List of Periodicals dealing with Germanic Languages and Literatures in the University Library and in Libraries of the Colleges and Institutes of the University* (1956); the next *Schiller. Bicentenary Lectures*, edited by Frederick Norman (1960). This was positively reviewed in *Germanistik*, which calls the volume 'eine schöne Bereicherung' and continues: 'Im ganzen zeugen die englischen Aussagen [...] von einem frisch offenen und sachlich zielbewußten Blick für die trotz allem noch erkennbare Modernität von Schillers Wesen und Größe' (*Germanistik*, 2 (1961)). *British Book News* wrote that the published essays 'round off a symposium which is an impressive tribute both to Schiller and to the research in German studies carried on at the British universities'. For the *Germanic Review* 'the book is stimulating, sometimes fascinating reading for the present and a historical document for the future'. The *Deutsche Literaturzeitung* went even further:

> Die von dem 1950 gegründeten und seither sehr rührigen Institute of Germanic Languages and Literatures der Londoner Universität veröffentlichten Beiträge sind keineswegs eine bloße Nachlese zum Schillerjahr, sondern zählen zu den gewichtigsten Früchten, die das durch die Gedenkfeiern angeregte wissenschaftliche Bemühen gezeigt hat (*Deutsche Literaturzeitung*, 82 (1961)).

Other titles in the Publications of the Institute of Germanic Studies series include: *Schiller in England, 1787–1960. A Bibliography.* Compiled under the direction of R. Pick (1961); *Probleme mittelalterlicher Überlieferung und Textkritik*, ed. by Peter F. Ganz and Werner Schröder (1968); *Essays in German and Dutch Literature*, ed. by W. D. Robson-Scott (1973); *Three Essays on the 'Hildebrandslied'*, by Frederick Norman, ed. by Arthur T. Hatto (1973) (in memory of Frederick Norman); *Germanistik in Festschriften von den Anfängen (1877) bis 1973* (1976);[1] *Karl und Hanna Wolfskehl: Briefwechsel*

1 *Germanistik in Festschriften* was the eventual outcome of the project initiated by the Institute many years earlier with which Maurice O'C. Walshe had been heavily involved. When the enormity of the undertaking became apparent, Maurice Walshe negotiated with

mit Friedrich Gundolf, 1899–1931 (1977), one of eight volumes discussed in the radio programme *Lesezeichen* on Wednesday, 25 June 1977, 17.15–18.00 on Südfunk 2; *Modern Swiss Literature. Unity and Diversity,* ed. by John L. Flood (1985); *Berlin. Literary Images of a City / Eine Großstadt im Spiegel der Literatur*, ed. by Derek Glass, Dietmar Rösler and John J. White (1989); *Two into One. Germany 1989–1992. A Bibliography of the 'Wende'*, compiled by Bill Abbey (1993); *Spannungen und Konflikte menschlichen Zusammenlebens in der deutschen Literatur des Mittelalters. Bristoler Colloquium 1993*, ed. by Kurt Gärtner, Ingrid Kasten and Frank Shaw (1996); *Rilke und die Moderne. Londoner Symposion*, ed. by Adrian Stevens and Fred Wagner (2000); and *'Verwisch die Spuren!' Bertolt Brecht's Work and Legacy. A Reassessment*, ed. by Robert Gillett and Godela Weiss-Sussex (2008).[2] The year 2015 saw the publication of the one-hundredth volume in the Germanic Publications series, namely *Protest and Reform in German Literature and Visual Culture, 1871–1918*, ed. by Godela Weiss Sussex and Charlotte Woodford.

Although a considerable number of the publications were published entirely at the Institute's own expense (its links with the firm of W. S. Maney in Leeds go back to the early 1950s), many were also published in conjunction with (frequently) Continental publishers in order to reduce costs and increase the size of the market, as the UK market for specialist German publications was small. Several volumes were, for example, co-published with German academic publishers such as the Erich Schmidt Verlag in Berlin, Max Niemeyer in Tübingen, Hans-Dieter Heinz in Stuttgart and, more recently and regularly, iudicium in Munich.

the Herzog August Bibliothek Wolfenbüttel to complete the project jointly. The resulting volume was published by Metzler in Stuttgart.

2 For a full list of titles, see http://www.modernlanguages.sas.ac.uk/publications/germanic-studies-publications.

Research Centres

The 1990s saw additional developments in the Institute's activities: on 8 November 1995 'the Board [of the Institute] approved a proposal to set up and locate the national Research Centre for German and Austrian Exile Studies at the IGS'. The Centre brought together the London Research Group for German and Austrian Exiles and the Research Centre for Germans and Austrians in Britain at the University of Aberdeen:

> The work of the Centre focuses on the history of German-speaking emigrés who found refuge in Britain, their personal recollections and experiences, their reception in British society, and their enrichment of the life of their new country of residence in such varied spheres as the professions, industry and commerce, literature, art and culture, politics, publishing, the media, and the world of leisure and entertainment. The concept of German-speaking exile extends to those who came from the former Czechoslovakia, Hungary, Poland and other European countries, as well as Germany and Austria.[1]

According to the then Honorary Director of the IGS, Mr Edward Batley, 'the founding of the Centre at the Institute was warmly supported by the Directorate of the School [of Advanced Study], and also by the University of London School of Slavonic and East European Studies and the German Historical Institute'. It was Mr Batley who suggested to Professor Hamish Ritchie, Professor of German at the University of Aberdeen, that the latter's archive of exile literature be moved from the University of Aberdeen to London and specifically to the Institute. Professor Ritchie was fully in favour of this idea right from the start, realizing that his collection would complement the exile collection already in the Institute's holdings. In the stalwart spirit of Leonard Willoughby and Robert Pick, who in 1950 had themselves transported, cleaned and installed furniture in the original Institute, Mr Batley even brought crates of Professor Ritchie's books from Sheffield (his home) to the Institute by car. Mr Batley and Professor Ritchie were aware of the Centre for German-Jewish Studies being set up at the University of Sussex under Professor Edward Timms, but believed that their joint concept of Exile Studies was broader and covered a longer historical

1 Taken from the Centre website at http://modernlanguages.sas.ac.uk/research-centre-german-and-austrian-exile-studies. This echoes the initial mission statement: 'It is also the task of the Centre to evaluate the positive human and cultural achievements of German-speaking exiles and to mark the special contribution which they made, not only to the cause of humanity generally but also specifically to Gt. Britain, to literature, the visual and the performing arts, the theatre, education, art history, architecture, cinema, philosophy, psychology, religion, sociology, law, publishing, banking, medicine and journalism'.

period (there had been German-speaking exiles to this country well before Hitler). Moreover, in London there was already a group of dedicated and productive exile researchers scattered throughout other London institutions to whom the Institute could offer a kind of home. These included Richard Dove, Charmian Brinson, Anthony Grenville, Marion Malet, Jennifer Taylor and Hamish Ritchie himself, who was the first President of the Centre and an Honorary Research Fellow, the post of Honorary Secretary being held by Dr Anthony Grenville (University of Westminster). Thanks to the Institute's Development Officer Brigid Knapper, the new Centre won a research grant of a few thousand pounds to pump-prime its activities. Dr Emil Brix was in London in the mid-1990s as Director of the Austrian Cultural Institute (then again as Austrian Ambassador from April 2010 to January 2015); with his wife he attended the occasional Foundation Day at the Institute's invitation and they were presented to Princess Anne, Chancellor of the University of London.[2] Dr Brix gave considerable support to the Research Centre for their work on Austrian Exile Studies in the form of both financial aid and contacts in Vienna and elsewhere. Moreover, in 1997–98 the Exile Centre made a successful application to the British Academy for funding for a joint project with the University of Greenwich, the *Austria Centre 1939–1947*. Other researchers joined the original core; audiences expanded and the Centre initiated and edited a successful new journal dedicated to the subject of Exile Studies.[3] The Research Centre proved attractive to postgraduate students, becoming an important source for research theses and supervisors. Furthermore, seminars took place on the poetry of German and/or Austrian exiles living in London. Even at this early stage it was envisaged that other designated Research Centres would follow.

An article in the *Frankfurter Allgemeine Zeitung* entitled 'Deutsche im englischen Exil' (29 January 1992) highlights the work of the original London Centre and the considerable contribution made to British culture by German and Austrian refugees:

> In London ist ein Forschungszentrum für Exilstudien gegründet worden. Es ist dem Germanic Institute in London angegliedert. In der unmittelbaren Nachbarschaft dieses Instituts im Universitätsviertel Bloomsbury befand sich während des Krieges das 'Bloomsbury House', wo Hilfsorganisationen die Emigranten nach ihrer Ankunft mit dem Nötigsten versorgten. Die Generation der Emigranten hat in den kulturellen Beziehungen zwischen England und Deutschland wichtige Spuren hinterlassen. Aus ihr sind zum Beispiel so bedeutende englische Germanisten wie Peter Stern, Siegbert S.

2 Foundation Day is the annual celebration of the grant by King William IV of the University's first charter on 28 November 1836.

3 For a list of Exile Centre publications, see http://modernlanguages.sas.ac.uk/research-centre-german-and-austrian-exile-studies/exile-centre-publications.

> Prawer und Charlotte Jolles hervorgegangen. Das neue Forschungszentrum will die vielfältigen Zeugnisse des Exils sammeln, bevor es dafür zu spät ist. Nach den Methoden der 'oral history' wird die Lebensgeschichte der noch lebenden Emigranten auf Tonband aufgenommen und ausgewertet.
>
> Auch frühe Zeugnisse sollen erschlossen werden, wie etwa die heute über viele Bibliotheken verstreuten deutschsprachigen Exilzeitungen in London: 'Die Zeitung', 'Der Zeitspiegel' und 'Die Einheit'. Eine reichhaltige Quelle sind auch 'Pem's Personal Bulletins', private Rundbriefe des Journalisten Paul E. Marcus, der sich im Berlin der zwanziger Jahre einen Namen mit Feuilletons über Theater, Film und Kabarett gemacht hatte. Ferner soll das Exil bildender Künstler wie Oskar Kokoschka, Ludwig Meidner und Kurt Schwitters erforscht werden. Das beeindruckendste Denkmal des Exils jedoch steht ebenfalls im Herzen Bloomsburys: Es ist das aus Hamburg übergesiedelte Warburg Institute, dessen einzigartige Bibliothek Anhänger in aller Welt gefunden hat. In der Schriftenreihe des Germanic Institute (Band 64) sind einige Erträge der Exilforschung nachzulesen (*England aber, wo liegt es? Deutsche und österreichische Emigranten in Großbritannien 1933–1945*, hrsg. von Charmian Brinson, Richard Dove, Marian Malet und Jennifer Taylor, Iudicium Verlag, München 1996).[4]

The new Centre also embroiled the Institute in (slight) controversy, one which showed how sensitive the topic of exile remains. On 16 May 1996 Professor Ritchie gave a talk to the Friends entitled 'Exile is No Laughing Matter – or Is It?' which discussed humour as a way of hitting back, as an instrument for the powerless. He remarks:

> When the second London exile conference was arranged for September of this year, it went out under the title, in inverted commas: 'Hitler's Gift to Britain'. The inverted commas indicated that this was a reference back to the reaction in the press at the time in the thirties, and to a more recent article in a national newspaper. But inverted commas are not strong enough and this title gave offence in some quarters (*Newsletter*, p. 6).[5]

Fortunately, no offence was given by a talk on a similar subject some years later: on 21 February 2013 Daniel Snowman, author of *The Hitler Emigrés: The Cultural Impact on Britain of Refugees from Nazism* (2002), gave the

4 The importance of the Centre is also pointed out by Jennifer Hogarth, Archivist at the IGS, in a contribution to the *British Records Association Newsletter* entitled 'The Germanic World in London' (Series 2, No. 2, Winter 1998). After a brief account of the Institute's history, events and holdings (including photos from World War I and Berlin before and after the Wall), Ms Hogarth particularly highlights the Exile archives as a depository for 'letters, diaries, photo albums' of 'those who lived through the persecution and exile inflicted by the Nazis'.

5 In his lecture Professor Ritchie also mentions Martin Miller and his parody of Hitler's speeches (broadcast on the BBC German Service on 1 April 1940), as well as Miller's work with the *Laterndl*. The Millers and other exile writers collaborated with the BBC.

second Martin Miller and Hannah Norbert-Miller Lecture on the topic '*The Hitler Emigrés* Revisited'.

The Martin Miller and Hannah Norbert-Miller Trust

In 2009 the Martin Miller and Hannah Norbert-Miller Trust was established to support and promote the work of the Centre, being made possible by a generous donation from the Millers' son, the music producer Daniel Miller. Martin Miller (2 September 1899–26 August 1969) was an actor and director who spent the early years of his career in theatre and cabaret in Austria and Czechoslovakia. A member of the Jewish League of Culture in Berlin in 1938–39, he emigrated to Britain in March 1939 to escape the persecution of the Jews. In London he co-founded the emigré cabaret and theatre at the Austrian Centre, the *Laterndl*; and from 1940 onwards played a number of roles in British films and on the British stage, building a successful career in this country. His wife, Hannah Norbert-Miller, trained at the Reinhardt Seminar and had a promising career in Austria, but also fled to Britain just before the outbreak of war and joined the *Laterndl*. She married Martin Miller in 1946 and after the war embarked on a distinguished broadcasting career in the BBC World Service, also performing in a number of television and radio plays.[6] As well as enabling the Centre to offer bursaries for doctoral study and visiting fellowships at the Institute, sponsoring its triennial conferences and funding the biennial Miller Memorial Lecture referred to above, the Trust has funded the cataloguing and promotion of the Martin Miller and Hannah Norbert-Miller Archive. This contains audio tapes (now digitized) which include Martin Miller's well-known anti-Nazi radio sketches broadcast by the BBC German Service in 1940; songs; review scripts; publicity material; images; correspondence with such luminaries of the British stage and screen as Richard Attenborough and Michael Redgrave or German and Austrian exile intellectuals such as Erich Fried, Hugo Frederick Garten[7] and Franz Theodor Csokor; and much more. From June to August 2013 *Theatrical Lives from Vienna to London*, an exhibition showcasing treasures from the Miller Bequest, was held in Senate House and accompanied by a launch event; this was followed in May 2014 by a similar exhibition and event, *Exile Lives Told*

6 For full biographies see http://www.modernlanguages.sas.ac.uk/library/germanic-archives/archive-collections/martin-miller-and-hannah-norbert-miller-archive. A blog about the Martin Miller and Hannah Norbert Miller Archive and its treasures can be found at http://norbertmiller.wordpress.com.

7 Mentioned on p. 119 as the author of the catalogue of the Gerhart Hauptmann Exhibition at the IGS.

Figure 24: Hannah Norbert-Miller and Martin Miller in Goethe's Iphigenia.

Through the Archives, held in Senate House Library.[8] This featured material from across the Institute's Exile collections that illustrated the themes of refugee employment, organizations, cultural life, politics and internment in the late 1930s and early 1940s.

Exile Collections

Thanks to Daniel Miller's continued support of the Exile Centre, the Miller Trust has enabled the Germanic Studies Library to purchase material in the field of Exile Studies and to fund the cataloguing of other exile-related material held by the IMLR. Indeed, *Exile Lives Told Through the Archives* drew on common themes and material identified whilst these other Exile collections were being catalogued. They include correspondence; literary manuscripts; autobiographical writings by individual German-speaking exiles, official documents, publicity material for exile-related organizations such as the Polish Relief Fund and the Heinrich-Heine-Club (London);

8 For full accounts of both events and the contents and significance of the various archives, see the *Friends Newsletter* for 2013 and 2014.

manuscripts by Fritz von Unruh; and records of activities organized by the inmates in the internment camps on the Isle of Man.[9] Amongst the exile-related highlights in the Germanic Studies Library are a number of more extensive archives containing personal papers. These include the correspondence of Yvonne Kapp from her time as Personal Assistant to the Director of the Czech Refugee Fund between 1939 and 1940, minutes and papers of the Fund and Yvonne Kapp's correspondence with Helene Brecht-Weigel;[10] and the stage, studio and private photographs of figures associated with the Brecht Circle, for example Elisabeth Hauptmann and Helene Weigel, to be found in the archive of Margaret Mynatt.[11] The archive of the Austrian exile artist Margarete Berger-Hamerschlag, who first came to the UK in 1935, contains her theatre, costume and fashion designs as well as her correspondence, diaries and literary writings;[12] and that of the Austrian exile

9 For a full account see the *Friends Newsletter 2014*, pp. 24–26.

10 Yvonne Kapp (1903–1999) was educated at King's College London. She joined the Communist Party of Great Britain in 1936; worked with Basque and Jewish refugees from 1937 to 1938; and was appointed Assistant to the Director of the British Committee to Refugees from Czechoslovakia, which in 1939 became the Czech Refugee Trust Fund. In 1940 the Home Office dismissed her from this post following allegations that she was a member of the Communist Party. With Margaret Mynatt, her former colleague at the Trust Fund, she co-authored the pamphlet *British Policy and the Refugees* (1941). From 1941 to 1946 Yvonne Kapp worked as Research Officer for the Amalgamated Engineering Union and between 1947 and 1953 for the Medical Research Council. An editor and translator for the publishers Lawrence and Wishart (an independent, radically left-wing publishing house founded in 1936), she also wrote a biography of Eleanor Marx (1855–1898), active Socialist and youngest daughter of Karl Marx. For a fuller account of the archive, see the *Friends Newsletter 2015*, p. 6.

11 Margaret Mynatt (1907–1977) was born in Vienna; moved to Berlin in 1929; joined the Communist Party and became involved with Bertolt Brecht and his circle, working, amongst other plays, on *Die Heilige Johanna der Schlachthöfe* (written between 1929 and 1931). In 1933 she moved to London, where she became Head of Tribunals for the Czech Refugee Trust Fund (1938–41). Like Yvonne Kapp, she was dismissed by the Foreign Office in 1941. Mynatt went on to become Head of Reuters Soviet Monitor (1951), Manager of the independent distributor Central Books (1951–66) and a director at the publishers Lawrence and Wishart (1966–77). At the time of her death, she was editor-in-chief of the *Collected Works of Marx and Engels*, the largest collection to-date (fifty volumes) of translations into English of works by Karl Marx and Friedrich Engels. It was compiled and issued between 1975 and 2005 by Progress Publishers (Moscow), Lawrence and Wishart (London) and International Publishers (New York).

12 Margarete Berger-Hamerschlag (1902–1958) studied at the Kunstgewerbeschule in Vienna in 1921; and married the modernist architect Josef Berger in 1922. In 1936 they moved to Palestine, where Josef Berger had architectural commissions, then, unable to return to Vienna due to the political situation, they emigrated to the UK in the same year. In London, Margarete Berger-Hamerschlag worked as a portrait and landscape painter, illustrator, fashion- and costume-designer. From about 1950 she taught in youth clubs as post-war austerity made it hard for her to sell her work. Her experience in youth clubs resulted in a successful book, *Journey into a Fog* (1955). For a fuller fuller account of the archive, see the *Friends Newsletter 2015*, p. 6.

writer Robert Lucas the scripts of his anti-Nazi satirical features, which were broadcast on the BBC's German Service during World War II.[13] The Herbert Löwit Archive includes the correspondence between exiled Sudeten German trade unions tracing the history of the split within the Czech-German Social Democrat Party in exile in wartime London.[14]

Ingeborg Bachmann Centre for Austrian Literature

The IGS did not rest on its laurels but was active in launching new initiatives. The year 2002 saw the foundation of the Ingeborg Bachmann Centre for Austrian Literature, thanks in part to the support of the Erste Bank, the Österreichische Nationalbank, the Austrian Cultural Forum and Österreich Kooperation. The Austrian Cultural Forum and the Bithell Bequest Fund (Institute of Germanic Studies) continue to sponsor its activities. The brainchild of Professor Rüdiger Görner and the then Director of the Austrian Cultural Forum, the Centre, the first Director of which was Dr Martin Liebscher, takes as its figurehead Ingeborg Bachmann, whose poem 'Abschied von England' expresses the challenge presented by other cultures and the difficulties of comprehending them:

'Abschied von England'

Ich habe deinen Boden kaum betreten,
schweigsames Land, kaum einen Stein berührt,
ich war von deinem Himmel so hoch gehoben,
so in Wolken, Dunst und in noch Ferneres gestellt,
daß ich dich schon verließ,
als ich vor Anker ging.

13 Robert Lucas (born Robert Ehrenzweig; 8 May 1904–9 January 1984) had studied Chemistry and Physics at the Technical University in Vienna and the University of Vienna; and then gone on to work for the Social Democrat publisher Vorwärts-Verlag and to write political cabaret. He emigrated to the UK in 1934 after the Social Democratic Workers' Party of Austria was banned. Until 1938 Robert Lucas was the London correspondent of the Viennese newspaper *Neue Freie Presse*, after which he worked for the BBC German Service. For a fuller account of the archive, see the *Friends Newsletter 2015*, p. 7 and the *Friends Newsletter 2016*, pp. 4–5.

14 Herbert Löwit, born in Teplitz (now Teplice) in North West Bohemia, was a member of the Socialist youth group 'Rote Falken'; his family were active Socialists and members of the Deutsche Sozialdemokratische Arbeiterpartei in der Tschechoslowakischen Republik (DSAP). As Jews, they fled to England when Germany occupied Czechoslovakia in 1938. In 1941 Herbert Löwit joined the Czechoslovak Independent Brigade until he was demobbed in 1945, playing a crucial role in the surrender of Dunkirk, since his command of German, Czech and English enabled him to function as the telephone link between the headquarters of the Germans and the Czechs. After the war he worked, amongst other things, as German teacher in adult education.

Du hast meine Augen geschlossen
mit Meerhauch und Eichenblatt,
von meinen Tränen begossen,

hieltst du die Gräser satt;
aus meinen Träumen gelöst,
wagten sich Sonnen heran,
doch alles war wieder fort,
wenn dein Tag begann.
Alles blieb ungesagt.

Durch die Straßen flatterten die großen grauen Vögel
und wiesen mich aus.
War ich je hier?

Ich wollte nicht gesehen werden.

Meine Augen sind offen.
Meerhauch und Eichenblatt?
Unter den Schlangen des Meers
seh ich, an deiner Statt,
das Land meiner Seele erliegen.
Ich habe seinen Boden nie betreten.

The remit of the Centre is the exploration of Austria's contribution to modern German-language literature by means of its writers-in-residence programme, lectures, seminars, workshops and reading groups. Its main focus has been twentieth-century Austrian literature, above all developments from 1945 onwards.[15] To mark the tenth anniversary of the Ingeborg Bachmann Centre, the year 2012 saw the publication of a bi-lingual collection of essays and poems by all the Centre's writers-in-residence to date; and in 2015 the Centre was renamed the Ingeborg Bachmann Centre for Austrian Literature and Culture to reflect the needs and interests of the public and academics in a changing scholarly landscape.[16]

15 See the IBC website at http://modernlanguages.sas.ac.uk/ingeborg-bachmann-centre-austrian-literature.

16 In 2016 the Institute's Advisory Council approved a proposal to offer a home to the Ernst Bloch Centre for German Thought. Founded by Dr Peter Thompson at the University of Sheffield, the Centre is headed by Dr Johan Siebers (Associate Fellow of the IMLR).

Making Waves: The Institute's Reputation at Home and Abroad

We have already seen that the IGS, its research events and its publications enjoyed considerable resonance in the UK and abroad. Throughout its existence, it was also called upon to provide expert advice in matters generally Germanic. For example, its archives contain some correspondence (April/May 1960) between Frederick Norman and a Dr Viktor Lehmann, a solicitor in Red Lion Square acting for a lady whose husband (d. 1928) was the maternal grandson of Samuel Naylor (1809–1865), who had corresponded with Ottilie von Goethe. Dr Lehmann's client had in her possession some fifty letters from Ottilie von Goethe (Naylor's letters were in Weimar) that she wanted to go to the Goethe-Schiller Archive in Weimar and Dr Lehmann was seeking advice.[1] While Professor Norman was obviously angling for the letters to stay in the UK and be edited and published by an English scholar such as Elizabeth Mary Wilkinson, it is not clear what happened as the correspondence ends (or is not preserved). The archives also contain a letter dated 2 February 1982 from the Deputy Director, John Flood, to a Miss Pamela White of the Manuscript Department at Christie's about a letter from 1591 (from an Austrian officer requesting assistance in arranging transport and the payment of wages) which he had transcribed and translated for her. The Deputy Director's expertise was called upon again a year later: a letter of 6 January 1983 to a Dr Robson Lowe concerns three letters which Professor Flood had transcribed and translated for him, the first of which was from Archduke Charles of Austria. Indeed, the Institute, especially its library staff, were constantly being called upon to answer the public's questions about matters German – and not just the public's! Around 1990 the German Embassy asked the Institute to explain why the German name for their country is *Deutschland*, since a member of the public had enquired about the origin of the word and the Embassy had not known!

Just how renowned and valued the Institute had become is illustrated by a piece on the IGS published on 22 April 1988 by the *Neue Zürcher Zeitung* and entitled 'Ein Haus der deutschen Literatur in London. *Porträt des Institute of*

1 On Naylor see L. A. Willoughby, *Samuel Naylor and 'Reynard the Fox': a Study in Anglo-German Literary Relations* (London; New York: Milford, 1914). The Leonard Ashley Willoughby and Elizabeth Mary Wilkinson Papers include a letter to Leonard Willoughby from Karl Breul (Schröder Professor of German, University of Cambridge) dated 27 December 1914, thanking him for the copy of his 'capital study on "Samuel Naylor and Reynard the Fox", which I have read with much interest. Any good study on Anglo-German literary relations is sure of a special welcome with me, and I say to you vivat sequens!'.

Germanic Studies', which gives a very full and complimentary account of the IGS's activities. Günter Kowa writes:

> Versteckt hinter der vornehm-schlichten Ziegelfassade eines georgianischen Reihenhauses, geht am Russell Square in London ein Institut der Londoner Universität seit Kriegsende still seiner akademischen Tätigkeit nach. 'Institute of Germanic Studies' liest man auf dem kleinen Türschild. Für das Studium deutscher Literatur ist dies ein Ort von besonderer Bedeutung in der angelsächsischen Welt.
>
> Vom Kellergeschoss bis in den dritten Stock durchwandert der Besucher ein Labyrinth von Räumen, die mit ihren bis unter die Decke reichenden, vollgepackten Bücherregalen zunächst an eine besonders wohlsortierte Bibliothek denken lassen. [...]
>
> [...] Internationalen Ruf haben sich aber die vom Institut veranstalteten Symposien erworben [...]. In der gewissermassen neutralen Atmosphäre am Russell Square kommen Teilnehmer aus West- und Ostdeutschland, aus Österreich und der Schweiz zusammen, von angelsächsischen Ländern ganz abgesehen. [...]
>
> [...] Aus ihrer [the founders of the IGS] akademischen Idee entstand am Russell Square ein Haus zu Studien der deutschen Literatur, wie es in der angelsächsischen Welt ohne Beispiel ist.

Moreover, the IGS and the tradition of scholarship it represented continued to attract admiring attention in the German-speaking press. Writing in the Zurich *Tages-Anzeiger* (13 May 1998), Stefan Howald seems captivated:

> 'Traut vereint: Der Dichter und sein Attentäter. The Institute of Germanic Studies dient seit 50. Jahren dem Kulturaustauch mit dem deutschsprachigen Raum. Eine Fundgrube und eine Oase der Gelehrsamkeit':
>
> [...] Als ich das Institute of Germanic Studies vor ein paar Jahren zum erstenmal besuchte, frappierte mich freilich die Zeitschriftenabteilung im ersten Stock. Über 100 Periodika liegen hier auf, literaturwissenschaftliche ebenso wie allgemein kulturelle, von 'Akzente' und dem 'Bargfelder Boten' über 'German Literature in India' und den 'Michigan Germanic Studies' bis zu den 'Schweizer Monatsheften' oder der 'Zeitschrift für Germanistische Linguistik'.

An account follows of the founding and subsequent activities of the IGS, after which Howald continues:

> Im Arbeitsraum gruppieren sich neben der Zeitschriftenablage ein paar Sessel um einen Tisch wie zum Teestündchen, daneben steht ein langgestreckter, massiver Arbeitstisch, auf allen Seiten behütet von hohen Büchergestellen.

Figure 25: The Willoughby Room, 29 Russell Square, looking onto Russell Square.

> Die ebenso familiäre wie konzentrierte Arbeitsatmosphäre versetzt einen zurück in frühere Zeiten.

He records the bequests to the Institute from Germanists and draws attention to the computerization of the IGS catalogue, which had brought with it some astonishing finds:

> eine einmalige Geschichte des Rheins von 1688; eine Beschrebung von Kreta aus dem Jahre 1669, mit herausfaltbaren Stadtplänen; oder ein gebundener Band mit Originalmanuskripten, offenbar Gedichten aus dem schwäbischen Dichterkreis. [...] In einem Band mit Liedern aus den Befreiungskriegen von 1814 wurden vier Seiten eingebundene Originalmanuskripte mit Musik 'von einem deutschen Barden 1819' entdeckt. Ein Fund ist besonders faszinierend: Eine Ausgabe von August von Kotzebues Theaterstück 'Der hyperboreische Esel oder Die heutige Bildung' von 1804 ist mit handschriftlichen Einträgen von Karl Ludwig Sand aus dem Jahr 1814 versehen, jenes Burschenschafters also, der Kotzebue 1819 aus politischen Gründern erdolchte. [...] Auch hier [amongst the holdings of works by Goethe und Schiller] gibt es Raritäten: Einer Ausgabe der Farbenlehre von 1810 ist ein praktisch einmaliger Separatband mit kolorierten Kupfertafeln beigegeben. [...] Einen Band legt mir William Abbey besonders sorgfältig in die Hände: Eine Ausgabe von Schillers 'Don Karlos' aus dem Besitz des Regisseurs Leopold Jessner. Bei genauerer Betrachtung stellt sie sich als eigentliches Regiebuch heraus, mit Anstreichungen und Anmerkungen. Für seine Inszenierung 1921 am Berliner

Staatstheater hat Jessner auf eingeklebten Seiten Szenenbilder skizziert, Aufmärsche notiert und die Figurenbewegungen mit Farben markiert.[2]

On Thursday, 20 May 1999 the *Frankfurter Allgemeine Zeitung* published an article in a similar vein by Robert Seidel, which includes the Institute of Germanic Studies amongst the cultural highlights in Bloomsbury: 'Neben dem Theaterland liegt das Reich der Bücher. Streifzüge durch das Londoner Viertel Bloomsbury'. Seidel's stroll through England's academic and cultural institutions contains a lengthy description of the Universities of Oxford, Cambridge and London; an account of the British Museum and the British Library; and culminates in praise of Bloomsbury as an academic quarter with its many institutes, such as the Warburg. On the founding of the School of Advanced Study he says:

> Für Bloomsbury hat es die Folge, daß dort für viele Fachbereiche Forschungs- und Diskussionszentren entstanden sind, die jenseits des täglichen Lehrbetriebes Gelegenheit zur Begegnung von Kollegen und Gästen bietet. Beispielhaft hierfür ist das Institute of Germanic Studies am Russell Square, das die größte Spezialbibliothek für deutsche Sprache und Literatur in London birgt. Das ausgedehnte Areal des aristokratischen Gebäudes mit den schweren Holztischen, dicken Teppichen und streng blickenden Dichterporträts erinnern an einen Zeitungsleseclub des 19. Jahrhunderts, und wenn eine der zahlreichen literarischen Veranstaltungen stattfindet, hallen die hohen Räume wider von den unverwechselbaren Geräuschen britischer Geselligkeit, die fast immer mit einem Glas Sherry beginnt. (Seite R6)

In 2000 the Institute celebrated its fiftieth anniversary, an event that also did not go unremarked in the German press: another article by Stefan Howald appeared in the *Frankfurter Rundschau* on 12 April 2000. He praises the IGS and its achievements – though not without irony at the parlous state of language learning and Higher Education in the UK:

> 'Auch Oasen sind bedroht. Das "Institute of Germanic Studies" in London feiert seinen 50. Geburtstag'
>
> Im Januar warnten BMW-Verantwortliche den britischen Industrieminister Stephen Byers, für die von BMW übernommene Rover-Fabrik im englischen Longbridge sei es fünf vor zwölf. Dem Minister wurde es mit 'at the eleventh hour' übersetzt, und er interpretierte, BMW plane 'in letzter Minute' eine neue Rettungsaktion. Das Beispiel eines möglichen Missverständnisses wurde letzte Woche an einer Tagung in London zur gegenwärtigen Situation von Deutsch als Fremdsprache diskutiert. [...] Spezialisierte Sprachkenntnisse,

2 Leopold Jessner (3 March 1878–13 December 1945) was a producer and director of German Expressionist theatre and cinema. Since he was both Jewish and a Socialist, he was forced to emigrate to the USA in 1933.

Wissen über die deutsche Kultur, geraten erst recht ins Hintertreffen. Handlungsbedarf also für das *Institute of Germanic Studies* in London. Dieser Tage feiert es seinen 50. Geburtstag.

1950 in Räumen eines Gebäudes im traditionsträchtigen Bloomsbury Quartier eröffnet, zog es drei Jahre später in das jetzige Domizil, ein imposantes, fünfstöckiges ehemaliges Wohnhaus von Anfang des 19. Jahrhunderts, in der Nähe des *British Museum*. Das Institut konzentrierte sich von Beginn an auf deutschsprachige Literatur und Kultur. Als Zentrum für das Fortgeschrittenenstudium der Germanistik in ganz Großbritannien, hat es unverzichtbare Arbeit im akademischen Bereich geleistet. Kernstück des Instituts ist die Bibliothek, mit rund 90 000 Büchern, Flugschriften und anderen Dokumenten, darunter vielen Erstausgaben und Raritäten. Eindrucksvoll auch die Zeitschriftenabteilung mit 350 Periodika, dazu kommen ein Archiv zur Exilliteratur und andere Spezialsammlungen.

Die Räume, vom Fußboden bis zur Decke von Büchern umstellt, sind eine Oase englisch-deutscher Gelehrsamkeit. Hier lässt sich Goethe in Originalausgaben studieren, finden sich anonyme Shakespeare-Übersetzungen aus dem 18. Jahrhundert, seltene Wörterbücher aus fünf Jahrhunderten oder einmalige Prozessdokumente von Hexenverfolgungen, annotierte Bücher aus dem Nachlass von Friedrich Gundolf und ein eigenhändig illustriertes Regiebuch von Leopold Jessner zu einer Schiller-Inszenierung.

Oasen sind immer bedroht. Das *Institute of Germanic Studies* sieht sich inmitten eines dreifachen Umbruchs. Da ist die Umkrempelung der englischen Bildungs- und Universitätslandschaft, in der Privatisierung den Druck auf Spezialinteressen erhöht. Da ist die Klimaveränderung zwischen den beiden Nationen, in der die deklarierte Europafreundlichkeit der neuen Labour-Regierung immer wieder durch die Instrumentalisierung antieuropäischer und antideutscher Reflexe aufgehoben wird. Und da ist der Umbau und die finanzielle Ausdünnung deutscher Kontaktorganisationen wie des Goethe-Instituts. Der neue Direktor Rüdiger Görner, zugleich *Director of German Studies* in Birmingham, will die Probleme dynamisch angehen.

Bereits zeigt sich ein neuer Schwung in verstärkten Aktivitäten und dem Gewinn neuer Sponsoren, zum Beispiel für Forschungsstipendien. Dabei soll der Kulturbegriff ausgeweitet worden. Das Jubiläum wird mit einem weitläufigen Programm begangen, zu dem auch die Tagung 'German as a Foreign Language' gehörte, die vergangene Woche zusammen mit dem Deutschen Akademischen Austauschdienst (DAAD) und Goethe-Institut in London organisiert wurde.

A particularly personal tribute to the Institute, its international reputation and the 'home' it provided for scholars from across the globe comes from Nine Miedema, now Professorin für Deutsche Philologie des Mittelalters at the Universität des Saarlandes in Saarbrücken:

Figure 26: From left to right: Jane Lewin (Asst. Secretary), William Abbey (Librarian), L. J. Watts (Caretaker), Karin Hellmer (Administrative Secretary).

Ich war damals vom 1. April bis zum 30. September 2000 ohne Bezüge beurlaubt und habe den größten Teil dieser Zeit in London verbracht. Die Beurlaubung hatte ich beantragt, da ich meine Arbeiten am Habilitationsprojekt (Konrad von Würzburg als Sangspruchdichter. Studien und Texte zum Wandel des Autorbildes eines der zwölf Alten Meister) vorantreiben wollte; während der Beurlaubung hatte ich keine Lehrverpflichtung, konnte mich also ganz der Forschung widmen. Die Habilitation habe ich dann im Jahr 2002 eingereicht, es hat mir also viel geholfen, in Ruhe in London arbeiten zu können ...

Ich war damals (glaube ich) die erste (oder zumindest eine der ersten), die eines der Gäste-Arbeitszimmer im IGS am Russell Square benutzen durfte, und erinnere mich sehr gerne daran, wie privilegiert ich mich fühlte, da im Herzen Londons praktisch "in" einer Bibliothek ein Arbeitszimmer benutzen zu dürfen, und dann auch noch die British Library um die Ecke zu haben. Ich war damals sehr angetan, dass das IGS auch im Bereich der Mediävistik eine gute Handbibliothek hatte – auch wenn einige der Bände, die ich gebraucht habe, zwar aus dem 19. oder frühen 20. Jahrhundert stammten, aber noch gar nicht aufgeschnitten waren – sie waren also noch nicht gerade oft benutzt worden ... Die Unterstützung seitens des Personals im IGS war großartig, sowohl was die leitenden Wissenschaftler als auch was das Bibliotheks- und das administrative Personal anging, und es war hilfreich für die Kontakte, dass es im Institut (wie ja heute auch noch) oft Vorträge gab. Ich habe das IGS, zu dem ich vom in Belsize Park gemieteten Zimmerchen aus oft zu Fuß hingelaufen bin (u.a. quer durch Regent's Park ...), als eine Oase empfunden, in der meine Ideen so reifen konnten, dass ich sie in überarbeiteter Form dann als Habilitationsschrift einreichen konnte![3]

3 Quoted with the kind permission of Professor Miedema.

Friends of the Institute of Germanic Studies

Even into the Vale of Tears that currently passes for Higher Education in the UK some light must fall; and in the case of the IGS its source are the Friends of the Institute, founded, at the instigation of Professor John Flood, in 1986:[1]

> The Friends of Germanic Studies were established to promote those activities which were beyond the means of the Institute's slender budget, and now directly support research in the languages, literatures, and cultures of the German-speaking countries. Since they were established in 1986, the Friends have sponsored lecture series, special publications, visiting fellowships as well as studentships in modern German literature.[2]

Frank Fowler, then Professor of German at Queen Mary & Westfield College and Vice-Chairman of the Committee of Management of the IGS from 1985 to 1992, was the first to sign up. One hundred and thirteen Friends were recruited during the first six months and together donated £4,500. Ten years later, in 1996, there were three times as many patrons and life members; the number of Friends who donated annually had risen by 60%; and some £28,000 had been raised. The first Annual General Meeting was held at the Institute on Thursday, 4 June 1987, the birthday of Leonard Willoughby, and attended by thirty-one Friends and six members of staff. It was on this occasion that Professor Flood gave his talk on the history of the Institute, subsequently published in *London German Studies IV*. The first issue of the annual *Friends of the Institute Newsletter* appeared in 1987–88. Traditionally, the Friends' AGM includes a lecture of general interest which is subsequently published in the *Newsletter*. One such was, for example, the paper given by Ian Wallace (Bath) on 15 May 1997 entitled 'East German Writers Look Back at the GDR: Two Recent Examples', which was dedicated to the memory of Philip Brady (d. 15 May 1997), Reader in German at Birkbeck College and long a staunch supporter of the Institute. More recently, in May 2011 Joyce Crick introduced the Friends to 'Benjamin Britten's Texts. Two German Poets'; and in 2012 Dr Benedict Schofield of King's College London spoke on 'Bestsellers, "Worstsellers", and the Question of Canonicity: Gustav Freytag's *Die Ahnen* and Theodor Fontane's *Vor dem Sturm*'. In 2013, to the great delight of colleagues and the Friends, the former Institute Librarian Bill Abbey returned to give the annual lecture on 1 May. He spoke on '"The greatest dramatic genius ... since Shakspeare [*sic*]": Kotzebue's Reign on the London

1 Following the merger with the IRS, the Friends were reconstituted as the Friends of Germanic Studies at the IGRS, thereafter IMLR.

2 Friends of Germanic Studies website: http://www.igrs.sas.ac.uk/about-us/germanic-friends.

Stage'. In addition to the lectures given at the Friends' AGM, the *Newsletter* publishes the Sylvia Naish Lecture, an annual review of events at the Institute, book reviews, announcements of upcoming conferences and short articles of general academic interest, frequently drawn from the contributors' current research, such as Kevin Hilliard's 'The Making of a Nihilist' on the wager between Goethe's Mephistopheles and Faust (2011); Margaret Gajewski's 'The Tannhäuser Bacchanale and a Street Named Grahn' (2012); Ruth P. Dawson's 'Catherine the Great: A Celebrity in Eighteenth-Century Germany?' (2008); or Bernd Ballmann's 'Lockenwickel und Nadelkissen: Zu Heinrich Heine, "Lyrisches Intermezzo", 34' (2006). More than a mere "newsletter", then, the Friends' publication provides a window onto, and record of, the enduring richness and diversity of Germanic Studies in this country.

Moreover, the *Newsletter* has communicated many key events in the life of the IGS: in 1995, for example, it reported that the IGS had been awarded funding from HEFCE to make its Library catalogue available online (a process which took up a considerable amount of Librarian Bill Abbey's time); and to appoint a qualified archivist (on a short-term contract) for 'a serious effort to be made on describing the Institute's rich holdings of archive materials, notably correspondence to and from distinguished German authors and papers bearing on the history of German studies in Great Britain'.[3] The *Newsletter* for 2002 announced that income from the Friends' scheme had totalled over £120,000; and that it was able to offer two short-term fellowships: 1) the Frederick Norman Fellowship to enable a British Germanist to conduct research at the Institute in the area of medieval motifs in modern German literature; 2) the Friedrich Gundolf Fellowship for Germanists working in the field of Anglo-German literary relations. In 2003 the then Director of the IGS, Professor Rüdiger Görner, was able to announce another feather in the Institute's cap: namely, that the Claussen-Simon-Stiftung had just awarded it a grant to set up a Research Lectureship in German Literature (including an element of comparative literature) for three years, with a possible extension for another three. This was the first-ever award made by the Stiftung to a *foreign* academic institution. Various editions of the *Newsletter* also recorded the bequest to the IGS of the Keith Spalding library and its delivery in July 2003; the acquisition of the Archives of the Anglo-Austrian Society and the Anglo-Austrian Music Society (2006); the donation by the Royal Academy of Music of about five hundred German and Austrian theatre programmes and playbills, most of which date from between 1893 and the 1930s and come

3 According to the *Development Plan 1998–2003*: 'The Follett/JISC-funded project has allowed the Institute to appoint a professionally qualified archivist for the first time ever and much has been achieved: the configuration and setting up of a database, the establishment of authority files, an accessions register and an enquiry log, and the cataloguing of several of the individual collections mounted on the Institute's Web page'.

from theatres in Vienna and Berlin (including nearly one hundred and fifty from the Burgtheater);[4] and the formal establishment, in November 1995, of the IGS's Research Centre for German & Austrian Exile Studies, headed by Professor J. M. Ritchie (Sheffield).

However, the *Newsletter* has also been the bearer of sadder tidings, such as the retirement in September 2002 of Professor John Flood, who had served as Deputy Director of the IGS for twenty-four years; or the deaths of such luminaries as Professor Elizabeth Mary Wilkinson, former President of the English Goethe Society and staunch supporter of the IGS in its early days; Professor Kenneth Graham Knight, Secretary-Librarian of the Institute from 1960 to 1965; Professor Tony Harper (Strathclyde, d. 2004); Professor J. P. Stern (d. 1991); Professor Frank Fowler, who had been Vice-Chairman of the Committee of Management of the IGS between 1985 and 1992 and died on 29 October 2005; former Honorary Director of the IGS Professor Claus Victor Bock (d. 2008); Professor Frank Shaw (Bristol, d. 2011); Dr Bernhard Stillfried (2011), former Director of the Austrian Cultural Institute in London; former Honorary Director of the IGS Professor Siegbert Salomon Prawer (1925–2012); Mr Timothy McFarland (University College London, d. 2013); Professor Michael Batts (University of British Columbia, former President of the Internationale Vereinigung für Germanistik and a University of London graduate; d. 2014); and many more colleagues who had helped to build Germanic Studies in the UK and Ireland after the war and are sorely missed. The obituaries, many of them moving personal tributes to respected, cherished colleagues and friends, also allow us rich insight into the history of scholarship and academia in a more generous era, into personalities and service to the subject untrammelled by current financial constraints and commercial pressures.

Throughout their existence the Friends have given staunch support to the IGS Library, one example being the Save-a-Book Appeal, launched in 1992, through which Friends are invited to sponsor the restoration of a volume in particular need of attention. The initial appeal identified twenty-five books in need of restoration, amongst them: Eichendorff's *Aus dem Leben eines Taugenichts* (Berlin: Simion, 1842); Hermann Dunger, *Engländerei in der deutschen Sprache* (Berlin: Allgemeiner Deutscher Sprachverein, 1909); Franz Grillparzer, *Der Traum, ein Leben* and *Weh' dem, der lügt!* (both Wien: Wallishausser, 1840); Heinrich Heine, *Poems/Translated by Julian Fane* (Vienna: From the Imperial Court and Government Printing Office [i.e. not published], 1854); Henry Crabb Robinson, *Ein Engländer über deutsches Geistesleben* (Weimar: Böhlau, 1871). Other titles rescued over the years include: Clemens Brentano, *Honor, or, The Story of the Brave Casper and the*

4 For a full account see the *Friends Newsletter 2007*, pp. 6–8.

Fair Annerl. Translated from the German (London: Chapman, 1847); Gerhart Hauptmann, *Das Meerwunder. Mit 18 Zeichnungen von Alfred Kubin* (Berlin: Fischer, 1934); and George Henry Noehden, *A Grammar of the German Language*, 6th edn (London: Longman, 1830).[5] In addition, the *Friends Newsletter* 1996–97 reports that the Institute had received donations totalling £2,500 from the Bayerische Landesbank, the Hamburgische Landesbank and Deutsche Morgan Grenfell (the last including a pledge to increase its gift for a further three years). These donations were to benefit the book fund.

In 2005 the Friends of Germanic Studies at the IGRS launched a welcome new initiative in the form of PhD Studentships open to candidates in any field of Germanic Studies and to be supervised at the Institute. By October the following year two students had taken up studentships and were working on very diverse fields: Steffen Stadthaus was writing on '"Deutsche Jugend wohin?" Eine Untersuchung des Generationsdiskurses nach dem Zweiten Weltkrieg am Beispiel von Zeitschriften der "jungen Generation"', while Isabel Schropper was working on 'Desperate for Work or Love: the Emigration of Austrian Women to Great Britain 1945–1960'. Two further students sponsored by the Friends are about to submit their doctoral dissertations: Sharon Baker on 'From Satire to Silence: Hans Sachs's Commentary on Civic Decline'; and Nicola Sayers on 'Gold in the Rubble: a Utopian Mining of Contemporary American Nostalgia Culture'.

5 Nicola McLelland discusses Noehden's *Grammar* in *German Through English Eyes*. Professor McLelland also gave the Keith Spalding Lecture on the topic 'German through English Ears: How and Why the English Learnt German, 1600–2000' in February 2013.

Benefactors and Bequests

The Bithell Bequest

In 1959 the Library acquired 2,000 volumes from the library of Jethro Bithell, including many first editions of works published in the 1920s and 1930s. Several hundred more books were subsequently donated by his second wife Mrs Alice Emily Bithell.[1] Jethro Bithell (1878–1962) had been educated at Wigan Mining School and then studied Modern Languages at Manchester University, graduating with a first-class degree in 1900. He subsequently studied German and Scandinavian literature at the Universities of Munich and Copenhagen. From 1902 to 1904 he lectured in Modern Languages at Salford Technical College; from 1904 to 1910 he was Lecturer in German at Manchester University, before being appointed in 1910 as Head of the Department of German at Birkbeck College, London, where he remained until his retirement in 1938, publishing prolifically and being appointed Reader in the University of London in 1921.[2] Jethro Bithell had held hopes for the establishment of a Bithell Chair of German if the funds from his bequest were sufficient; its holder was also to be Director of the IGS. Jethro Bithell's estate had been held in trust for his wife; when she died in November 1974 his entire estate and hers, too, came to the IGS. In recognition of the Bithells' generosity, on 21 May 1975 Professor Bock proposed the institution of an annual Bithell Memorial Lecture, the subject to be contemporary German literature or language, or English-German comparative literary studies, a proposal endorsed by the Committee of Management, but without any stipulation as to subject.[3] Thus the first Bithell Memorial Lecture was held on 13 November 1975, when the force behind the founding of the Institute,

1 Alice Emily Bithell, née Eastlake (1894–1974), was a former student of Jethro Bithell who had written a PhD dissertation under his supervision entitled 'The Influence of English Literature on the German Novel and Drama, 1880–1900' (1937).

2 Jethro Bithell was a particularly productive author of textbooks, including the *Handbook of German Commercial Correspondence* (1908); *Pitman's Commercial German Grammar* (1912); *A German Course for Science Students* (1925, with Arthur Cyril Dunston); *Advanced Prose Composition* (1929); *A Modern German Course, for Students of History, Geography, Economics and Literature* (1928, also with Arthur Cyril Dunston); *Germany. A Companion to German Studies* (1932; revised at least five times before Jethro Bithell's death and in 1972 by Sir Malcolm Pasley); *Modern German Literature 1880–1938* (1939); *An Anthology of German Poetry 1830–1880* (1941); *An Anthology of German Poetry 1880–1940* (1951); and so forth. Many went through several editions. See Nicola McLelland, *English Through German Eyes*.

3 The Bithell Lectures, from 1986 onwards given every two to three years, have always been published. A full list is available at http://modernlanguages.sas.ac.uk/publications/bithell-memorial-lectures.

Emeritus Professor Leonard Willoughby, spoke on '"Wine that maketh glad . . .". The Interplay of Reality and Symbol in Goethe's Life and Work'.[4] Of his title he had the following to say:

> As to the wine bit in my title: Well, Bithell himself was a man of frugal habits (for which our Institute has indeed cause to be grateful). And Birkbeck College, in which he spent most of his working life, had its origins in that puritanical work-ethos of adult education – Mechanics' Institutes, Working Men's Colleges and the like – of which my own father, where not entirely self-educated, was a grateful product. It was partly due to their inspiration that, as well as being a craftsman (he was a master-hatter, who made those silk Toppers we rarely see nowadays except at weddings and Ascot), he could take me on his knee and recite *Don Quixote* in the original, and also fill me with a love of Goethe's *Egmont*. But there was a period in the life of Birkbeck College – and that long before it moved to its present spacious quarters within the University's precincts, when it was still cramped in Bream's Buildings off Chancery Lane (next door to the offices of the *Daily Mirror*) – a period when it was the height of every London academic's ambition to be invited to a formal dinner there. For they were a gourmet's delight, and we would have rated at least four stars in the Michelin. [...] As with most things of aesthetic quality, the delectable results were entirely due to the inspiration and knowledge, the love and concern, of one single individual: the then Secretary and Clerk to the Governors, a man by the name of Trouphorne. Even during the War he was able, in the darkest of days, to produce bottles of that 'which maketh glad the heart of man'. Any suggestion that he achieved this by trafficking on the 'BLACK MARKET' would be sheer calumny! As my own experience may testify. For during those very same years I too acquired an unprecedented popularity. Popularity of a kind I have enjoyed neither before nor since. It had, alas!, nothing to do with any, much needed, improvement in my character as I might have been gratified to think. It had solely to do with the fact that I had laid down so many bottles of wine that they lasted for the duration. And this I had been able to do, not because I was rich: one can't be rich on a professor's salary, or one certainly couldn't then! But because I imported by the barrel, and bottled myself. My corking machine eventually went to University College (though I doubt whether they've ever used it). And the price per bottle of my favourite Rhône wines worked out at 'one and seven-pence' (1*s*. 7*d*) – old currency! Work *that* out for yourselves.[5]

The broad appeal of the topic is evident from the range of those who attended: a nun; a representative from the Department of Energy; colleagues from the Institute of Education, from the Wellcome Institute and from Ealing Technical College; and even from the department store Peter Jones

4 The reference is to Psalm 104, verse 15: 'And wine *that* maketh glad the heart of man, *and* oil to make *his* face to shine, and bread *which* strengtheneth man's heart'.

5 Willoughby, '*Wine that maketh glad . . .*', pp. 10–11. One shilling and seven pence are worth roughly seven-and-a-half pence in today's money.

in Sloane Square. Who said public engagement in Higher Education was a new concept?

The Bithell Memorial Lecture series went on to boast a distinguished list of speakers: for example, Professor Eric Blackall of Cornell, who gave the Bithell lecture on 3 May 1984 on 'Faust's Last Speech'; Lord Annan; Leonard Forster; Bryan Magee; Marcel Reich-Ranicki, author and doyen of the literary talk show *Deutsches Literarisches Quartett*; the journalist and broadcaster Matt Frei (2010); the theatre director Peter Stein; and Richard von Weizsäcker. On the recommendation of Mr Edward Batley, the then Honorary Director of the Institute, former Bundespräsident Richard von Weizsäcker[6] had been awarded an Honorary Doctorate by the University of London, which he received from its Chancellor Princess Anne on the University's Foundation Day (28 November) in 1995. The Chief Rabbi in London at the time, Hugo Gryn, was another of the six Honorary Doctorands. Representatives from the German, Austrian and Swiss Embassies attended the ceremony; and so well did the occasion go that the idea arose of inviting the former Bundespräsident back to give the Bithell Memorial Lecture, which he did in 1996. Klaus Balzer, President of the German Board of Commerce in London and Chair of the IGS Advisory Board at the time, was very helpful in obtaining financial support for the visit. Just before the lecture, when Dr von Weizsäcker was 'sheltering' at the Institute, he was asked whether he might consent to meet the Institute's caretaker, Mr Watts, who was a great admirer of his. Dr von Weizsäcker agreed, to the delight of Mr Watts, who was also thrilled to have a photograph of the two of them together as a memento of the occasion. The two visits by the former Bundespräsident assisted in making the Institute even better known and helped to ensure its survival in an increasingly tough funding climate.

The Bithell Bequest was also used to set up two prizes, both awarded by the Institute, for the first time in July 1977: the Jethro Bithell Prize, awarded for the best overall performance in German in the University of London BA examinations; and the Alice Emily Bithell Prize, awarded for the best overall performance in Modern (i.e. post-medieval) Literature and intended as the 'modern' counterpart to the Priebsch Prize established in 1937 and awarded by the Board of Studies in Germanic Languages and Literatures to reward the best performance in medieval literature. Following the demise of the federal BA degree, the Jethro Bithell Prize has been awarded to the best candidate in a University of London MA examination (with a substantial German component, i.e., 50% of the overall assessment for the MA), with the Alice Emily Bithell Prize being awarded for the best performance in Modern Literature papers in the BA examination across the University of London

6 Richard von Weizsäcker (1920–2015) was Mayor of West Berlin from 1981 to 1984 and Bundespräsident from 1984 to 1994.

Figure 27: Former West German President Dr Richard von Weizsäcker and Edward Batley, then Director of the IGS, on the occasion of the 1996 Bithell Memorial Lecture.

Colleges (any BA course with a minimum German component of 50% being eligible).

In addition, the Honorary Director (Professor Claus Bock) proposed a series of publications which would include the name of Bithell in the title in order to denote that it was separate from the regular series of Institute publications. The purpose of the new series would be to encourage younger members of the profession; it was originally intended to consist of 'condensed' versions (*c.* 100–150 pages) of theses on Germanic subjects which had been accepted by British and Irish universities.[7] The prestigious 'Bithell Series of Dissertations' was launched in 1978; from 1989 onwards the series was published jointly with the Modern Humanities Research Association (MHRA), before being taken back under the sole control of the Institute in 2013.[8] The Bithell Series is still going strong. The first volume to appear was *E.T.A. Hoffmann and the Rhetoric of Terror* by Elizabeth Wright (1979); the most recent volumes include *Bridal-Quest Epics in Medieval Germany* by Sarah Bowden (vol. 40; 2012), *Phantom Images* by Catherine Smale (vol.

7 In practice, after at least three years of writing their theses few authors were willing to cut them down by at least fifty per cent, so in most cases relatively few revisions have been made in the published versions.

8 The Bithell Series was passed to the MHRA with considerable misgivings. The work involved in selection and preparation of the volumes for press remained with the Institute, but whilst the agreement had the advantage that most of the costs were borne by the MHRA, the Institute received none of the income.

Figure 28: Front cover of Volume 45 of the 'Bithell Series of Dissertations'.

41; 2013), *Intercultural and Intertextual Encounters in Michael Roes's Travel Fiction* by Seiriol Dafydd (vol. 42; 2015), *Society and its Outsiders in the Novels of Jacob Wassermann* by Katharina Volckmer (vol. 44; 2016) and *'mit worten lûter unde glanz': Metapoetics in Konrad von Würzburg's 'Trojanerkrieg'* by Esther Laufer (vol. 45; 2016). Theses accepted for publication in the Bithell Series cover an enormous variety of topics in German Studies, ranging from *Landscape and Landscape Imagery in R.M. Rilke* by John Sandford (vol. 4; 1980); *The Authority of the Source in Middle High German Narrative Poetry* by Carl Lofmark (vol. 5; 1981); *Spinoza in Germany from 1670 to the Age of Goethe* by David Bell (vol. 7; 1984); *History and Poetry in Novalis and in the Tradition of the German Enlightenment* by Nicholas Saul (vol. 8; 1984); *Philosophy, Letters, and the Fine Arts in Klopstock's Thought* by Kevin Hilliard (vol. 12; 1987); *Sexuality and the Sense of Self in the Works of Georg Trakl and Robert Musil* by Andrew Webber (vol. 15; 1990); *The Correspondence of Edward Gordon Craig and Count Harry Kessler, 1903–1937* by Lindsay Newman, sometime Librarian of the Institute (vol. 21; 1996); *Divided Loyalties: East German Writers and the Politics of German Division 1945–1953* by Peter Davies (vol. 24; 2000); *The Reception of English Puritan Literature in Germany* by Peter Damrau (vol. 29; 2006); and *Single Combat and Warfare in German Literature of the High Middle Ages. Stricker's 'Karl der Große' and 'Daniel von dem Blühenden Tal'* by Rachel E. Kellett (vol. 33; 2008).[9]

Keith Spalding Bequest

Keith Spalding was born in Darmstadt in 1913 as Karl Heinz Georg Spalt, the only son of a Protestant family. A committed pacifist, in 1932 he published *Kultur oder Vernichtung. Ein Handbuch des Pazifismus*, which was seized and publicly burnt by the Nazis in May 1933. At the end of 1932 he rejected an 'invitation' to become a member of the NSDAP and in early 1933 escaped by train to Vienna. He came to England in 1934 and was offered a home in Coventry by a Baptist minister and his wife. He read French, German and History at Birmingham, graduating with an Upper Second in 1937. In May 1940 he submitted his PhD dissertation on 'Social Factors in German-Swiss Literature', written under Roy Pascal. Keith Spalding was interned on the Isle of Man from June to October 1940. In November 1940 he joined the British Army and served until 1946, helping in the reconstruction of Germany after the war, before taking on an Assistant Lecturership at Swansea in 1946 and moving to Bangor as Head of Department in 1950. In 1953 he became Professor of German and Teutonic Philology, remaining at Bangor until his retirement in 1980. His first book was an *Introduction to the German Language through Lyric Poetry* (London: Harmony Press [1940]); almost the entire print run was destroyed by German air raids. His first substantial academic publication was an edition of the *Ackermann aus Böhmen* (1950; published by Blackwell). From the 1950s onwards Professor Spalding focused increasingly on lexicography and the history of the language, helping to revise the Muret-Sanders Dictionary as *Langenscheidts Großes Enzyklopädisches Wörterbuch* (1962–75) and compiling the *Historical Dictionary of German Figurative Usage* (Oxford: Blackwell, 1952–2000), a collection of figurative expressions in German from 1750 onwards. He also edited works by Adalbert Stifter (e.g. *Abdias* (1966)) and Goethe (e.g. *Hermann und Dorothea* (1968)); and in 1958 published a textbook, *Advanced German Unseens*. In 1955 he had set up an exchange between Bangor and the University of Tübingen and in 1972 the latter awarded him an honorary doctorate; while in 1975 he was awarded the Großes Bundesverdienstkreuz of the Federal Republic of Germany. Professor Spalding, a staunch supporter of the IGS, died in November 2002, having, on the occasion of his eightieth birthday in 1993, presented the Institute of

9 For a full list of titles, see http://www.modernlanguages.sas.ac.uk/publications/bithell-series-dissertations.

Figure 29: Keith Spalding in his young years (portrait by P. W. Söchtig).

Germanic Studies with a substantial sum to be used to establish a fund the income from which was to support research on subjects within its purview, particularly Anglo-German relations. The Fund endowed an annual lecture on an Anglo-German topic. The first *Keith Spalding Lecture* was given on 9 March 1995 by Professor John Flood, then Deputy Director of the Institute, on 'How Reynard the Fox Went to Earth in Russell Square: an Anglo-German Odyssey'. It was based on a manuscript from the Institute's Priebsch-Closs Collection which had once belonged to Augustus Frederick, Duke of Sussex and son of King George III. Other distinguished speakers have included Professor W. J. Jones (London) on 'Germanic Virginity or Teutonic Virility? Attitudes to Language among Earlier German Purists'; Dr Philip Brady (Reader in German at Birkbeck College and broadcaster) on 'Autolysis versus Underpants: Literary Angles on the "Wende"'; Professor Martin Durrell (Manchester); Professor Nigel Reeves, OBE (Aston); Dr Gottfried Wagner (great-grandson of the composer); Professor Hans-Joachim Kreutzer (Regensburg); Professor Ekkehart Krippendorff (Berlin); Dr Anthony Julius (London); and, in 2003–04, Dr Manfred Osten (General Secretary of the Alexander von Humboldt Foundation). The most recent lectures have been given by Professor Nicola McLelland (Nottingham) on 'German Through English Ears: How and Why the English Learnt German, 1600–2000' (2013);

Figure 30: Sylvia Naish.

and Dr Jill Bepler (Herzog August Bibliothek Wolfenbüttel) on 'Why Pay for an Education in Germany? Wolfenbüttel and its Academy for the Nobility, 1687–1715' (2104).

The Sylvia Naish Bequest

The 'Bithell Series of Dissertations' was one initiative aimed at supporting postgraduates; another was possible due to a generous bequest from Sylvia Naish (1913–1996), herself an accomplished linguist and translator fluent in French, German and Greek (and with a working knowledge of Italian, Spanish and Turkish), though she had worked as a charity administrator all her life. She had joined the Friends of the Institute of Germanic Studies in 1988 and often attended conferences and workshops put on by the Institute. Mrs Naish had been particularly keen to support young scholars, so the Institute used her bequest in 1996 to help with grants for graduates from the German-speaking countries to visit Britain. The IGS also used the money to establish the annual Sylvia Naish Lecture, to be given by a postgraduate registered at a British university. The first was delivered on Thursday, 22 February 2001 by Kristin Semmens (St John's College, Cambridge) on 'Touring the Past, Politicizing the Present: Tourist Culture in the Third Reich'; and recent lectures include, in 2013, 'Vorrede zu Vorreden: Jean Paul's Pretexts for Literary Parody' by Seán Williams (Jesus College, Oxford); in 2014 'A Hidden Idiom of Cultural Memory? Gender and Attempts to Manage the Memory of National Socialism' by Katie Stone (Clare College, Cambridge); and, in 2015, 'One Eye is not Enough: Stereoscopic Writing after WWII' by Melanie Dilly (University of Kent). The Sylvia Naish Fellowships were intended to help postgraduates from the UK or a German-speaking country to spend up to two months at the IGS for the purposes of carrying out research into any area of German language or literature. The first holder of the award was Andreas Anglet (Cologne), who worked on European cultural history between 1900 and 1930. His report on his stay at the Institute was published in the *Friends Newsletter* in 2001; the Sylvia Naish Lectures are published in the following *Newsletter* as well.

The William Robson-Scott Bequest

The William Robson-Scott Travelling Scholarship was established in memory of Professor W. D. Robson-Scott, Honorary Director of the Institute of Germanic Studies from 1968 to 1973, and is intended to help research students to travel abroad in order to carry out research bearing on the languages and literatures of the German-speaking countries, the Netherlands, or Scandinavia.

The Robertson Prize

Finally, one ought not to forget the Robertson Prize, named after John George Robertson (1867–1933), from 1903 Professor of German Language and Literature at the University of London, and from 1924 Director of the Department of Scandinavian Studies and editor of the *Modern Language Review*. Professor Robertson (after whom one of the reading rooms in the old IGS premises at 29 Russell Square was named) had been responsible for introducing Dutch and Scandinavian Studies into the University of London. The Prize was awarded by the University of London for 'the best book in the field of Germanic Studies [i.e. German, Dutch, Scandinavian but not English] published in Britain during the preceding three years'. The University Senate was advised on the award by a small committee of four or five people from within the University that generally included a representative from the Institute. Books awarded the Robertson Prize include Henry and Mary Garland's *Oxford Companion to German Literature* (1976) and Nicholas Boyle's *Goethe: The Poet and the Age* (vol. 1, 1991; vol. 2, 2000).

National Postgraduate Colloquia and Awards

The Sylvia Naish Bequest constitutes one plank in the platform of support offered to postgraduate students by the IGS and its successor institutes; and it was once again the *Friends of the Institute Newsletter* for 1987–88 that had announced another important new initiative, one highlighted in the appraisal recently undergone by the IGS: 'A major new venture of particular interest has been the institution of a national forum for postgraduate students from all universities to meet and discuss their research. The first such colloquium took place at the Institute in February 1987'.[1] Since 1988 the National Postgraduate Colloquia in German Studies have taken place twice a year, alternating between London and a university outside the capital. Thus the fifty-second National Postgraduate Colloquium was held in October 2012 at St John's College, Cambridge; the fifty-third took place at the IGRS in London in March 2013; the fifty-fourth at the University of Birmingham in November 2013; the fifty-eighth at the University of Kent in November 2015. The programmes have always been innovative and wide-ranging: the twenty-first colloquium (5 April 1997), for instance, included papers on, amongst other topics, 'For or Against Nature? Monstrous Forms in Medieval Literature'; 'Caspar David Friedrich: Art, Philosophy, Nature and the Inner Self'; 'Form in Fontane: A Narratological Analysis of *Graf Petöfy*'; and '*Frauensprache im Männerstaat*? Evolution of Female Fascist Discourse'; while the fifty-eighth included such themes as 'Typography and the City: Kurt Schwitters, Hanover, and the "Systemschrift"'; '"Also mein allerliebster redette Ihre Sapho mit dem Kriege": the Seven Years' War in Anna Louisa Karsch's *Sapphische Lieder*'; '*Die Elixiere des Teufels* and the Problem of Identity'; and 'Symbole und Motive des Boxens in der deutschprachigen Literatur'. Moreover, in 1997–98 an Intercollegiate German Postgraduate Group was established to foster informal contact between postgraduates at the Institute and at various London Colleges. Now the IMLR Graduate Forum meets informally once a month during term time to present and discuss work in progress. In recent years the Institute has also offered a comprehensive programme of training in research skills and methods to graduate students in the School of Advanced Study and universities in London and beyond.

1 This initiative came from the then Honorary Director, Professor Roy Wisbey (KCL), acting on a suggestion from Dr Andrea Reiter. (Southampton) The National Postgraduate Colloquium website is at http://www.modernlanguages.sas.ac.uk/graduate-study/research-training/national-postgraduate-colloquium-german-studies.

The Institute Library and its Donors

Denn es genügt schon meinem Sinn,
Wenn ich umringt von Büchern bin.[1]

Right from the conception of the IGS the Library has stood at the heart of its activities. Relatively soon it developed a clear acquisitions policy: 1) to provide bibliographical material and critical editions of works by standard authors indispensible to research; and 2) to specialize in certain fields not yet represented in other London libraries (cf. *First Annual Report*). In addition, colleagues in London used to write to Robert Pick, the first Secretary-Librarian, to suggest possible purchases. For example, on 14 November 1950 Leonard Forster wrote to suggest that the Institute Library collect not only the works of standard authors but also those of standard critics such as Jacob Grimm, Wilhelm Dilthey, Ernst Troeltsch and Johan Huizinga. A major strength of the Library, one particularly cherished by its users, was its comprehensive collection of periodicals and its innovative practice of indexing individual articles from them.[2] For colleagues and organizations beyond Germanic Studies the Institute Library also came to be viewed as the natural repository for archival material, so that in 1977 we find correspondence about the IGS housing the Minute Book of the London Medieval Society (established in 1943), in which the eminent German medievalist Arthur Hatto had played no small role. The idea came from his distinguished colleague at Queen Mary College, Dr Rosemary Combridge. Indeed, from the start donations and fortunate purchases contributed to building up the Library's holdings and its ownership of some internationally significant collections.[3]

The Priebsch-Closs Collection

In the late 1940s the Institute acquired from Professor and Mrs August Closs roughly 2,500 books that had belonged to Robert Priebsch (1866–1935), Professor of German Language and Literature at University College London

1 Sebastian Brant, *Das Narrenschiff* (Basel: Johann Bergmann von Olpe, 1494).

2 Unfortunately, this practice had to be abandoned around 1990 because of lack of staff and because the computerized union catalogue of institute libraries was not designed to include individual articles.

3 Another important collection is that of material relating to the history of German Studies in the UK, an initiative prompted by Professor Frederick Norman at the annual meeting of the Conference of University Teachers of German in Great Britain and Ireland that was held at the University of Cardiff in 1965.

from 1898 to 1931.[4] It is not precisely known how Robert Priebsch acquired the rare books in his collection; but the idea of obtaining the Priebsch Collection for the Institute emanated from Professor Willoughby, the first Honorary Director, and Dr Robert Pick, the first Secretary-Librarian. Amongst Professor Priebsch's books were first and early editions of Classical and Romantic writers; rare works by less-known German authors from the same periods; and numerous translations from German, illustrating the influence of German thought and literature on English literature and the stage in the eighteenth and nineteenth centuries. Another significant addition to the Library holdings were the thirty sixteenth-century works and 108 seventeenth-century books acquired in 1967 from Professor August Closs (1898–1990),[5] who had arrived from Austria in 1924, become Reader in German at the University of Bristol in 1931, first Professor of German at Bristol in 1948 and a Patron of the IGS in 1987.[6] The *Friends of Germanic Studies Newsletter 1991–92* records that more of Professor Closs's books came to the Library after his death in 1990.[7] His daughter, Professor Elizabeth Closs Traugott, felt that the IGS was the most appropriate place for the bulk of his papers and library; hence in August 1990 approximately three thousand volumes, countless letters, postcards (many of them sent by Closs's students during their year abroad) and other manuscripts were transferred from Bristol to the Institute, where they joined Professor Closs's earlier donation of over 2,300 titles mainly from the eighteenth and early nineteenth centuries.

Amongst the treasures in the Priebsch-Closs Collection are manuscript fragments of various lengths; a huge, bound manuscript of Latin sermons (*c.* 1450); and the original handwritten records of two witch trials, that of Catharina Stroblin, a farmer's wife from Schernfeld (near Eichstätt,

4 August Closs was Robert Priebsch's son-in-law, having married the latter's daughter, Hannah, in 1931. The information in this section is taken mainly from Flood, 'The Institute of Germanic Studies and its Library', pp. 272–73; and his essay in this volume, 'The Priebsch-Closs Collection of the Institute of Germanic Studies'. In 1937 a 'Robert Priebsch Prize in books' had been endowed by a committee formed to commemorate his services, which had transferred the princely sum of £166.7s.6d to the University of London for this purpose. The fund yielded an annual income of £5.00. The Prize was awarded to the best Medieval German paper in the BA Honours examination until after 2000. Its value was increased: first to £10, then to £30, then to £50 towards the end of the twentieth century.

5 Professor Closs had already sold 273 sixteenth-century items to Princeton University in 1969. A letter from Siegbert Prawer to the Institute's Librarian, Mr V. J. Riley, dated 21 April 1967, informs him that Professor Closs was prepared to accept £700 for the seventeenth-century part of his collection.

6 A Patron is an individual who makes a substantial one-off donation to the Friends of the IGS (currently £250), or those whose cumulative donations reach £250.

7 The following is taken from the *Friends of Germanic Studies Newsletter*, pp. 9–11; and from additional information supplied by Professor John Flood.

Bavaria), who was tried on 24 November 1617 and on 26 January 1618 'durch das Schwert hingerichtet, und verbrannt'; and that of Appolonia Neuberin (aged thirty-two), a brewer, who was tried on 10 May 1623 and 'durch das Schwert hingerichtet und sodann verbrannt' in June 1623. Also found in the Collection are seventeenth-century travel guides, some of which praise the beauties of Germany whilst others document engagement with Europe and the Mediterranean: the health-conscious tourist might wish to consult François Blondel, *Außführliche Erklärung und augenscheinliche Wunderwirkung deren heylsamen Badt- und Trinckwässern zu Aach* (Aix-la-Chapelle: J. H. Clemens, 1688), while the cruise afficionado could turn to *Das edle Fluss-Perle, oder der Gold-trächtig und fürtreffliche Ströme-Printz, der Rhein* (1689). For journeys further afield, the traveller might profit from the *Kurtze Beschreibung der Insel und Reichs Creta oder Candia* (Nuremberg: Johann-Philipp Miltenberger, 1669); *Des berühmten englischen Theologi Gilberti Burnets [...] durch die Schweitz, Italien, auch einige Orte Deutschlands [...] gethaner Reise [...] curieuse Beschreibung* (Leipzig: Johann Friedrich Gleditsch, 1687) (see p. 206); and Casimir Freschot's *Des Königreichs Dalmatien historische und geographische Vorstellung* (Leipzig: Johann Friedrich Gleditsch, 1688).

Further evidence of cultural exchange is provided by the translations of German works into English, including Schiller's *Fiesco, or the Genoese conspiracy* (1796); his *Cabal and love* (1795); *Maria Stuart* (1801); Rilke's *Selected Poems* (translated by Ruth Speirs and published in 1943 by the Anglo Egyptian Bookshop in Cairo); a Welsh translation of *Wilhelm Tell*; and *Reynard the Fox. A Saxon Poem of the 15th Century*, an English verse translation by Dietrich Wilhelm Soltau (1745–1827) of the Low German *Reynke de Vos*. Other items demonstrating the intensity of cultural exchange between England and Germany in previous centuries include: Amalia (Prinzessin v. Sachsen), *Original Beiträge zur deutschen Schaubühne* (Dresden u. Leipzig, 1836–1844) (vols. I, II, III, V, VI, VII); Amalia (Princess of Saxony), *Six Dramas Illustrative of German Life* (London, 1848), with drawings; Sir Ralph A. Anstruther (Bart), *Griselda. A Drama in 5 Acts*, translated from the German (London: Black & Armstrong, 1840; Dresden & Leipzig: Chr. Arnold), and bearing the dedication on the title page: 'To G. L. Anstruther from her affnte [*sic*] Brother the Translator'; Gotthold Ephraim Lessing, *Minna von Barnhelm. The Disbanded Officer or the Baroness of Bruchsal. A comedy, as performed at the Theatre Royal in the Hay-Market* (by James Johnstone, see Prologue III–VI) (London, 1786) (this was the first English translation of *Minna von Barnhelm*); *Robinson Crusoe. Das Leben und Begebenheiten des . . . Engelländers Mr. R. C. .... von ihm selbst beschrieben*, die 2te Hamburgische Auflage (Hamburg: Thom. v Wierings Erben . . . 1721); Thomas Carlyle, *Leben Schillers*, aus dem Englischen eingeleitet durch

Goethe (Frankfurt am Main, 1830), Titelkupfer: Carlyles Wohnung (note in the original typed catalogue: 'Prachtexemplar aus der Bibliothek Percy Fitz-Gerald, Freund und Biographer Ch. Dickens'); Charles Dickens (Boz), *Oliver Twist*, aus dem Englischen v. H. Roberts mit Federzeichnungen nach Cruikshank (Leipzig: J. J. Weber, 1838), 1. Bändchen (3 Bände); *Faustus. Lives and exploits of notorious characters. George Barnwell. Richard Turpin. . . . Dr. Faustus* (London: F. Brown, 1845) (Collection of Chapbooks. The Wonderful [History?] of Dr. Faustus and the Devil being the third), frontispiece: the Devil fetches Dr. Faustus; Klopstock, *The Messias* I & II Vol. attempted from the German (London: Dodsley, 1763) (very rare) (in handwriting: '1st Eng. trans. by Mary Collyer'); and Scotland's answer to Kaspar Hauser: Thomas Charles Colyear, Earl of Portmore, *Ausführliches Leben und besondere Schicksale eines wilden Knaben von zwölf Jahren, der zu Barra, einer Schottländischen Insel von zweyen berühmten Aerzten gefangen u. auferzogen worden* (Frankfurt und Leipzig, 1759). Other holdings from the eighteenth and nineteenth centuries in the Priebsch-Closs Collection include first editions of works by such eminent German authors as Gotthold Ephraim Lessing (*Nathan der Weise* (1779)); Ludwig Tieck (*Franz Sternbalds Wanderungen* (Berlin, 1798)); Friedrich Schiller (*Wilhelm Tell* (Tübingen, 1804)); Heinrich von Kleist (*Penthesilea* (Tübingen, 1808)); and Franz Grillparzer (*Weh dem, der lügt* (Vienna, 1840)).

Another major strength of Professor Closs's collection is lyric poetry, especially from the periods immediately following both World Wars.[8] However, his collection contains earlier gems as well, such as Friedrich von Bodenstedt, *Für Strassburgs Kinder. Eine Weihnachtsbescheerung von Deutschlands Dichtern. Zeitgedichte* (Berlin: F. Lippenhelde, 1870). A further strong point are early works of Germanistik: an edition of the *Edda* from 1818; Jacob Grimm's *Reinhart Fuchs* (1834); Ludwig Uhland's *Walther von der Vogelweide, ein altdeutscher Dichter* (1822); Johann Jacob Bodmer and J. J. Breitinger's *Fabeln aus der Zeit der Minnesänger* (Zürich: auf Kosten der Gesellschaft, bey Orell, 1757) (see p. 171). Titelkupfer von R. Füssli;[9] Jacob Grimm's *Deutsche Mythologie* (1835); *Specimens of the German Lyric Poets: consisting of translations in verse, from the works of Bürger, Goethe, Klopstock, Schiller etc. interspersed with biographical notices & ornamented with engravings on wood by the first artists* (London: Boosey & Sons, 1822); J. F. R. W. Jerusalem, *Über die Teutsche Sprache u. Literatur. An Ihro Königliche Hoheit die verwittwete Frau Herzogin von Braunschweig und Lüneburg* (Berlin, 1781); and the curious, but potentially handy, *Der curiose und in allen nöthigen Wissenschaften Nützliche Dollmetscher Oder Allgemeines*

8 See the essay by John Flood in this volume.

9 The engraving is by Rodolf Fueßli (poss. Hans Rudolf Fueßli der Jüngere (1709–1793)). The work is the first critical edition of Ulrich Boner's *Der Edelstein* (*c.* 1350).

Figure 31: Frontispiece of Ulrich Boner's Fabeln aus den Zeiten der Minnesinger.

Zeitungshandbuch by Johann Andreas Erdmann Maschenbauer (Augsburg, 1748). Finally, amongst Professor Closs's papers are documents relating to the very first town-twinning after the Second World War, that between Bristol and Hannover in 1947, in which Professor Closs had been closely involved and for which he was honoured by being accorded the Freedom of the City of Hannover.

The Keith Spalding Bequest

The library of Keith Spalding was bequeathed to the IGS on his death in 2002 and delivered in July 2003. Dictionaries from all periods figure largely in the Spalding Bequest, the oldest being the seventh edition of Heinrich Decimator's *Sylvae vocabulorum et phrasium* (1591); Theodor Arnold, *Neues Deutsch-Englisches Wörterbuch* (Leipzig, 1770) and J. C. A. Heyse's *Allgemeines Wörterbuch zur Verdeutschung und Erklärung der in unserer Sprache gebräuchlichen fremden Wörter und Redensarten* (Oldenburg, 1804). His library also included an edition of Quintilian from 1504.

The Friedrich Gundolf Collection

Professor C. V. Bock, who had himself carried out a considerable amount of research on Friedrich Gundolf (1880–1931), was instrumental in attracting what was to become one of the Institute's most valuable acquisitions, and in 1959 the Institute acquired 1,500 books from the author's estate at a cost of £120. German poet and academic, Gundolf had been Professor at Heidelberg from 1916 until the late 1920s, and had in 1899 joined the George-Kreis, publishing his first poems in Stefan George's literary magazine *Blätter für die Kunst*.[10] *The First Ten Years* (15 January 1960; a report by Robert Pick to the Honorary Director) relates that the Gundolf Collection had passed into the possession of the Institute by Deed of Gift and included one hundred files containing manuscripts of Friedrich Gundolf's biographical and critical works; fifty manuscripts of his poetic works; and sixty files of his correspondence with the George-Kreis. Shortly before the report was written two pages from a Gundolf manuscript had sold for DM255. Pick proposes the establishment of a research fellowship at the IGS to work on the collection and, in conjunction with this, suggests a request be made for a special grant for the acquisition of other collections with the hope that '[t]he Institute could try and do on a small scale

10 Stefan Anton George (12 July 1868–4 December 1933) was a German poet, editor and translator at the centre of an influential literary and academic circle, the George-Kreis, which included many leading young writers of the day. The group cultivated mystical and political as well as cultural interests.

what Marbach and Weimar are now doing in a big way'. In fact, it was Institute policy to acquire secondary literature on Gundolf and the George-Kreis to complement the Gundolf Archive. Mention is made in the *IGS Development Policy 1972/77* of the 'extremely important Gundolf collection', 'one of the Library's most treasured possessions', which to this day attracts frequent enquiries. The Gundolf Archive is not the only such collection in the Library,[11] which also holds, *inter alia*, the Berthold Auerbach Collection (acquired in 1987)[12] and Archive of Germanic Drama; the Archive of the Anglo-Austrian Society; the Archive of the History and Development of German Studies (an initiative of Professor Frederick Norman, who proposed its establishment at the CUTG conference in 1965); the Exile Archive;[13] the Archive of Martin Miller and Hannah Norbert-Miller on Exile Theatre; the Papers of Professor J. P. Stern;[14] and Rudolf Majut Papers.[15]

Other Benefactors

The Institute wished to build on the Priebsch Collection in order to develop a strong focus on Anglo-German literary relations, especially Shakespeare

11 For the full list of archives held by the Institute see Appendix 2 and http://modernlanguages.sas.ac.uk/library/germanic-archives/archive-collections.

12 Berthold Auerbach (1874–1960) was a theatrical agent in Berlin. He knew Leopold Jessner. Auerbach worked first for E. Drenker & Co.; then, after their closure, for the official State agency for stage and film, the *Paritätischer Stellennachweis der Deutschen Bühnen*, with which he remained until 1933, when, being Jewish, he was dismissed. Though unemployed, he stayed in Berlin from 1934 to 1939, when he and his wife decided to leave Germany to join their daughter in England. They were not allowed to bring out their two sons. After arriving in England, Auerbach was interned in the camp on the Isle of Man for a few months. For a full biography see http://modernlanguages.sas.ac.uk/library/germanic-archives/archive-collections/berthold-auerbach-germanic-theatre.

13 See http://modernlanguages.sas.ac.uk/library/germanic-archives/archive-collections/exile-archive.

14 Professor Joseph Peter Maria Stern (1920–1991) was Professor of German at University College London from 1972 to 1986, Honorary Director of the IGS from 1981 to 1985 and an authority on nineteenth- and twentieth-century authors, particularly Friedrich Nietzsche, Franz Kafka, Rainer Maria Rilke and Thomas Mann.

15 Rudolf Majut (1887–1981) was born in Vienna into a family of Jewish origin. In 1912 he obtained his doctorate with a thesis on the German playwright Georg Büchner. He had planned to make a career as an academic and started his *Habilitation*, but was dismissed from teaching in 1933 due to his Jewish descent. In 1939 Majut came to England at the personal invitation of Dr George Bell, Bishop of Chichester, ending up in Leicester, where he first taught German in a secondary school and later took up the post of Lecturer at Leicester University, to which he bequeathed his library of some six thousand books. His wife, Dr Hermine Majut, a mathematician, posthumously published his work and often attended events at the Institute. For more detail see http://modernlanguages.sas.ac.uk/library/germanic-archives/archive-collections/rudolf-majut-papers.

in Germany. Thus it collected translations of Shakespeare's works that had been published in Germany since the mid-eighteenth century and owns, for example, a first edition of Schiller's translation of *Macbeth* (1801). In 1954 Professor W. Walker Chambers (Glasgow) gave the Institute sixteen different early translations of Goethe's *Werther*, which included the *Sorrows of Werther* (London: Dodsley, 1780, 1784, 1785 & 1786) and other translations published up until 1815. They supplemented the fifteen translations into English, French, Spanish and Italian in the Priebsch Collection. Professor Chambers also gave the Institute a two-volume collection of plays, *German Theatre* (London, 1800), which contains six translations altogether, amongst them Schiller's *Die Räuber* and two plays by Kotzebue. Another of his gifts was *Plays from the German* (London, 1793), which includes *Iphigenie* and *Nathan der Weise*. The Library also possesses English translations of three plays by Kotzebue (*The Corsicans, La Perouse, Pizarro*), all published in London in 1799. Moreover, in 1954 the Library purchased seventy-five rare editions of works by Lessing and his contemporaries from the publishing house of Max Niemeyer in Tübingen. In 1958 Professor William Rose (LSE) was another benefactor, giving copies of plays by Schiller, Wedekind and Ibsen that contained detailed annotations by Leopold Jessner from his time as Director of the Berliner Staatstheater between 1919 and 1925; as well as a complete bound set of the *Hamburger Nachrichtenblatt der alliierten Militärregierung* of 1945 (printed single-sided so that it could be posted up).

From Professor Max Liddell of Trinity College Dublin the IGS Library has Luther's pamphlet *Ursach und antwort das iūgfrawē klöster göttlich verlassen mügen* (Basel: Adam Petri, 1523). During World War I Professor Liddell had been in the internment camp at Ruhleben (then a village ten kilometres west of Berlin) along with Professor Frederick Norman, the third Honorary Director of the Institute. In 1979 Professor Leonard Forster sold to the Institute, for the sum of £400, 223 volumes, mainly of poetry from the immediate post-war period. The Library also acquired early editions of Expressionist authors from the library of Professor William Robson-Scott, as well as the library of Dr Mary Beare of Westfield College (d. 1985), which displays a strong focus on Hans Sachs and the sixteenth century, including printed material from that time. From Thomas Mann's librarian Ida Herz (1894–1984) came, in 1984, 400 volumes from Mann's own library. Most are about Thomas Mann; many are signed by him or include handwritten dedications from Thomas Mann to Ida Herz.[16] The Library also contains Dr H. F. Garten's correspondence

16 The Herz Archive also includes a typed copy of the obituary for Thomas Mann written for the British weekly political and literary-review magazine *Time and Tide* (August 1955) by the English historian and broadcaster C. V. Wedgwood, great-great-great granddaughter of the potter Josiah Wedgwood (and Special Lecturer at University College London from 1962 to 1991). Also in the Archive is the programme for the tribute meeting for Thomas Mann

with Gerhart Hauptmann; and William Rose's correspondence with Richard Dehmel, Else Lasker-Schüler, Thomas Mann, Franz Werfel, Carl Zuckmayer and Stefan Zweig. The year 1988 saw the transfer from the Westminster Mayfair library of about four hundred volumes, including many first and early editions of Expressionist works. In 1989 over one thousand volumes came from the Verband der Verlage und Buchhandlungen in Baden-Württemberg e. V.. Other treasures in the Library holdings include a perfect copy of Johann Heinrich Zedler's sixty-eight-volume *Grosses Universal-Lexikon aller Wissenschaften und Künste* (1752–54) (purchased for £200); Burkhard Waldis's translation and adaptation of Aesop's *Fables*, the *Esopus* (first published 1548; Institute's copy: Frankfurt am Main, 1565); and early German translations of Petrarch. The working library of the Embassy of the Deutsche Demokratische Republik in London came to the IGS in 1990.[17] In 2007 the *Friends Newsletter* reports on the acquisition of another new collection: the Royal Academy of Music had passed to the Institute Library about five hundred German and Austrian theatre programmes and playbills, the majority of which date from between 1893 and the early 1930s, for example, from the Kammerspiele of the Deutsches Theater Berlin (whose director between 1907 and 1911 was Max Reinhardt, amongst others). In fact, most of the programmes come from Berlin and Vienna and include nearly one hundred and fifty examples from the Burgtheater.

Other Holdings

The medieval side of the Institute's Library was built up systematically (with a strong focus on Wolfram von Eschenbach) and includes early nineteenth-century editions of Middle High German texts, microfilm and

organized by the PEN–Zentrum Deutscher Autoren im Ausland, the Honorary President of which Thomas Mann had been. It was held in the Beveridge Hall, Senate House, on Friday, 18 November 1955. The programme includes a photo, taken by Katia Mann, of Thomas Mann delivering the address at the Goethe Dinner arranged by the English PEN Club in 1949 and a *Nachruf* by the Austrian-Jewish exile author, translator and contributor to the BBC's European Service during the Second World War, Dr Hans Flesch-Brunningen, President of the PEN–Zentrum between 1953 and 1958. The meeting included a reading from *Der Erwählte* by Hannah Norbert (see the section on the Martin Miller and Hannah Norbert-Miller Trust); 'Thomas Mann – as seen by an English writer' by C. V. Wedgwood; and a recital by the Austrian exile pianist Peter Stadlen of Beethoven's Piano Sonata No. 32 in C Minor, Opus 111. In Chapter 8 of Mann's *Doktor Faustus*, Adrian Leverkühn's music teacher Wendell Kretzschmar delivers a lecture on why Beethoven had omitted to write a third movement for the sonata. As for Ida Herz's extensive correspondence with Mann and her other papers, these went to the Thomas Mann Archive at Zurich in 1960. On her see Friedhelm Kröll, *Die Archivarin des Zauberers. Ida Herz und Thomas Mann* (Cadolzburg: ars vivendi, 2001).

17 In 1996/1997, an exceptional year, the Institute Library acquired over 1,650 volumes, that is, 73% of its acquisitions, through donations.

facsimiles.[18] Between 1953 and 1954 the Institute started its collection of Festschriften. Another focus was the collection of dictionaries of New High German to 'facilitate survey of German lexicography'; also dialect dictionaries, grammars and linguistic atlases. Hence the Institute bought the Grimms' *Deutsches Wörterbuch* for £200 in 1950. It also owns original editions of Justus Georg Schottelius, *Ausfuehrliche Arbeit von der teutschen Haubt Sprache : worin enthalten gemelter dieser Haubt Sprache Uhrankunft, Uhraltertuhm, Reinlichkeit, Eigenschaft, Vermoegen, Unvergleichlichkeit, Grundrichtigkeit, zumahl die Sprach Kunst und Vers Kunst teutsch und guten Theils lateinisch Voellig mit eingebracht, wie nicht weniger die Verdoppelung, Ableitung, die Einleitung, Nahmwoerter, Authores vom teutschen Wesen und teutscher Sprache, von der Verteutschung, item die Stammwoerter der teutschen Sprache samt der Erklaerung und derogleichen viel Merkwuerdige Sachen* (1663) (three copies, one donated by Professor K. G. Knight); Johann Christoph Adelung, *Mithridates, oder, Allgemeine Sprachenkunde : mit dem Vater Unser als Sprachprobe in beynahe fünfhundert Sprachen und Mundarten* (Berlin: Vossische Buchandlung, 1806–17); the *Deutsche Sprachlehre für Schulen* (1792, 1803 & 1816); the *Aelteste Geschichte der Deutschen, ihrer Sprache und Litteratur bis zur Völkerwanderung* (Leipzig: J. G. Göschen, 1806); the *Grammatisch-kritisches Wörterbuch der hochdeutschen Mundart : mit beständiger Vergleichung der übrigen Mundarten, besonders aber der Oberdeutschen* (Leipzig : J. G. I. Breitkopf, 1793–1801); Johann Georg Scherz, *Johannis Georgii Scherzii J.U.D. et P.P. argentoratensis Glossarium germanicum medii aevi : potissimum dialecti suevicae* / edidit illustravit supplevit Jeremias Jacobus Oberlinus (Strasburg, 1781–84); and the *Wörterbuch der deutschen Sprache* / veranstaltet und herausgegeben von Joachim Heinrich Campe (Braunschweig: Schulbuchhandlung, 1807–11).

By 2000 the Library held approximately ninety thousand volumes (books and journals). The oldest journal was a volume of the *Monatliche Unterredungen einiger guten Freunde von allerhand Büchern* (1696). The library also contains a complete set of microfiches covering all the works mentioned in Karl Goedecke's *Grundriss zur Geschichte der deutschen Dichtung* (1859), thus in effect a complete set of all the major works of German literature. It was donated by the Deutsche Forschungsgemeinschaft. Also in the library is an extensive set of microfiches of Reformation pamphlets.

18 See John Flood, *A Handlist of Facsimiles of Medieval Manuscripts of Interest to Students of German Literature in the Libraries of the University of London* (University of London, Library Resources Co-ordinating Committee, 1979). This is now in the Germanic Studies Library, Senate House: IGS REF COLL 4th floor Middlesex North Gallery; shelfmark A 240.016 Flo RR.

Space and Budget

One perennial problem with the Library very soon manifested itself: the acute lack of shelf space on which to house its steadily growing collections. Amongst the papers in the IGS archives is the draft of a report on the Library (unfortunately undated and unsigned, but probably written by K. G. Knight). As well as bemoaning the 'difficulty in finding suitable, well-trained staff for bibliographical projects', it complains:

> Where to house our ever growing library is another problem. We can get some thousands of books into the cellars and I think the Institute, if it is careful, can manage to exist in its present surroundings for another eight to ten years. After that there will be so much material that this will be quite impossible (p. 2).

However, the Library faced a further grave problem, one which has continued to haunt it, since 'within the twelve years since its [the Institute's] foundation, prices have risen alarmingly particularly the prices for new German books, and also second-hand German books which are truly colossal' (p. 5). On a more optimistic note, the draft remarks on the potential of the Institute's own publications and proposes an annual volume to include lectures given at the Institute, the 'London German Studies', a sub-series of 'Publications of the IGS'.[19]

Similarly, a memo dated 15 June 1961 from F. Norman notes the following:

> Our first overflow from books must be in the large cellar which is lockable. Later we must devise means to have bookshelves along the walls in the passage downstairs. This will see us through for a very long time. In fact, after examining the book storage problem, I have come to the conclusion that a far greater problem for us is the Staff accommodation which is difficult and wasteful in this house.
>
> As we must decorate and get lower store ready almost immediately in order once more to free the mantlepiece [*sic*] in the main library, I think you should now approach Professor Forster and ask him to see that the books which we have now stored for a very long time are removed.

A letter of 19 December 1962 (unsigned, but certainly from Frederick Norman) requests that the Institute be permitted to take over the ground and first floor of 28 Russell Square at some point in the next few years as:

> it will be able to accommodate about 25,000 books on that [ground] floor. The first floor of 28 Russell Square would take not less than 10,000 books so that

19 'London German Studies' came into existence in 1980, when the first volume was published; vol. XV was published in 2016. For a full list of IGS titles, see http://modernlanguages.sas.ac.uk/publications/germanic-studies-publications.

> the Institute of Germanic Languages and Literatures would be reasonably well supplied [with space] until about the year 2000. By that time the University will be ready to pull down all those buildings anyway and I don't think I need worry very much at my age about what is to happen in the 21st century!
>
> [...] The question of storing books in our University Depository [in Egham, Surrey] is bound to arise and if anybody enquires whether we wish to, the answer must be: We are a library in which nobody can borrow and in which every book must be present all the time for staff and visiting scholars and postgraduates. There would be no sense at all in running our postgraduate Institute if we sent any books away. A book which we do not wish to keep on the premises, we do not wish to keep at all.[20]

However, on 28 December 1962 the Principal wrote to Professor Frederick Norman politely turning down his request that the Institute be permitted to take over the ground and first floors of 28 Russell Square, which the School of Slavonic Studies was to retain under the new accommodation arrangements. Thus the lack of space continues to be highlighted: for example, in the Report on the Library from the Librarian Lindsay Newman to the Director, dated 7 March 1965.

Further persistent problems were inadequate staffing (at that time one librarian with a degree in German; one trainee librarian with a degree in German; and occasional assistance from an untrained postgraduate) and hence an inadequate catalogue; largely unclassified stock; a backlog of donations and bequests that had not even been sorted; and the constant moving around of books in order to accommodate new acquisitions. Indeed, on 11 June 1965 the Librarian Lindsay Newman and the Director Frederick Norman wrote jointly about the Library to members of the Committee of Management, pointing out that the catalogue was 'inconsistent, ill-arranged, in part obsolete and confusing. It is not possible to be sure whether or not a specific volume is in stock'; that the 'books are largely unclassified; there is no subject-index [...] it is difficult for readers or the library staff to find books'; that to classify the whole library would take one qualified librarian with a clerical assistant, both full-time, at least two years (if doing no other work); that the Library received approximately fifteen hundred new acquisitions per annum and had a backlog of some five hundred donations and bequests; and that the grossly understaffed Institute Library needed a basic permanent staff of three as well as someone for two years to sort out the disorder that reigned there. Despite these problems, the Library was such a valuable resource that a list of proposed suggestions to be made to the Working Party on Friday, 12 February 1971 notes the following:

20 Unfortunately – and most inconveniently – about 80% of the IGS Library's holdings are now held in storage in Egham, so since the move to Senate House a long-held, much-cherished principle has perforce been abandoned, an attempt at relocation in the 1980s having successfully been rebuffed.

> A number of members of the Institute have pointed out that a large proportion of the regular users of the building is made up of postgraduate students who must visit the Institute in the intervals of their work as college assistant lecturers, etc. They would like to be able to use the facilities of the building at evenings and weekends.

Much later, in the 1980s or early 1990s, the Institute experimented with extended opening until 8 p.m. one evening a week, but the experiment was not a success as hardly anyone took advantage of the facility, yet someone had to be present in the Institute office at all times to let readers into the building.

In 1972 Library expenditure on books amounted to £2,500. The total IGS budget was approximately £20,000 per annum and it was proposed to increase the Library budget to £3,500 by 1976–77 due to the rising cost of German books, not least since in 1972 the Library had been hit by the renewed devaluation of Sterling and revaluation of the Deutschmark. Suggestions for book purchases and Library activities were made on the assumption that financial stringency would continue, which was probably wise, as the revised estimates of library expenditure from 1974–75 similarly note that the Library had been adversely affected by the exchange rate since the Pound had again fallen against the Deutschmark and purchases from Germany formed between eighty and ninety per cent of all transactions. A minimum increase in the Library's allowance of £550 was needed. In the session 1977–78 proposed expenditure on books amounted to £8,110; the years 1981 to 1982 saw a modest increase to £8,350. These figures made no allowance for the rise in book prices, which was running at approximately 20% per annum. In addition, the cost of periodicals was growing at an alarming rate: journal subscriptions were rising at least as fast as book prices and the number of journals was increasing rapidly, with the result that an ever-increasing proportion of the funds available were spent on periodicals. This in turn meant that the funds available for books were ever smaller. Books and periodicals were purchased largely out of the Bithell Bequest Fund, the money provided by Senate for the Institute library being used to cover staff salaries.

The years 1977 to 1978 saw an attempt to solve the problem of inadequate space when, at the instigation of Professor C. V. Bock, the Bithell Twentieth-Century Room was built in the basement. Unfortunately, however, this solution did not prove entirely satisfactory as from the start the room was prone to flooding. Indeed, the BA Board of Examiners' meeting in July 1981 saw one of those mid-summer downpours with which the guttering could not cope. Board members and Institute staff formed a chain to rescue books from the Bithell Room; and the caretaker L. J. Watts heroically stripped off his shirt in an attempt to staunch the flood! In addition, the Bithell Room also proved only a temporary solution to the problem of space, so in about 1981 Dr Flood resolved the space problem by proposing the clearance of a large cellar then used as a junk room and installing compact shelving to create a new periodicals room. A year or two later compact shelving was similarly installed in part of the basement corridor (for nineteenth-century literature) and in another basement store room (to accommodate stocks of IGS publications). Compact shelving increased the usable space by fifty per cent.

In the *IGS Annual Report 2001–2002* we encounter familiar concerns about the Library, the major ones being the clearing of the backlog in cataloguing and the upgrading of catalogue entries for books and journals, as well as the disposal of duplicates etc., since 'in the medium term, these are all steps that will allow the Library to cling on in the existing building for a little longer'. The process of cataloguing had led to the discovery of new material: Carl Philipp Conz's *Gedichte, erste Sammlung* (Tübingen, 1792) (not previously catalogued); and a complete set of Friedrich Perthes's journal *Vaterländisches Museum* (1810–11), which contained in its final issue an early German account of William Blake. Eighteenth-century editions of medieval works had been re-catalogued and moved to secure storage. By contrast to the disappointment registered in an earlier Librarian's report, extensive use was now being made of the Priebsch-Closs Collection. Moreover, the following was noted:

> It is also evident that many readers are coming to the Institute because they have located material that is not easily available elsewhere. Clearly, the Library must maintain the depth and currency of its collections in order to go on attracting readers, but that takes money: money to buy books and journals in the first place, money for the staff to catalogue and process them.

Thus, sadly, some journal subscriptions were abandoned to avoid their cost consuming too much of the Library budget. However, journal subscriptions continued to be a priority and it was not uncommon for a journal that had ceased publication to be replaced by another. It was proving impossible to buy Festschriften, exhibition catalogues and conference proceedings as widely as had once been the case. Greater selectivity was also exercised in the purchase of secondary literature:

> In the current circumstances, it is difficult to respond adequately to new trends in research or to keep up, even in selective fashion, with new monographs in fields once considered the highest priority. Yet it is particularly in respect of secondary literature that the Library experiences most demand from readers.[21]

21 From the outset the Institute had tried to have a clearly defined acquisitions policy and to this end had, in the early years, included John Wilks, the Librarian of University College

To balance this regrettable state of affairs, in the same year over six hundred titles had been received as gifts or through bequests; and over sixteen thousand volumes had been received in this way during the previous twenty years. In 2001 to 2002 the Institute was still awaiting the outcome of an application to the Vice-Chancellor's Development Fund, which, if successful, would enable it to create a detailed inventory of the Gundolf Papers.

For over fifty-five years the Institute Library and its staff provided a secure, peaceful, scholarly haven for Germanists from all over the world, offering continuity in ways both reassuring and challenging, as IGS Librarian Bill Abbey points out in the *Friends Newsletter* of 2006:

> Change is in the air but, for the moment at least, much is carrying on as it always has: the Germanic Studies Library is still occupying the same premises at 29 Russell Square and, when the clouds burst, those premises still leak and rainwater threatens the books in the Bithell Room – some things *never* change. [...] That the building is not bursting at the seams is thanks to the safety valve provided by the store in the Senate House basement, to which lesser-used and outdated titles can be relegated without affecting the integrity of the core collection.

Nonetheless, it is a tribute to the dedication and professionalism of the Library staff that none of the problems which may have beset the Library over the years was ever manifest to Library users. On the contrary: the Institute Librarian, Mr Bill Abbey, was the calming font of wisdom and knowledge who helped visiting scholars and countless anxious PhD students find necessary and valuable material for their research and was thus undoubtedly at least co-responsible for the successful completion of many a dissertation or monograph.

Although the Institute Library was intended as a *Präsenzbibliothek* rather than a lending library, this policy was not invariably adhered to. A letter of 15 November 1972 from V. J. Riley to the Design Department of the BBC

London, on the Committee of Management and the Library Sub-Committee. From the start it was recognized that the Institute enjoyed neither the funds nor the space to cover secondary literature and hence it was considered the role of the University Library in Senate House and the College libraries (especially those nearby, such as University College, Birkbeck and King's) to make necessary provision. In 1975 the University set up the Library Resources Co-ordinating Committee (LRCC), which was supported by a large number of subject sub-committees, including one for German, whose responsibility it was to consider the best means of ensuring adequate provision for the subject within the University as a whole. The German Sub-Committee, which included representation from all the Colleges teaching the subject and from the British Library, met regularly and discussed whether to support a particular library's plan to purchase an especially expensive item (e.g. a dialect atlas) or whether it made better sense for that item to be placed elsewhere, such as in the Institute or a College where there was particular interest or expertise in an author or topic. The German Sub-Committee also achieved some degree of rationalization in the purchase of periodicals. The Library Resources Co-ordinating Committee lasted for about ten years.

concerns books that had been borrowed the previous year and not yet returned. In a rather more opaque incident, on 5 January 1978 Catherine M. Kent (the Senior Library Assistant) wrote to Brentford Police about sending the Library Assistant Miss Carol Stephens to identify three books in their Property Found Department. The books, dating from 1650, 1663 and 1744, included Johann Michael Moscherosch's *Wunderliche und warhafftige Gesichte Philanders von Sittewald* (1650). No indication is given as to how the books might have made their way to Brentford or, indeed, the Property Found Department.[22] Finally, on 22 February 1974 V. J. Riley wrote to the John Rylands Library, University of Manchester, about a book (Johann Neubauer, *Altdeutsche Idiotismen der Egerländer Mundart, mit einer kurzen Darstellung der Lautverhältnisse dieser Mundart . . .*, 2nd edn (Vienna: Graeser, 1898)) borrowed on 24 July 1954 and not yet returned. He wrote again on 25 July 1974, still not having received a reply. In a letter dated 29 November 1974 he acknowledges return of the book, which had been bound in Manchester for the first time by way of apology and the restoration of good relations. A letter from the John Rylands says the book had eventually turned up on a shelf in Inter-Library Loans with a note dated 1959 telling ILL to return it to the Institute of Germanic Languages and Literatures. Fortunately, all ended amicably.

The Germanic Studies Library is now based in the Middlesex North Reading Room in Senate House Library.

22 At the Institute there was no security whatsoever and hence the Library relied on trust. Even after electronic security equipment became available, the Institute simply could not afford to install it.

The IMLR

The year 2013 saw the name of the Institute of Germanic & Romance Studies changed to Institute of Modern Languages Research.[1] However, the storm of discussion and protest generated on the German-Studies Jiscmail list by the change in name, which eradicated all obvious links to the old Institute of Germanic Studies, was eloquent testimony to the profound affection and respect in which the IGS was held by Germanists of all generations across the globe and to the central role it had played in German Studies at home and abroad. Whilst yet again called upon to demonstrate its resilience and adaptability, German at the new IMLR continues to flourish and the promotion of the discipline through lectures, conferences, readings, workshops and other ventures remains undiminished. One striking example is the conference *German in the World*, organized with colleagues from King's College London and Queen Mary College, University of London, and held at the IMLR in June 2014. Its intention was to explore and highlight the significance of German as a global language and Germany as a major international player in both economic and cultural terms; and to stimulate new directions for the subject. Speakers included colleagues from Europe, South Africa, Japan, India and the USA, from neighbouring disciplines and from the cultural and diplomatic sector.[2] So successful was the conference that the German Department at King's College London have been running a seminar series entitled *German in the World* to continue the discussion generated by the event.

Other initiatives in which the IMLR has been involved include the research network for Literature and Biological Thought in the Nineteenth and Twentieth Centuries, led jointly by the IMLR and the Department of German, University of Cambridge. It was inaugurated with a day-long workshop at the Institute on 20 March 2014 in which colleagues from the UK, Germany and Switzerland participated. Continuing the theme established in 2010 by the event 'Shakespeare – a German Writer?', in June 2014 the IMLR hosted a conference on 'Adapting, Performing and Reviewing Shakespearean Comedy in a European Context'.[3] The facilitation of translation and interaction between languages and cultures remains at the heart of IMLR activity, as illustrated by the series of encounters or conversations between authors, their translators and publishers held at the Institute and hosted jointly with the University

1 This change was partly a result of the of HEFCE review of the School of Advanced Study.

2 See the *Friends Newsletter 2014* for a full report on the conference.

3 For a full account of 'Adapting, Performing and Reviewing Shakespearean Comedy in a European Context' see the *Friends Newsletter 2014*.

of Nottingham. The first took place on 4 December 2014 and featured the Iranian-born German-language writer Sudabeh Mohafez in conversation with one of the Institute's Sylvia Naish Visiting Fellows, Kate Roy, who was working on the translation of a work by the author.[4] Other encounters have taken place between Karen Leeder, Angela Krauß and Margaret Vince; Annett Gröschner and Katy Derbyshire; and Ulrike Ulrich and Marielle Sutherland. This initiative has subsequently branched out to other languages with similar encounters between Antonella Annedda and Jamie McKendrick and Ana Luisa Amaral and Margaret Jull Costa. A further example of 'translation', this time across disciplines, is the *Dinggedicht* competition organized by the Institute and the DAAD to complement *Germany – Memories of a Nation*, an exhibition which ran at the British Museum between October 2014 and January 2015. Students of German at all levels were invited to write a poem on one of the objects exhibited at the Museum; and the Institute received no fewer than 160 entries. As Godela Weiss-Sussex remarks in the *Friends Newsletter* for 2015, this 'was all the more heartening at a time when the learning of modern languages, and especially German, is at a low point' (p. 1). A second competition for all learners of German was jointly organized by the IMLR and the DAAD in 2015; and a third is being planned at the time of writing.

In 2016, under the new Director, Professor Catherine Davies, the IMLR received a great boost to its research profile. A four-year research project, run together with the Universities of Manchester and Durham and entitled *Cross-Language Dynamics: Reshaping Community*, was approved by the AHRC's Open World Research Initiative (OWRI) programme and will be supported by funding totalling £3.9 million. Unfortunately, however, for all the lip service paid to Britain's role in Europe the future of German Studies in secondary and higher education in the UK remains uncertain;[5] and German, like other Modern Languages, will always be subject to the vagaries and political agendas of respective governments as reflected in their – at times distinctly perverse – decisions on the role and funding of Higher Education. However, none of this detracts from the uniquely valuable role played by the Institute of Germanic Studies (and its successors the IGRS and the IMLR) as the international home of Germanistik in its broadest sense for over sixty years,[6] or from the vision of its founders and subsequent Directors, the drive,

4 The event was sponsored in part by the Keith Spalding Bequest Fund. The podcast is available at http://www.sas.ac.uk/videos-and-podcasts/culture-language-and-literature/encounters-writers-and-translators-conversation-.

5 The vote on 23 June 2016 in favour of Great Britain's leaving the European Union adds a further layer of uncertainty to the future of Modern Language teaching generally in our schools.

6 The value of the Institute's work, its service to and status at the centre of German – and

generosity and utter dedication of its staff, its fostering of scholarship and intellectual exchange, its success in opening German, Austrian and Swiss culture to a broader public and the place it holds in Germanist hearts – something to which a slender account such as this cannot hope to do justice.

Modern Languages – in the UK were confirmed by the review of the Institute conducted in January 2015 as part of the School of Advanced Study's rolling programme (See the *Friends' Newsletter 2015*, p. 1 and pp. 26–28).

Appendix 1

Staff at the Institute of Germanic Studies

(Honorary) Directors of the Institute of Germanic Studies

Professor Leonard Ashley Willoughby (1950–53)
Professor Edna Purdie (1953–56)
Professor Frederick Norman (1956–65)
Professor Siegbert Salomon Prawer (1965–68)
Professor William Douglas Robson-Scott (1968–73)
Professor Claus Victor Bock (1973–81)
Professor Joseph Peter Stern (1981–85)
Professor Roy Albert Wisbey (1985–89)
Professor Martin William Swales (1989–93)
Mr Edward Malcolm Batley (1993–99)
Professor Rüdiger Görner (1999–2004)

Directors of the Institute of Germanic & Romance Studies

Professor Naomi Dinah Segal (2004–11)
Professor Bill Marshall (2011–14)

Directors of the Institute of Modern Languages Research

Professor Catherine Davies (2014–)

Deputy Directors of the Institute of Germanic Studies

Mr Maurice O'Connell Walshe (1965–79)
Professor John Lewis Flood (1979–2002)

Secretary-Librarians of the Institute of Germanic Studies

Dr Robert Pick (1950–60)
Dr Kenneth Graham Knight (1960–65)

Institute Librarians

Lindsay M. Newman (1965–66)
Victor John Riley (1966–80)
William (Bill) Abbey (1981–2009)
Dr Martin Liebscher (2009–11)
Andrea Meyer-Ludowisy (2011–; Western European Studies Librarian, SHL)

Archivists

Jennifer A. Hogarth (1996–98)
Dr Clare George (2012– ; Miller Archivist)

Institute Secretaries/Administrators

Ruth Singh (née Ruff) (1965-68)
Margaret Appleton (1968–72)
Karin Hellmer (1972–2004; Asst. Secretary 1970–72)
Jane Lewin (2004–; Asst. Secretary 1981–2004)

Appendix 2

ARCHIVES OF THE LIBRARY OF GERMANIC STUDIES

Collection Name	Dates Covered
Additional Archive Material [ADD]	*c.*1848–1998
Archives of the IGS/IGRS/IMLR [IGS]	1939–2015
Archive of the Anglo-Austrian Society & Anglo-Austrian Music Society [AAS]	*c.*1944–*c.*89
Julius Bab [BAB][1]	1930
Berthold Auerbach Collection & Archive of Germanic Drama [BAA][2]	1881–2002
Clair Baier Archive [CBA][3]	*c.*1934–76
Mary Beare Papers [MBE][4]	*c.*1936–83
Margarete Berger-Hamerschlag Papers [MBH][5]	*c.*1902–*c.*2008
Jethro Bithell Papers [JBI][6]	*c.*1912–76
P. V. Brady Papers [PVB][7]	*c.*1960–93
Karl H. Breul Papers [KHB][8]	*c.*1883–*c.*1925
E. M. Butler Papers [EMB][9]	1919–59
August Closs Papers [Closs/ACL][10]	*c.*1850–1990
Elizabeth Closs-Traugott Papers [Closs/ECT][11]	
Hannah Closs Papers [Closs/HCL][12]	
Conference of University Teachers of German [CUTG]	1963–96
Herbert F. Cook Papers [HFC][13]	1940s–70s
Archive of the English Goethe Society [EGS]	*c.*1774–*c.*2001

1 Julius Bab was a German dramatist, critic and co-founder of the Kulturbund Deutscher Juden.

2 Berthold Auerbach was a Jewish-German theatrical agent in Berlin in the 1930s.

3 Clair Baier was Head of the Department of German at Hull.

4 Mary Beare was Reader in German, Westfield College.

5 Margarete Berger-Hamerschlag was a painter, illustrator, author and teacher.

6 Jethro Bithell was Reader in and Head of German, Birkbeck College, London. Another collection of Bithell papers is held in the Brotherton Library, University of Leeds.

7 Dr Philip Valentine Brady was a broadcaster and Reader in German, Birkbeck College, London.

8 Karl Breul was Schröder Professor of German, University of Cambridge.

9 Eliza Marian Butler was Schröder Professor of German, University of Cambridge.

10 August Closs was Professor of German, University of Bristol.

11 Elizabeth Closs-Traugott is the daughter of Professor August Closs.

12 Hannah Closs was the wife of August Closs and daughter of Robert Priebsch.

13 Herbert F. Cook was a schoolteacher and author of language-teaching books.

M. Ettisch [MET][14]	1945–69
Exile Archive [EXS]	*c.*1900–*c.*2003
Leonard W. Forster Papers [LWF][15]	*c.*1933–*c.*91
Hans Franck [HFR][16]	1935–63
Nicholas Furness/Otto Lehman-Russbueldt Papers [FLR][17]	1947–95
H. F. Garten Papers [HFG][18]	1936–75
Len Goldman Audio Recordings [LGO][19]	1945–80
Friedrich Gundolf Archive [FGU][20]	*c.*1902–33
Clement Harris Diaries [CHA][21]	1889–97
History and Development of German Studies [HGS]	1909–95
Sylvia Harris Papers [SHA][22]	1953–80
Ida Herz Papers [Herz][23]	*c.*1921–*c.*81
James Blair Leishman Papers [JBL][24]	*c.*1927–*c.*61
Herbert Löwit Papers [HL][25]	*c.*1919–2006
London Medieval Society [LMS]	1945–77
Robert Lucas [RLU][26]	1893–1995
Norman McCann Collection [NMC][27]	1893–1960

14 A collection of photographs of Berlin.

15 Leonard Forster was Schröder Professor of German, University of Cambridge.

16 Hans Franck was a writer.

17 Nicholas Arthur Furness completed his doctorate at the University of Innsbruck in 1952 with a thesis on Georg Büchner. In 1954 he joined German Department at the University of Edinburgh; in 1969 he succeeded Professor Eudo Mason in the Chair. His research expertise lay in Expressionist Theatre, especially the works of Ernst Toller. Otto Lehman-Russbüldt was one of the co-founders of the Bund Neues Vaterland (after WWII renamed the Deutsche Liga für Menschenrechte), of which he was Secretary-General from 1922 to 1926. In 1933 he emigrated to the Netherlands and then the UK, having been one of the thirty-three Germans on the first *Ausbürgerungsliste* issued by the National Socialists. In exile he worked for German refugee newspapers and between 1941 and 1946 was editor of the *Rundbrief des Flüchtlings*.

18 Hugo Frederick Garten was an exile, teacher, lecturer, journalist and author.

19 Len Goldman was a political activist.

20 Friedrich Gundolf was a German poet and academic.

21 Clement Harris was an English pianist and composer.

22 Sylvia Clare Harris was Lecturer in German, Birkbeck College, London.

23 Ida Herz was an exile and Thomas Mann's librarian.

24 James Blair Leishman was a scholar and translator of Hölderlin and Rilke.

25 Herbert Löwit was an exile, a wartime member of the Czechoslovak Independent Brigade and later a teacher.

26 Robert Lucas (né Robert Ehrenzweig) was an Austrian-Jewish exile writer, correspondent for the Austrian newspaper *Neue Freie Presse* and from 1938 worked for the German Service of the BBC.

27 Norman McCann was an impressario and collector of theatre programmes and musical memorabilia.

Reginald John McClean Papers [RJM][28]	1923–69
Rudolf Majut Papers [RMA][29]	1918–66
Martin Miller and Hannah Norbert-Miller Archive [Miller][30]	*c.*1933–*c.*97
Mynatt/Kapp Papers [MYK][31]	*c.*1921–*c.*99
Kathleen Nichol's Photograph Album [KNI][32]	1935
Frederick Norman [FNO][33]	1952
Pavel and Eli Novak Papers [PN][34]	2003
Pictorial Collection [PIC]	*c.*1625–1998
Placzek/Philipp Papers [PLA][35]	1966–2000
Robert Priebsch Papers [Closs/RPR][36]	
George Brychan Rees Papers [GBR][37]	1967–68
William Rose Papers [WRO][38]	1900–62
Seemann Slide Collection [EAS][39]	1911–39
Keith Spalding Papers [KS][40]	*c.*1932–*c.*93
J. P. Stern Papers [JPS][41]	1944–91
Herbert Thoma Papers [HTH][42]	*c.*1400–1975
Timm Ulrichs' Publicity Material [TUL][43]	*c.*1970–90

28 Reginald John McClean was Professor of German at Birkbeck College, University of London.

29 Rudolf Majut was an exile and Lecturer in German, University of Leicester.

30 The Millers were exiles, directors, actors and broadcasters.

31 Margaret Mynatt was an exile, activist and editor; Yvonne Kapp an editor, author and translator.

32 Kathleen Nichol is unknown, apart from the fact that she visited Nazi Germany in 1935.

33 Frederick Norman was Professor of German at King's College London and Honorary Director of the IGS between 1956 and 1965.

34 Pavel and Eli Novak were Czech refugees.

35 Adolf K. Placzek was a librarian, Professor at the Columbia Graduate School of Architecture, architectural historian and exile; Ernst Philipp was a cousin of Adolf Placzek, a refugee, soldier in the British Army and maths teacher.

36 Robert Priebsch was Professor of German, University College London.

37 George Brychan Rees was a scholar.

38 William Rose was Professor of German, London School of Economics.

39 This contains educational material from the German publisher E. A. Seemann.

40 Keith Spalding was an exile and Professor of German and Teutonic Philology at Bangor.

41 Joseph Peter Maria Stern was an exile and Professor of German, University College London.

42 Herbert Hans Karl Thoma was an exile and Senior Lecturer in German, King's College London.

43 Timm Ulrichs is a German artist and was, between 1972 and 2005, Professor für Bildhauerei und Totalkunst at the Institut für Kunsterzieher Münster (from 1987 onwards the Staatliche Kunstakademie Münster).

Gilbert Waterhouse Papers [GWA][44]	1911–68
Leonard Ashley Willoughby and Elizabeth Mary Wilkinson Papers [WW][45]	*c.*1930–80
Franz Wurm [FRW][46]	1988
Marianne Wynn Papers [MW][47]	1958–*c.*2001
Herbert David Ziman [HDZ][48]	*c.*1915–40

44 Gilbert Waterhouse was Professor of German, Queen's University, Belfast and Trinity College, Dublin.

45 Professor Willoughby was Professor of German, University College London and first Honorary Director of the IGS; Professor Wilkinson was Professor of German, University College London.

46 Franz Wurm was a Swiss poet and translator.

47 Marianne Wynn was Professor of Medieval German, Westfield College.

48 Herbert David Ziman was a literary journalist. The collection contains postcards and bank notes.

Appendix 3

History of 29 Russell Square

RUSSELL SQUARE commemorates the Russell family, Dukes of Bedford, who constructed it. About 1777 No. 29 was briefly let to William Hanbury [1725–1778] rector of Church Langton in Leicestershire. Sometimes called 'the clergyman-gardener' or 'God's harrower', Hanbury is best remembered today for his 'Essay on Planting and a Scheme for Making it Conducive to the Glory of God and the Advantage of Society'.

By 1806 No. 29 Russell Square had been sold to George Cowie, a gentleman of independent means, who sold it on about 1824 to George Brown [1790–1865]. A decade or so earlier, Brown had served with distinction in the Peninsular Campaign – the British army's successful attempt to stiffen Spanish opposition to French revolutionary and Napoleonic aggression. He was knighted in 1852 and advanced to the rank of general. Forty years after seeing action in the Peninsular, at past sixty years of age, he commanded the Light Division in the Crimea. From 1860 to 1865 he was commander-in-chief in Ireland.

From 1832 No. 29 Russell Square was home to George Meek, who owned an estate at Brantridge in Sussex. About 1852 he sold on to Samuel Beale, chairman of the Midland Railway and member of parliament for Derby from 1857 to 1865. He lived here with his second wife, Mary, the daughter of John Johnson of Field House, Chester.

Records for 1873 show No. 29 Russell Square sheltering Henry John Simmons, senior partner with Simmons & Simmons, solicitors, of Threadneedle Street. When Simmons died shortly before the turn of the century he bequeathed the property jointly to his two sons, Edward and Percy. As the former was domiciled elsewhere, Percy it was who made No. 29 his home.

Sir Percy Coleman Simmons [1875–1939] became a member of the London County Council in 1907 at an election which threw the 'old progressives' into power. He was chief whip of the Municipal Reform Party from 1914 to 1921; and during his long term of membership of the L.C.C. served as chairman of various departments including the fire brigade and the theatre and music-halls. In 1919 he became one of the four members who represented the interests of the City of London at County Hall. He is best remembered today for the leading part he played in the Waterloo-Charing Cross Bridge controversy. Sir Percy was in favour of a new six-line railway bridge at Waterloo. His opponents desired to retain the old bridge and to erect a new one at Charing Cross. Sir Percy won the day. He was a liveryman of the Needlemakers' Company and during the First World War served in the R.A.F. He died at Chelwood Corner, Nutley, Sussex, two weeks after the outbreak of the second [*sic*] World War, aged 64.

By 1920 No. 29 Russell Square was in use as the accounts department of the London War Pensions Committee. By 1926 – the depths of the Depression – it had become the London office of the Official Receiver for Bankruptcy. Shortly after the end of the second World War it was acquired by the University of London for the Institute of Germanic Languages and Literature, which survives here today as the Institute of Germanic Studies.[49]

49 This is taken verbatim from the IGS Archives. No authorship is given. The former Deputy Director Professor John Flood wrote: '[…] the one-page history of 29 Russell Square was sold to us by a woman who was a freelance architectural historian. […] I recall her coming in and asking if we would like to buy it for £50. It used to hang on the wall of the main staircase'. He also recalls receiving, on more than one occasion in the 1980s, correspondence addressed to the 'Official Receiver' and the 'Institute of Ceramic Studies'! The *History of 29 Russell Square* contains one factual error: the University first allocated 29 Russell Square to Birkbeck College; only after Birkbeck had relinquished it did it become available for the Institute. My thanks to Professor Flood for pointing this out.

The Priebsch–Closs Collection

John L. Flood

The Priebsch–Closs Collection

At the time of its merger with the Institute of Romance Studies (established in 1989) in 2004, the Institute of Germanic Studies (founded in 1950) had at its core a library comprising some 75,000 books, 25,000 volumes of periodicals with around 300 current subscriptions, and 22,000 microfiches (including full-text reproductions of 15,000 post-1650 titles by 2,500 authors), a large collection of theses (principally those submitted for degrees of the University of London) and substantial archive holdings amongst which the papers of the literary historian and poet Friedrich Gundolf (1880–1931) held pride of place.

Of particular importance among the treasures of the library is the Priebsch–Closs Collection, numbering some 2,390 volumes. The nucleus of this was the personal library formed by Robert Priebsch (1866–1935), Professor of German at University College London from 1898 to 1931, lovingly maintained and augmented by his son-in-law August Closs (1898–1990) who had arrived in Britain from Austria in 1924 and would become Reader in German at the University of Bristol in 1931 and Professor there from 1948 to 1964.[1] Priebsch spent the last four years of his life mainly in Vienna, so Closs must have assumed responsibility for the collection in 1931 and it passed formally into his ownership on Priebsch's death in 1935. The collection comprised several medieval manuscripts, incunabula and other early printed books, with many first editions of German Classical and Romantic authors, early German translations of Shakespeare and notable holdings of translations of plays from and into German. Unfortunately, the integrity of Priebsch's original collection was seriously compromised already in 1969 when Closs sold 273 sixteenth-century items to Princeton University.[2] The richness of this part of the collection, especially in the areas

1 An account of Priebsch's career is given in the essay 'Taught by Giants' in the present volume. For further details of the lives of Priebsch and Closs see their respective entries in the online version of the *Oxford Dictionary of National Biography*. Real insight into Priebsch's character and interests emerges from his published correspondence with his senior colleague Elias von Steinmeyer (1848–1922): *Robert Priebsch, Elias von Steinmeyer: Briefwechsel*, selected and edited by August Closs (Berlin: Erich Schmidt, 1979), and excellently reviewed by George C. Schoolfield in *Germanic Notes*, 17 (1986), 60–62. See also the review by Werner Schröder, in *Beiträge zur Geschichte der deutschen Sprache und Literatur* (1983), 308–11.

2 A list of these may be found at http://libweb2.princeton.edu/rbsc2/misc/Priebsch-Closs.pdf.

Figure 32: August Closs.

of theology, historiography and poetry, may be gauged from a roll-call of some of the better known names represented: Johannes Agricola (1494–1566), Heinrich Cornelius Agrippa von Nettesheim (1486–1535), Erasmus Alberus (1500–1553), Nikolaus von Amsdorf (1483–1565), Johannes Aurifaber (*c.*1519–1575), Johann Aventinus (1477–1534), Sebastian Brant (1457–1521), Hieronymus Braunschweig (*c.*1450–*c.*1512), Caspar Brusch (1518–1559), Johannes Bugenhagen (1485–1558), Heinrich Bullinger (1504–1575), Johannes Dietenberger (1475–1537), Hieronymus Emser (1478–1527), Desiderius Erasmus (1466–1536), Matthias Flacius Illyricus (1520–1575), Nicodemus Frischlin (1547–1590), Johann Geiler von Kaysersberg (1445–1510), Joseph Grünpeck (1473–1532), Argula von Grumbach (1492–1568), Henry VIII (1491–1547), Ulrich von Hutten (1488–1523), Albert Krantz (*c.*1448–1517), Martin Luther (1483–1546), Philipp Melanchthon (1497–1560), Thomas Murner (1475–*c.*1537), Wolfgang Musculus (1497–1563), Johannes Oecolampadius (1482–1531), Julius von Pflug (1499–1564), Willibald Pirckheimer (1470–1530), Erasmus Sarcerius (1501–1559), Caspar Schwenckfeld (1490–1561), Johannes Sleidanus (1506–56), Georg Spalatin (1484–1545), Johannes Trithemius (1462–1516), Jörg Wickram (*c.*1505–*c.*1560), Jacob Wimpheling (1450–1528), and Huldreych Zwingli (1484–1531). It is possible that an occasional item from Priebsch's collection may have found its way into the library of his old College, University College London. Other items may have passed through his son-in-law to the library of the University of Bristol.[3] However, the remainder of the library – principally the seventeenth-, eighteenth- and nineteenth-century books, some medieval manuscripts and a residue of thirteen incunabula and about thirty sixteenth-century titles –, came to the Institute of Germanic Studies, which on Closs's death also received his papers, including his extensive correspondence with colleagues and authors, among them Gottfried Benn, Stefan George, Rainer Maria Rilke, Thomas Mann, J. R. R. Tolkien, E. M. Forster, as well as 120 letters from L. P. Hartley which Closs had himself proposed to publish. A further strength of the collection is lyric poetry, especially from the periods immediately following both world wars, and Closs had been personally acquainted with many of the poets; hence the books frequently contain dedications to him and letters from their authors. The Priebsch–Closs Collection also includes various autograph letters and manuscripts from such luminaries as Wilhelm von Humboldt (*c.* 1799); Theodor Storm (1867); Schiller and Goethe; Friedrich and Caroline de la Motte Fouqué (1814, 1827); Friedrich Schlegel (undated); Christina G. Rossetti (1865); Charles Darwin; Stefan Zweig (1909); Sigmund Freud; Albert Einstein; T. S. Eliot; George Bernard Shaw; Heinrich Mann; John Galsworthy and many others. Some of these may have been acquired by Priebsch himself, others by Closs; in most cases, it is now impossible to say which collector was responsible. The same applies to some of the books. Closs certainly added items to the collection regularly, but it is seldom possible to be sure which items were originally acquired by Priebsch and which by Closs.

The Institute purchased some of the books from Closs and his wife, Priebsch's daughter, the novelist Hannah Closs (1905–1953), at an early date in its existence, and a further 108 seventeenth-century books were acquired from him in 1967. The Institute also holds numerous other early books which, while not technically part of the Priebsch–Closs Collection, are kept with it. For instance, these include early German translations of the *Chronicon Urspergense* (by Caspar Hedio, Strasbourg, 1539), Vitruvius's *De Architectura, Von der Architektur* by Walther Hermann Ryff (Basel, 1575), and Petrarch's *De rebus memorandis* (Frankfurt am Main, 1566), all acquired in 1959 from the library of Friedrich Gundolf. Other items kept with the collection for convenience include several seventeenth-century books (including three

3 For example, according to information kindly provided by Michael Richardson (University of Bristol Library), in November 1944 Closs sold to the library a collection of twenty-seven printed essays and dissertations dating from between 1864 and 1910. They are almost exclusively on topics in medieval German, and several of them relate specifically to the research interests of Robert Priebsch; these include Paul Jäckel, *Egenolf von Staufenberg* (Marburg, 1898) and Eugen Glaser, *Ueber das mhd. Gedicht 'Der Busant'* (Göttingen, 1904), which tends to suggest that these originally formed part of Priebsch's library.

copies of Justus Georg Schottelius's pioneering *Ausführliche Arbeit von der Teutschen HaubtSprache* (Braunschweig, 1663)), 350 eighteenth-century books, as well as a number of valuable books with handwritten dedications from Thomas Mann to Ida Herz (1894–1984), Mann's former librarian, who was a devoted visitor to the Institute over many years.

As is abundantly evident from his extensive correspondence with Elias von Steinmeyer during the years 1892 to 1922, Priebsch was utterly devoted to scholarship. As he wrote on 19 August 1898, his greatest joy on being appointed to University College as from October that year was that he would now have 'das geliebte British Museum' at his disposal, meaning the Museum's library (now the British Library) and above all its magnificent collection of manuscripts. For Priebsch was one of the most distinguished palaeographers of his generation.

Very little is known in detail about how Priebsch came to acquire the rarities in his collection. A passage in his letter of 13 December 1908 to Steinmeyer suggests that he kept a close eye on what London antiquarian booksellers had on offer:

> Deutscher Geschäftsgeist spürt jetzt hier eifrig nach Erstausgaben der deutschen Klassiker u. Romantiker, wovon früher vieles herübergekommen ist; mehrere junge Deutsche tun nichts anderes als von Früh bis Abend bei den hiesigen Antiquaren u. Trödlern herum zu stöbern u. haben soeben auch ihr eigenes Geschäftslokal aufgemacht mit Lessings *Nathan*, Werken von Lenz u. Klinger natürlich in Erstausgaben im Schaufenster. In L[ondon] ist eben alles zu haben, nur bezahlen muß man's können.[4]

Whether the copy of the first edition of Lessing's *Nathan der Weise*, referred to here, is the one which is now in the Priebsch–Closs Collection is not clear. A month later, on 13 January 1909, he jubilantly tells Steinmeyer: 'Meiner Bibliothek fügte ich vor kurzem ein schönes Stück bei: den ndd. [niederdeutschen] Rostocker Druck des Reineke Vos von 1549', but he does not reveal its provenance.[5] Several years later, on 21 December 1913, he writes:

> Meine bibliophilen Neigungen scheinen mit zunehmendem Alter zu wachsen; ich habe mir in den letzten Jahren manches schöne Stück erworben, besonders in Reformationsliteratur u. auch Incunabeln. Freilich mit Bezug auf Erstausgaben der Klassiker u. Romantiker habe ich niemals mehr solches Glück gehabt, als vor Jahren durch Ihre freundl. Vermittlung. Darf ich hoffen,

4 Closs (ed.), *Robert Priebsch, Elias von Steinmeyer: Briefwechsel*, p. 197.

5 Closs (ed.), *Robert Priebsch, Elias von Steinmeyer: Briefwechsel*, p. 198. This book is not in the Institute's collection, but, according to Closs's note (p. 297), now at Princeton, though Hubertus Menke, *Bibliotheca Reinardiana* (Stuttgart: Hauswedell, 1992), pp. 282–83, does not record it there; however, a copy of the 1553 index to the 1549 edition is recorded at Princeton (p. 285).

daß Sie an mich denken werden, falls Ihnen wieder einmal ähnliches bekannt wird?[6]

Steinmeyer had indeed already helped him to acquire a significant number of books from the library of a man called Hermann Beckh (1805–1866) who had been a substantial landowner at Rathsberg, near Erlangen (where Steinmeyer was Professor). Many years after their father's death, Beckh's two sons, one (Friedrich Beckh, 1843–1927) a politician, the other a local school professor (Dr Heinrich Beckh, 1858–1919), sold his library; some of the books – mostly those on law but also a collection of about five hundred ephemera dating from the 1848 revolution[7] – went to Erlangen University Library in 1908, but the rest were disposed of through the antiquarian book trade.[8] In a letter to Steinmeyer dated 6 October 1907 Priebsch mentions that 'Eine große u. eine kleine Kiste mit Büchern aus der Beckhschen Bibliothek ist für mich unterwegs', but precisely what was among them is not known. Priebsch was particularly keen to obtain a first edition of the Grimms' *Irische Elfenmärchen* (Leipzig, 1826) 'zu einem verständigen Preise' from the Beckh collection, remarking that he had paid nine Marks for an uncut copy of Wilhelm Grimm's *Altdänische Heldenlieder* (Heidelberg, 1811),[9] and adding, 'Falls dieselbe Bibliothek [i.e. Beckh's] außerdem noch Erst-Ausgaben der Romantiker oder Klassiker besäße u. diese gleichfalls zum Verkaufe ständen, sollten sie auch hierin in mir einen Käufer finden, soweit ich die Bücher noch nicht besitze'.[10] On 24 February 1908, having told Steinmeyer how pleased he was with the seminar library he had built up at University College, he added, 'Dabei ist meine plötzlich erwachte Sammlerleidenschaft keineswegs geringer geworden u. es vergeht selten eine Woche, ohne daß ich ein neues

6 Closs (ed.), *Robert Priebsch, Elias von Steinmeyer: Briefwechsel*, p. 237.

7 It is to be regretted that these were not acquired by Priebsch as they would have been a most welcome addition to the smaller, yet still significant collection of such material donated to the Institute by Professor Keith Spalding (1913–1997) in 1996. This material is mentioned by Susan Reed, 'Printing the Revolution: Berlin Broadsides from 1848', in *The Book in Germany*, ed. by M. C. Fischer and W. A. Kelly (Edinburgh: Merchiston Publishing, 2010), pp. 101–15. The Institute's collection comprises sixty-five items, of which four are duplicates. They include fifty-two single-sided broadsheets, intended for posting up on walls or columns, and thirteen small brochures, mostly of four leaves. Some of the items are in verse. Professor Spalding himself wrote about the collection in his article, 'The Idiom of a Revolution: Berlin 1848', *The Modern Language Review*, 44 (1949), 60–74.

8 See Steinmeyer's letter of 3 November 1907, in Closs (ed.), *Robert Priebsch, Elias von Steinmeyer: Briefwechsel*, p. 177.

9 An antiquarian bookseller in Vienna had a copy of this edition on offer for £411.95 on 1 July 2016, while another in Copenhagen wanted £623.11 for one.

10 Closs (ed.), *Robert Priebsch, Elias von Steinmeyer: Briefwechsel*, pp. 173–74 (July 1907). Both the *Irische Elfenmärchen* and the *Altdänische Heldenlieder* are in the Priebsch–Closs Collection.

Stück hinzufüge'.[11] A few months later, on 8 November 1908, he laments that his hobby is now not producing very much:

> Mein Steckenpferd hat seit Monaten noch recht kümmerliche Nahrung bekommen; es wird immer schwerer Frühausgaben zu bekommen, falls man nicht geradezu lächerliche Preise zahlen will.[12]

On 14 September 1914 we hear:

> Ich habe in letzter Zeit wieder einiges für meine Bibliothek erworben, die mir anfängt viel Freude zu machen (z.b. Scheibles Schaltjahr, das ich bei einem Juden, Oppenheim genannt, für 2Mk50 erstand, aber Grimmiana sind mir nicht mehr untergekommen.[13]

As a palaeographer, Priebsch constantly followed sales of manuscripts. Early in October 1910 he inspected manuscripts in the private library of Alfred Henry Huth (1850–1910) at Hungerford which included the thirteenth-century *Christherre-Chronik*, *Von den synnrychen erlúchten wyben* (the German translation of Boccaccio's *De claris mulieribus*) by the Ulm physician Heinrich Steinhöwel (1412–1482/3) (now Ms. 105 in the Spencer Collection in New York Public Library) and a manuscript of the *Sachsenspiegel*, and later he reports on the sale from this library of letters by Goethe and Schiller for substantial prices.[14] For his own collection he acquired several items from the disposal of the enormous library of Sir Thomas Phillipps (1792–1872) at Cheltenham – there are many mentions in the correspondence of Priebsch's dealings with Thomas Fitzroy Fenwick, Phillipps's grandson, while other books from there were purchased, on his recommendation, by University College. As Dorothy K. Coveney put it in the preface to *A Descriptive Catalogue of Manuscripts in the Library of University College London* (London, 1935), 'the small collection of palaeographical treasures in the possession of University College, London, owed its development very largely to the great enthusiasm of the late Professor Robert Priebsch for the study of palaeography'. Of particular interest among the University College manuscripts are Ms. Frag. Germ. 1, part of a fourteenth-century manuscript of Wolfram von Eschenbach's *Willehalm*, which is known to have been in the hands of a retired headmaster at Enns on the Danube in 1904 and was

11 Closs (ed.), *Robert Priebsch, Elias von Steinmeyer: Briefwechsel*, p. 186.

12 Closs (ed.), *Robert Priebsch, Elias von Steinmeyer: Briefwechsel*, p. 194.

13 Closs (ed.), *Robert Priebsch, Elias von Steinmeyer: Briefwechsel*, p. 242. A copy of Johann Scheible's *Das Schaltjahr: welches ist der teutsch Kalender mit den Figuren, und hat 366 Tag*, 5 vols (Stuttgart and Leipzig, 1846–47), is now in the Warburg Institute; whether this once belonged to Priebsch I do not know.

14 Letters of 8 October 1910 and 18 June 1911 (Closs (ed.), *Robert Priebsch, Elias von Steinmeyer: Briefwechsel*, p. 213, p. 221).

acquired by the College in 1921, and Ms. Frag. Germ. 2, a fragment of an early fourteenth-century manuscript of the heroic poem *Virginal* which Priebsch himself described in *Archiv für das Studium der neueren Sprachen und Literaturen*, 145 (1923), 30–41.

Priebsch took a very particular interest in his medieval manuscripts.[15] The items which came to the Institute include a single vellum leaf from the *Recognitiones Clementis* (J. P. Migne, *Patrologia graeca*, I, cols 1202–1474) from a ninth-century west German scriptorium, fragments of two late manuscripts (one fourteenth-century, the other fifteenth-century) of the well-known mystical tract *Buch der Ewigen Weisheit* by Heinrich Seuse (*c.*1293–1366), neither of which is recorded in Hofmann's census of Seuse manuscripts;[16] and the manuscript of a fourteenth-century mystical text which Priebsch edited under the title *Christi Leiden in einer Vision geschaut* (Heidelberg, 1936). Then there is the late fourteenth-century manuscript from Alsace containing several texts including a few lines from one of only seven surviving manuscripts of the poem *Heinrich von Kempten* by Konrad von Würzburg (*c.*1225–87), the most significant German poet of the second half of the thirteenth century, and a much more substantial fragment of the poem *Peter von Staufenberg*, a poem originally composed in Alsace around 1310 and thematically related to the story of Fair Melusine.[17] Another fragment is from *Der Busant*, an anonymous poem of the early fourteenth century, the subject of which is the love of the son of the King of England, who has been sent to study in Paris, for the daughter of the King of France. The most substantial manuscript from Priebsch's library is a collection of Latin sermons, apparently put together by an unidentified south German preacher for his personal use probably in Bavaria around 1460; running to some three hundred and forty leaves, the manuscript bears on its cover the arms of the Farnese family and is reputed to have belonged to Alessandro Farnese (1468–1549) who was elected as Pope Paul III in 1534.

Among post-medieval manuscript material are two seventeenth-century reports on the trials of Catharina Stroblin, a farmer's wife from Schernfeld (near Eichstätt), and of Appolonia Neuberin, a thirty-two-year-old brewer, for

15 On the manuscripts he owned which are now in the Institute's collection see John L. Flood, 'Die mittelalterlichen Handschriften der Bibliothek des Institute of Germanic Studies, London', *Zeitschrift für deutsches Altertum und deutsche Literatur*, 120 (1991), 325–30.

16 Georg Hofmann, *Seuses Werke in deutschsprachigen Handschriften des späten Mittelalters* (Fulda: Parzeller, 1969).

17 Priebsch mentions his ownership of this in his letter of 7 March 1913 to Steinmeyer (Closs (ed.), *Robert Priebsch, Elias von Steinmeyer: Briefwechsel*, p. 232). Fragments of medieval German manuscripts are already mentioned on 16 April 1905 (see Closs (ed.), *Robert Priebsch, Elias von Steinmeyer: Briefwechsel*, p. 271), but the text of this particular letter is not included in Closs's selection.

witchcraft; Stroblin was beheaded with the sword and burned on 26 January 1618 and Neuberin suffered the same fate in June 1623. A manuscript of much more recent date contains a remarkable English translation of the fifteenth-century Low German *Reynke de Vos* (*Reynard the Fox*), made by Dietrich Wilhelm Soltau (1745–1827). Soltau had left his native Hamburg when he was twenty-one to spend the next thirty-two years in Russia, trading in a variety of commodities in St Petersburg. During this time and after his return to Germany following the death of Catherine the Great he developed into a remarkably versatile translator, publishing German versions of important works from English (including Samuel Butler's *Hudibras* (1787), Charles James Fox's *A History of the Early Part of the Reign of James the Second* (1810), and James Thomson's *The Seasons* (1823)), Spanish (Cervantes' *Don Quixote* (1800–01; reissued down to 1920) and Cervantes' *Novelas ejemplares* (1801, and dedicated to Queen Charlotte, the consort of King George III), Italian (Boccaccio's *Decameron* (1803; reissued down to 1932)), and Portuguese (João de Barros' *Asia* (1821)). But perhaps his most successful translation was that of *Reynke de Vos* from Low German into High German which he published in 1802 and which was being reissued as recently as 1964. The moralizing story of Reynard, of which Thomas Carlyle wrote, 'It has been lectured on in Universities, quoted in Imperial Council-halls; it lay on the toilette of Princesses, and was thumbed to pieces on the bench of the Artizan; we hear of grave men ranking it only next to the Bible',[18] seems to have had a particular appeal to Soltau for, not content with translating it into High German, he also rendered it into English verse, which was no mean achievement. He produced a handwritten fair copy of his translation, embellishing it with delightful illustrations, for presentation to Adolphus Frederick (1774–1850), 1st Duke of Cambridge, the tenth child of King George III and Queen Charlotte. George III was also Elector of Hanover and eventually Adolphus Frederick, who had distinguished himself in the Napoleonic wars, was appointed Governor-General of the Kingdom of Hanover, a fact recorded when Soltau dedicated the printed edition of his translation, *Reynard the Fox. A burlesque poem of the 15th century* (Hamburg, 1826) to him. Adolphus Frederick resided in the palace of Herrenhausen at Hanover until 1837 and the manuscript was probably in the library there until then. At some point it was inherited by Adolphus Frederick's son George, 2nd Duke of Cambridge (1819–1904), whose bookplate adorns the inside cover.[19]

Priebsch also collected early scholarly editions of medieval texts made by such important figures as Friedrich Heinrich von der Hagen (1780–1856), the first Professor of German at Berlin, the Brothers Grimm (Jacob [1785–

18 Thomas Carlyle, 'German literature of the fourteenth and fifteenth centuries', *Foreign Quarterly Review*, 8 (July–October 1831), 347–91 (p. 385).

19 See John L. Flood, 'Dietrich Wilhelm Soltau und seine Übersetzungen des *Reynke de Vos*. Ein Beitrag zur Erforschung der deutsch-englischen Literaturbeziehungen um 1800', *Archiv für Geschichte des Buchwesens*, 45 (1996), 283–336.

1863], and Wilhelm [1786–1859]), and Karl Lachmann (1793–1851). Of particular interest also is his pristine copy of Christoph Heinrich Myller's *Der Nibelungen Liet: ein Rittergedicht aus dem XIII. oder XIV. Iahrhundert: zum ersten Male aus der Handschrift ganz abgedruckt* (Berlin: Spener, 1782), of which Frederick the Great of Prussia, to whom Myller presented a copy, famously opined, 'Derlei Zeugs ist keinen Schuß Pulver werth'.

The collection includes thirteen incunabula, one of which – an almanac for 1492 printed by Johann Bämler at Augsburg – is unique.[20] This was discovered stuffed into an old envelope along with various unrelated jottings when Closs's papers came to the Institute in 1991. Of the remaining incunabula, eight were printed in Germany, at Cologne (the eleventh of fifty-two fifteenth-century editions of the *Stella clericorum*, this one printed by Heinrich Quentell *c.*1489), Heidelberg (a variant edition of Heinrich Knoblochtzer's 1490 *Ordnung zu reden*), Nuremberg (Friedrich Creussner's 1479 edition of Robertus Carraciolus's *Sermones de timore divinorum iudiciorum*, and Peter Wagner's edition of Astesanus de Ast's *Textus canonum penitencialium* of *c.*1495) and Strasbourg (the Pseudo-Cyrillus *Speculum sapientiae*, printed by Strasbourg's second printer, Heinrich Eggestein, not after 1475, in a binding embossed with the crest of the Duke of Sutherland; Johannes Herolt's *Liber discipuli de eruditione christifidelium* of *c.*1476/77, and Petrus de Alliaco, *Quaestiones super libros sententiarum* of 1490, both printed by Georg Husner, and Herolt's *Sermones discipuli de tempore et de sanctis una cum promptuario exemplorum*, printed by Martin Flach in 1495, this being the thirty-eighth of forty-four recorded editions). The other incunabula were printed in Italy (Florence, Milan, and Rome).

Among the seventeenth-century books, for which the Institute paid August Closs £700 in 1967, are a number of miscellaneous topographical works such as François Blondel's *Außführliche Erklärung und augenscheinliche Wunderwirkung deren heylsamen Badt- und Trinckwässern zu Aach* (1688; the British Library has only the Latin editions of 1671 and 1688), dealing with the health-giving properties of the waters at Aachen, and *Das edle Fluss-Perle, oder der Gold-trächtig und fürtreffliche Ströme-Printz, der Rhein* (1689), a eulogy on the Rhine. Also there is Heinrich Ludolf Benthem's *Engländischer Kirchen- und Schulen-Staat* (Lüneburg, 1694), an important early German work on Britain. Rare travel books include the anonymous *Kurtze Beschreibung der Insel und Reichs Creta oder Candia* (Nuremberg, 1669), *Des berühmten englischen Theologi Gilberti Burnets ... durch die Schweitz, Italien, auch einige Orte Deutschlands ... gethaner Reise ... curieuse Beschreibung* (Leipzig, 1687), and Casimir Freschot's *Des Königreichs Dalmatien historische und geographische Vorstellung* (Leipzig, 1688).

20 ISTC ia00517280. See John L. Flood, 'Ein Almanach auf das Jahr 1492 mit einer Übersicht über die Augsburger Kalenderproduktion des 15. Jahrhunderts', *Gutenberg-Jahrbuch*, 67 (1992), 62–71.

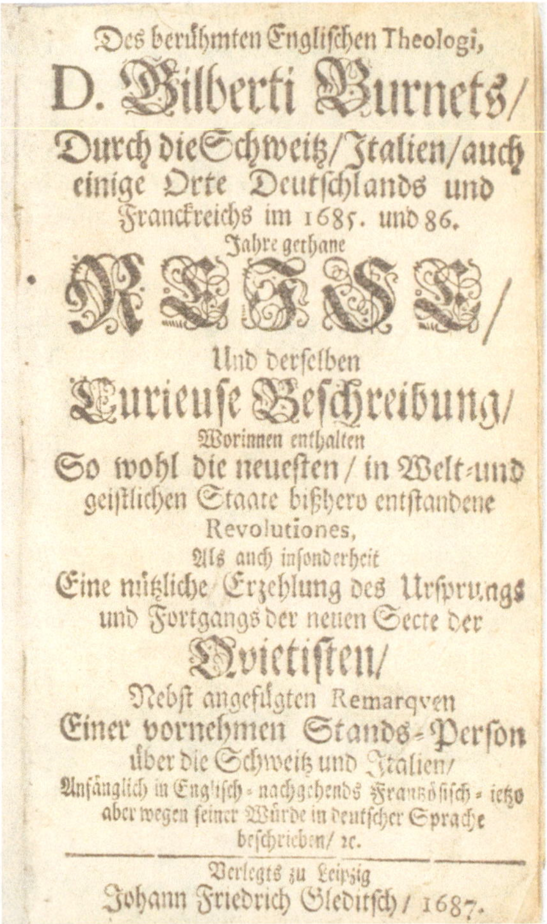

Des berühmten Englischen Theologi,
D. Gilberti Burnets/
Durch die Schweitz/Italien/auch
einige Orte Deutschlands und
Franckreichs im 1685. und 86.
Jahre gethane
REISE/
Und derselben
Curieuse Beschreibung/
Worinnen enthalten
So wohl die neuesten / in Welt-und
geistlichen Staate bißhero entstandene
Revolutiones,
Als auch insonderheit
Eine nützliche Erzehlung des Ursprungs
und Fortgangs der neuen Secte der
Quietisten/
Nebst angefügten Remarqven
Einer vornehmen Stands-Person
über die Schweitz und Italien/
Anfänglich in Englisch- nachgehends Frantzösisch- ietzo
aber wegen seiner Würde in deutscher Sprache
beschrieben/ 2c.
Verlegts zu Leipzig
Johann Friedrich Gleditsch / 1687.

Figure 33: Des berühmten englischen Theologi Gilberti Burnets . . . Reise *(Leipzig 1687). Copy from the Library of Friedrich Gundolf (his signature appears on the facing page).*

About 150 German authors of the sixteenth, seventeenth and early eighteenth centuries feature in the collection, though in most cases with but a single work. Writers represented by several items include Abraham a Sancta Clara (1644–1709), Aegidius Albertinus (1560–1620), Jacob Balde (1604–1668), Franz Callenbach (1663–1743), Friedrich von Canitz (1654–1699), David Fassmann (1683–1744), Hans Jacob Christoffel von Grimmelshausen (1622–1676), Johann Christian Günther (1695–1723), Christian Hoffmann von Hoffmanswaldau (1616–1679), Daniel Casper von Lohenstein (1635–1683), Heinrich Kornmann (*c.*1580–*c.*1640), Gottfried Wilhelm Leibniz (1646–1716), Ambrosius Lobwasser (1515–1585), Martin Luther (1483–1546), Philipp Melanchthon (1497–1560), Johann Michael Moscherosch (1601–1669), Martin Opitz (1597–1639), Benjamin Schmolck (1672–1737), Johann Balthasar Schupp (1610–1661), Christian Weise (1642–1708), Philipp von Zesen (1619–1689), and Julius Wilhelm Zincgref (1591–1635).

The oldest journal in the collection is *Monatliche Unterredungen einiger guten Freunde von allerhand Büchern ...* (1696ff.) edited by the polyhistor Wilhelm Ernst Tentzel (1659–1707). The publication takes the form of dialogues on the subject of a wide range of recent books.

Among the eighteenth and nineteenth-century holdings are many first and early editions of the German Classics and Romantics. These include first editions of Gotthold Ephraim Lessing's *Nathan der Weise* (1779), Ludwig Tieck's *Franz Sternbalds Wanderungen* (Berlin, 1798), Friedrich Schiller's *Wilhelm Tell* (Tübingen, 1804), Heinrich von Kleist's *Penthesilea* (Tübingen, 1808), Franz Grillparzer's *Weh dem, der lügt* (Vienna, 1840), Friedrich Hebbel's *Maria Magdalena* (Hamburg, 1844), and Gottfried Keller's *Die Leute von Seldwyla* (Braunschweig, 1856).

A special feature of the collection is the large number of translations from the German illustrating the impact of German thought on English letters in the eighteenth and nineteenth centuries. Among these are early English translations of Friedrich Schiller's *Kabale und Liebe* (1795), *Fiesko* (1796), and *Maria Stuart* (1801), and especially noteworthy are examples of translations by well-known British writers, including Matthew 'Monk' Lewis's *The Minister*, his version of Schiller's *Kabale und Liebe* (London, 1797), Sir Walter Scott's translation of Goethe's *Götz von Berlichingen* (London, 1799), and R. B. Sheridan's adaptation of August von Kotzebue's *Pizarro* (London, 1799). This part of the collection was significantly enriched in 1966 when William Walker Chambers (1913–1985, William Jacks Professor of German in the University of Glasgow), presented sixteen different early translations of Goethe's *Die Leiden des jungen Werthers*, which augment the fifteen English, French, Spanish and Italian translations already present in the Priebsch–Closs Collection. Among these is the very first English version, *The Sorrows of Werter* (London, 1779), anonymously translated from the French edition of 1776 and variously ascribed to Richard Graves and Daniel Malthus. This group of books is usefully augmented by a number of other early items reflecting the contemporary enthusiasm for *Werther*, including the anonymous *Eleanora: from the Sorrows of Werter: A Tale* (London, 1785); William James, *The Letters of Charlotte, during her Connexion with Werter* (London, 1786); Frederick Reynolds, *Werter: A Tragedy* (Dublin, 1786); Anne Francis, *Charlotte to Werter: A Poetical Epistle* (London, 1787); and Amelia Pickering, *The Sorrows of Werter: A Poem* (London, 1788). The Institute has a range of early translations of Shakespeare, including the first edition of Schiller's translation of *Macbeth* (Tübingen, 1801) as well as a very scarce Mannheim reprint of the same year.[21] Among other early translations into

21 In 1955 the Institute also acquired (from where is no longer known) a collection of the Shakespeare translations by Hedwig Schwarz (1898–1985), his most prolific German female translator. Of the seventeen or eighteen plays she translated between 1936 and about

German are those of John Barclay's *Argenis* (by Martin Opitz, Amsterdam, 1644), Defoe, Fielding, Milton, Sir Philip Sidney's *Arcadia* (originally translated by Valentinus Theocritus von Hirschberg in 1629 but reworked by Opitz, Leiden, 1642), Steele, Sterne, and Swift, while eighteenth-century dramatists are well represented with German translations of Centlivre, Cibber, Coffey, Colman, Congreve, Cumberland, Farquhar, Foote, Garrick, Goldsmith, Mason and Moore. The collection also contains early German translations of seventeenth- and eighteenth-century French writers including Beaumarchais, Bouilly, Corneille, Diderot, Dorvigny, Grafigny, Marivaux, Molière, Racine, J. B. Rousseau, and Voltaire.

Today, the Priebsch–Closs Collection is perhaps not valued as highly as it once was. For one thing, German Studies in Britain now tend to focus on the more recent periods of literature. For another, many of the books cherished by Priebsch and his son-in-law are now available in facsimile reprints or indeed digitally. Nevertheless, modern media, even facsimiles, let alone digital editions, cannot reproduce the thrill of handling the original editions such as a 1754 translation of Defoe's *Robinson Crusoe*.

1955, the Institute holds eleven. On her work see Hedwig Schwarz, 'Arbeit für Shakespeare durch Shakespeare-Bearbeitungen', *Shakespeare Jahrbuch*, 92 (1956), 175–83; Fritz Paul et al., *Europäische Komödie im übersetzerischen Transfer* (Tübingen: Narr, 1993).

Afterword

What emerges in these pages is the recurrence of a number of dilemmas having to do with (of course) funding, with the issue of physical space, and with the changing institutional structures of London University, and with the relationship of those structures to the intellectual heartland of German Studies. College Departments of German come into being, are advocated and defended, and are combined, rationalized, amalgamated. Time and again the Institute plays a central, meta-collegiate role; but the question arises as to how that centre is to be defined, how that centre can and should hold. Reading these pages, one has the sense, as with so many historical accounts, of *plus ça change*; but at another level one finds oneself fascinated by the perennial drama of the attempt, at the heart of all universities, to bring together institutional and intellectual aspirations. That story continues, of course. Perhaps, in these Brexit-dominated times, one historical juncture emerges with particular force. And that is the amazing process by which, in the years between 1943 and 1950, London University decides to set up a research institute devoted to German Studies. The times were hardly propitious; the war with Germany was vividly on everybody's mind, and the country was on its knees financially. Yet the miracle happened, the Institute came about, and the study of things German received an extraordinary shot in the arm. The history reviewed in this volume, then, gives one scope for many conflicting emotions – grief, certainly, but also, just as certainly, hope.

Professor Martin Swales
September 2016 Cambridge

Index

CPSIA information can be obtained
at www.ICGtesting.com
Printed in the USA
JSRC020147011219
2681JS00011B/143/P

9 780854 572632